NEHRU'S MANTLE

The Politics of Succession in India

NEHRU'S MANTLE
The Politics of Succession in India

MICHAEL BRECHER

FREDERICK A. PRAEGER, *Publishers*
New York · Washington

BOOKS THAT MATTER

Published in the United States of America in 1966
by Frederick A. Praeger, Inc., Publishers
111 Fourth Avenue, New York, N.Y. 10003

All rights reserved

Library of Congress Catalog Card Number: 66–17548

Printed in the United States of America

TO EVA

PREFACE

This book arose out of curiosity and deep intellectual concern. Long years of study led to a natural interest in the last phase of the Nehru era and the fascinating web of men and forces in Indian politics that were responsible for the Shastri succession. My teaching and research have, in recent years, stimulated an exploration into the process of decision-making, mainly but not exclusively in the sphere of foreign policy. During my current leave of absence from McGill University I have concentrated on this important and neglected field, both in India and in Israel.

The study of decision-making has attracted a great deal of attention in the literature of political science during the past decade or more. Models and hypotheses abound, but the gap between theory and empirical studies is vast. It is also disquieting, because of the abundant evidence that abstract assumptions and projections about decision-making are often sharply at variance with reality. The time has come, it seems to me, to divert more of our intellectual energies to explorations in depth of political decisions, great and small, while they are in motion, if possible, or by a careful reconstruction of the process, based on documentary materials and other sources. It was in this spirit, and with this conviction, that the present analysis of decision-making at the summit of Indian politics was undertaken.

The initial aim was to confine my research to one decision only—the Shastri succession to Nehru. But, as so often, interest once aroused is difficult to curtail, especially when an opportunity presents itself to examine at first hand other important decisions—in this case the controversies over food and language policy during Shastri's first year in office. What was designed as a paper, then, grew into a book; the decision without its consequences for India's political system seemed incomplete.

After this book had gone to the printers, Prime Minister Shastri died suddenly in Tashkent, hours after the conclusion of the Indo-Pakistani summit conference. India was again confronted with the challenge of succession, twice within nineteen months. Was the pattern of 1964 likely to be repeated or would the actors and the forces they represented respond differently? If the latter, what changes in behaviour would take place, and what would these changes presage for the working of India's political system in the future? These and related questions prompted me to return to Delhi to observe, document, and analyse the second succession. The comparison is not without relevance to an understanding of all-India politics and decision-making in politics generally.

While calmer reflection later may lead to a revision of certain judgements offered tentatively here, an effort has been made to document the complex flow of deeds and words, the multiple small decisions, day by day, and, as far as possible, hour by hour. The memories of the actors in these dramatic decisions, as with most men, are short-lived. I have therefore tried to benefit from the advantages of immediacy, direct observation, and the co-operation of many of the participants, with the goal of making available as complete a study as possible of these crucial decisions. I hope that other scholars can be encouraged to make similar studies and thereby help narrow the gap between the two complementary approaches to decision-making in politics.

This book owes much to many institutions and persons:

—The Rockefeller Foundation, which sponsored my research into India's foreign policy in 1964–5 and, therefore, made it possible for me to spend my 'leisure hours' exploring the Shastri succession and its consequences;

—The John Simon Guggenheim Memorial Foundation and the Canada Council, which are sponsoring my research into Israel's foreign policy during 1965–6, thus enabling me to return briefly to India to analyse the second succession;

—McGill University, which granted me a two-year leave of absence;

—Many Indian public figures whose names appear in these pages; but for their generous co-operation this study of political decisions in motion would not have been possible; detailed

notes of my interviews were drafted immediately upon their
conclusion, and the passages which have been quoted in this
book represent as accurate a recollection of their words as
possible; if, in any instance, I have misconstrued their words I
hereby offer my regrets;

—Mr. V. K. Krishna Menon, who kindly consented to a comprehensive dialogue on tape, from which his reflections on the
first succession, the working of Cabinet, and other topics are
drawn;

—Mr. Morarji Desai, who kindly made available his personal
correspondence with Nehru for research purposes and allowed
me to work through it with care for a week at his home;

—Mr. Neville Maxwell, distinguished correspondent of *The
Times* in Delhi since 1959, whose knowledge and understanding of the successions, as of other topics, were readily shared
during many hours of discussion;

—Professor W. H. Morris-Jones, Director of the Institute of
Commonwealth Studies, London, Professors Lloyd and
Susanne Rudolph of the University of Chicago, and a North
American political analyst with many years of experience in
India, who regrettably seeks anonymity; all read the first seven
chapters with the utmost care, despite heavy commitments, and
gave me the invaluable benefit of their insight and their
knowledge of Indian politics in regard to both the factual
detail and the analytical themes of this study;

—Mr. Richard V. Gorham and Mr. Howard Schaffer, who
provided valuable comments on the last two chapters; and to
Mr. and Mrs. Gorham for making it possible to draft the
account of the second succession in a friendly and sympathetic
atmosphere;

—members of the staff of the Oxford University Press, London,
who contributed helpful editorial comments.

Most of all, I owe a profound debt of gratitude to my wife.
As with all my previous research ventures, she provided unfalter-
ing encouragement and assistance at every stage of this project,
on this occasion despite adverse circumstances cheerfully borne.

Whatever merit this book may have owes much to the co-operation and help of these persons and institutions. None is responsible for any errors of judgement.

MICHAEL BRECHER

Jerusalem   1 October 1965
New Delhi   1 February 1966

CONTENTS

NEHRU'S MANTLE

The Politics of Succession in India

I
RATIONALE

THE problem of succession is central to all political systems: it is an inevitable consequence of Time and Man's mortality. The appearance of youth or vigour and the illusion of permanence, often combined with fear of the unknown, may shroud the issue for a decade or more. But ultimately, political pressure or ill fortune or disablement or death compels attention to the question of who and what will succeed the existing configuration of power: the political élite, and often the populace as well, cannot escape this responsibility. And on the process of succession often depends the stability, welfare, and progress, sometimes even the continuity, of the polity.

Different political systems have evolved diverse techniques to select a new ruler. Monarchy has relied on the seemingly simple and consistent principle of heredity through the ages, though history is replete with illustrations of dissension and conflict among sons and brothers of the deceased ruler for the prize of crown and glory: this is equally true of Egypt's Pharaohs and Rome's Caesars, of England's Tudors and France's Bourbons, of India's Moghuls and the Hans of China. Republics of the democratic type have long resorted to direct or indirect election, whether formally inscribed in a constitution or sanctioned by convention and custom. Those of an authoritarian type experience political change by cabal or *coup*, assassination or *putsch*, frequently by civil war, usually by violence in some form, overt or threatened: this applies to most states in recorded history. In ideologically-based régimes, too, succession is normally the result of force, whether through defeat and collapse in war, as with Fascist Italy and Nazi Germany, or through internal strife within the party hierarchy, as in the case of Soviet Russia. The pattern remains unclear in tutelary democracy (Pakistan) and mobilizing oligarchy (Ghana), but the evidence reveals the paramount presence of coercion.

The problem of succession is thus not unique to the contemporary world; indeed, it is as old as the history of political organization. Yet it has been accentuated by two striking characteristics of the present era: Gerontocracy and Charisma. The list of elderly men who have wielded political power for lengthy periods, in some cases extending back to the 1920s, constitutes an extraordinary club. Some have stepped down from the summit of power more or less voluntarily, such as Adenauer at 87 and Ben-Gurion at 77, in 196?, and Churchill at 80, in 1955. Two died without challenge to their authority, Stalin at 73, in 1953, and Nehru at 74, in 1964. Others were compelled to resign, notably Synghman Rhee of South Korea at 85, in 1960, and Khrushchev at 70, in 1964. One, Trujillo of the Dominican Republic, was assassinated at 71, in 1961. Yet many remain in power, most of them heading Communist or non-Communist authoritarian régimes: Ho Chi-minh (75), Tito (73), Mao Tse-tung, and Ulbricht (72); at the other extreme of the political-ideological spectrum are Chiang Kai-shek at 79, Salazar at 76, and Franco at 73; and ranged along the spectrum are de Gaulle at 75, Kenyatta of Kenya at 72, and Bustamente of Jamaica at 81. Here, then, is a microcosm of the mid-twentieth century: the club of Old Men represents all continents but one, most types of political system, virtually all major races and cultures, great, middle, and small powers, and economies in various stages of development.

Professor Rustow, who has aptly remarked ' clearly, ours is an age of gerontocracy ', discerns four sources of this phenomenon.[1] The first is ' the problem of a missing generation ', which explains the presence of old men in power in Germany, Italy, and South Korea, where middle-aged politicians had been killed, exiled, or made unacceptable through collaboration during a lengthy period of dictatorship or foreign rule; Adenauer, de Gasperi, and Rhee emerged from long years of obscurity on the ruins of Nazi, Fascist, and Japanese rule respectively. The second source is the seizure of power by young men who succeeded in perpetuating personal rule for a generation or more: such is the case of Salazar, Chiang, and Franco. A third is the attainment of vast power by nationalist or Communist leaders after prolonged struggle: noteworthy examples are Nehru and Ben-Gurion, and Tito, Mao, and Ho. The last is the belated triumph of dissent, the 'lonely political figure', whose policies are ultimately vindicated in the face of national disaster: Churchill in 1940 and de Gaulle in 1958 are the classic illustrations.

Some of these Old Men exercise (or exercised) power, in whole or in part, through charisma. But that gift of power through personality extends far beyond the gerontocrats to another significant club, the Nationalist Revolutionaries of Asia, Africa, and Latin America. There is some overlapping, notably Nehru, Ben-Gurion, Ho, and Kenyatta. But to these must be added an array of younger charismatic leaders of the new states: Sukarno and, perhaps, Prince Sihanouk, in Asia; Nasser, Nyerere, Nkrumah, and Bourguiba in Africa; and Castro in Latin America. The membership of these two clubs highlights the special character of the succession problem in the decades to come. But the magnitude of the danger of disorderly political change is awesome: the Nationalist Revolutionaries noted here are merely the charismatic expression of the most fundamental structural change in the global political system during this century —the creation of more than sixty new states in the anti-colonial revolution of the post-war world.

In most of these states the leadership may be neither old nor charismatic. Yet the problem of succession remains. Most of them are too new to have experienced the crisis, but the evidence thus far indicates a pre-eminent role for the military *coup* as a mechanism of change. Such has been the case in Burma, Pakistan, and the Sudan in 1958, South Korea in 1961, Burma and Togo in 1962, South Viet Nam in 1963, Algeria in 1965, Nigeria in 1966, and with abortive military *coups* in Tanganyika and elsewhere. Free elections have been held in only seven new states, India, Israel, Malaysia, Nigeria, Ceylon, the Philippines, and Turkey; and only in the last three have changes of the party in power occurred as a result of a national competitive ballot.[2]

A peaceful and orderly succession to an individual leader who had dominated the politics of his own country since independence has occurred in only two new states, Israel (1963) and India (1964). In both the leader was a gerontocrat with charisma in abundance. But there are two vital differences: the succession to Ben-Gurion is incomplete—he resigned but did not withdraw from the political arena; indeed, he declared to the world in the summer of 1965 that his successor, Levi Eshkol, was not fit to be Prime Minister[3] and formed a separate list for the *Knesset* (Parliament) elections later that year, in defiance of the majority in Mapai, the party he had dominated for thirty years;[4] secondly, few doubted the capacity of Israel's democratic system to survive the passing of Ben-Gurion from the political scene, but many had profound misgivings about India's democracy without Nehru. The magnitude of India's internal pressures and centrifugal tendencies, the narrowness of her democratic infra-structure, and the towering position of Nehru had created grave fears in India and abroad about the future of Indian politics.[5] Thus the succession to India's charismatic leader may be viewed as a unique phenomenon in the politics of the new states, with possible lessons for other countries in Afro-Asia yet to confront the problem of peaceful political change.

    This is one reason for exploring the succession to Nehru. Another is Nehru's dominant role in Indian politics for seventeen years and the uncertainty about the Indian political élite's ability to achieve a smooth succession, without shattering the system and its rules of behaviour. A third reason is the intrinsic interest in the drama itself and the light it sheds on the principal forces and actors in Indian politics in 1963-4. A study of the succession in India is also important because the process of selection had far-reaching consequences for the distribution of political power in the first year of the post-Nehru period. Fifthly, it provides insight into the last phase of Nehru as a political leader. And finally, it reveals some of the inner workings of the governing party in what may be termed a one-plus party system.

    There are various ways in which a political process as complex as the succession to Nehru can be explored. One viable method is to construct an elaborate analysis of the drama and its background, based upon a series of related functional questions, and then to examine the main consequences of the succession for India's political system. *When* did the process begin, i.e., at what point did the struggle for the succession enter the mainstream of Indian politics? *What* were the main interlocking developments in Nehru's declining phase which led to the decision in favour of Lal Bahadur Shastri? *Who* were the key actors and what forces did they represent? And finally, what ideas and institutions legitimized the process of decision and the decision itself?

II

BACKGROUND

At 9 a.m. on the 2nd of June 1964, 5 days and 19 hours after the death of Jawaharlal Nehru, the Congress Parliamentary Party met in extraordinary session in the Central Hall of Parliament and unanimously elected Lal Bahadur Shastri the party leader. Seven hours later, President Radhakrishnan invited Shastri to form a new government. With that act the succession to Nehru was complete. To those who participated in the drama of the six days that did not shake the world, no less than to those who observed it, this was a remarkably tranquil adjustment to the end of an era. People who had predicted dissension and turmoil, and there were many throughout the world, were proved prophets of gloom. Yet even those who had been optimistic were relieved, and even somewhat surprised, by the mature, sophisticated, and smooth internal transfer of power.

The cry of ' after Nehru, who? ', occasionally accompanied by the more significant question, ' after Nehru, what? ', was first heard in the mid-1950s, when India's leader was at the height of his power and vigour. It remained muted at first, a topic for salon discussion in New Delhi and good copy for aspiring journalists; indeed, it seemed to many an artificial creation of foreign correspondents, whose persistent prediction about India's likely descent into chaos did much to create panic in the chancelleries of the world during the last years of Nehru's India. The cry became more vocal when Nehru reached his 70th birthday in November 1959, amidst the first signs of tension and conflict with China.[1] But it was not until the Prime Minister's first serious illness in forty years, a kidney affliction known as pyelonephritis, in the spring of 1962, that concern about ' after Nehru ' became pointed—and justified. A thorough medical examination in London and a widely-publicized report of excellent health did not convince the cynics—or the knowing. The truth was that Nehru's illness had been serious and that, while his recovery had been swift, he had acquired a slight stoop and ' probably he will never be the same again '.[2] Thereafter, he was obliged to rest every afternoon, to follow a rigid diet, and to reduce his work schedule from 17 to 12 hours daily.

Another turning point in Nehru's twilight years was the Sino-Indian border war in October–November 1962. Many who knew him intimately testified that this deeply affected him [3]—' China's betrayal ', India's serious military reverse in NEFA (the North-East Frontier Agency) and Ladakh, Chinese occupation of 14,500 square miles of territory claimed by India, the shattering of a carefully-nurtured policy of *Panch Sheel* (the Five Principles of Peaceful Coexistence), the undermining of non-alignment and India's image in the world, and the enforced resignation of Krishna Menon from the cabinet. Menon, who recalls this period vividly, remarked: ' I think he collapsed; it demoralized him completely because everything that he had built up in his life was going.' [4] Mrs. Pandit, too, recalled the last eighteen months as a period of unrelieved sadness. Apart from declining health and vigour—his left foot was dragging, a sign of things to come—he no longer had any zest for life. When, on occasion, she tried to persuade her brother to rest, he replied, ' what for; to what end should I recover my strength? ' He was withdrawing almost totally from his surroundings during these months, rarely speaking to anyone; ' he was becoming totally alone '.[5]

There was good reason. Not only had his external policy suffered a massive jolt. India's internal problems seemed to be growing—after seventeen years of independence. The third Five-Year Plan was in difficulty; food was in short supply; foreign exchange reserves were virtually nil; communal tension had reared its head once more. And finally, the Congress, seemingly sick in body and spirit, was struck by what appeared to be a major blow.

In the spring of 1963 the Congress suffered three prestige electoral defeats, in Lok Sabha by-elections from Amroha, Farrukhabad, and Rajkot.[6] What is more, the victors were Nehru's most caustic and inveterate foes: Acharya J. B. Kripalani, now a lonely but respected Independent; Ram Mannohar Lohia, the Socialist Party leader, whose hatred of Nehru verged on the pathological; and Minoo Masani, the most articulate voice of India's right wing. All three, who had been defeated in the general elections the preceding year and who had been comrades in the nationalist movement, now returned to Parliament to pour scorn on an ageing and disillusioned Prime Minister. Reflecting the mood, Kripalani served notice of his intention to move a motion of No-Confidence when the Monsoon Session convened on 16 August, the first such formal challenge to Nehru's leadership since 1947. The result was a series of moves to cleanse the Congress—which led to the greatest reshuffle in the Union and State governments since independence.[7] The struggle for the succession was beginning to unfold, though no one realized it at the time.

It began in the middle of June with pressure from below, in the form of a petition by about 80 members of the All-India Congress Committee (AICC) for a special session to consider shortcomings in the party organization in the light of recent electoral defeats. The prime movers were Raghunath Singh, a general secretary of the Congress Parliamentary Party (CPP), and S. N. Mishra, leader of the left-wing 'Ginger Group'. At first, Congress President Sanjivayya and other party leaders resisted the pressure, but finally, on 5 July, the Working Committee yielded and called a special session of the AICC for 9 and 10 August; it was the first time this ranking policy-making organ was convened on the basis of a direct demand of its members.[8] In the interim, as if to nullify a possible rank-and-file revolt, the Working Committee authorized, and the President appointed, a seven-man committee headed by Labour Minister Nanda, to inquire into the election reverses.

Typical of the mood within the Congress and outside about the state of the Party, was a comment by the *Statesman* on 4 July: there are 'mounting signs of the organization, now big rather than great, falling apart. . . . Internal dissensions . . . now appear to have reached unprecedented proportions. . . . The Congress High Command [Working Committee] has reason to think hard before the whole set-up goes out of control.'[9] The Working Committee met again on 20 July and shifted responsibility to the Central Parliamentary Board; that body, in turn, merely issued a directive to the warring factions in Uttar Pradesh (U.P.) to desist from a head-on collision. Clearly, leadership was wanting. One newspaper was led to remark: 'The Congress High Command has reduced itself to a laughing stock . . . a group of frightened politicians unable or unwilling to come to grips with problems or policies . . .'; [10] among others, this referred to the U.P. crisis, factional quarrels in half a dozen other States, and corruption charges in Kerala and Orissa.

Behind the scenes, however, a novel and far-reaching purge was being conceived. Its official author was K. Kamaraj Nadar, Chief Minister of Madras and the foremost Congress politician in south India. The plan was simple yet revolutionary—some senior Congressmen in government were to resign their posts and take up full-time organizational work in order to revitalize the party. Kamaraj discussed the idea with Nehru in Hyderabad early in August. On the 8th the Working Committee adopted the proposal in general terms. Nehru took the lead the following day by seeking permission to resign but, as in 1954 and 1958, his colleagues proclaimed his indispensability as Head of Government.[11] They also turned down his suggestion that a small committee be created to implement the plan, insisting that he alone serve as judge and executioner. Of course, Nehru would not be acting in a vacuum—but in the context of constraints and expectations within the Congress.

The AICC dutifully endorsed its elders' recommendations on the 10th by passing the historic 'party before post' resolution embodying the Kamaraj Plan. Kamaraj revealed a little, but not much, of the background when he told the delegates that he had informed Nehru he would withdraw the proposal if Panditji insisted on resigning. And S. K. Patil, the Bombay City party leader who had seconded the resolution, echoed this sentiment by hailing Nehru as 'leader of leaders', who must 'remain there [as Prime Minister] till the country gets out of all difficulties'.[12] A few hours later, many Union Cabinet Ministers and State Chief Ministers submitted their resignations, and the Working Committee set up three committees to deal with organizational matters, corruption charges, and the collection of party funds. It was also announced that the five-man Central Parliamentary

Board would be enlarged to accommodate the resignees and that the Working Committee would meet again on the 20th.

Initial reaction was mixed. The *Statesman* led off with a savage commentary, terming 'Congressmen's resignation-wish comparable to the death-wish discerned in many morbid individuals by psycho-analysts of a particular school . . .'.[13] Within a day, however, it offered a more sober view: the plan 'has two virtues: boldness and simplicity. But whether it has others also is doubtful and in the long run it could well be dangerous'; shifting a few individuals, it added, could not solve the basic ailment, 'a flatulence resulting from lack of ideological exercise'.[14] The *Hindustan Times* suspended judgement,[15] as did the *Hindu*.[16] And the *Times of India*, in a clever editorial on 13 August, entitled 'Well Done If Well Done', remarked: 'It is too early yet to say hurrah for the Congress. . . . The Congress can renew itself as a great organization. Will it?'

Among the pundits, S. M. (Mulgaokar) entitled his weekly column, 'The Deeper Malady Where Kamaraj Will Not Help', asserting the existence of a wide gulf between the Congress and the people.[17] Krishan Bhatia was more blunt: 'No amount of political theatrics of the type now under contemplation will endear it to the people . . . [if it merely involves a shift of a few leaders in and out of power]'.[18] Subdued optimism was reflected in K. Santhanam's expression of hope that the plan 'is only the beginning of a movement of national purification of which the more important steps are yet to follow'.[19] All were agreed that Kamaraj had become 'Congress' Man of Destiny'.[20]

A game of political chairs—who should stay and who should resign—was played in deadly earnest between 11 and 23 August, particularly in the light of Nehru's remark to the Congress Parliamentary Party that important ministers would be asked to resign. Pressures of all kinds mounted day by day—geographic, ideological, caste, and factional. On the 21st, Kamaraj received an urgent summons in Madras from Nehru, a day earlier than their scheduled meeting; and he told newsmen that he had no concrete plan at that stage.

The Kamaraj Plan was activated on 24 August, when Nehru meted out the sentence before the Working Committee. First

came the Gandhian rationale: the decision, he said, 'was based
principally on making it clear that the Congress does not approve
of people being attracted by office and the power that it brings'.
Then the acknowledgement of the need to balance two considerations—strengthening the party and minimizing the harm to
government. And then the list of men who were to take the path
of renunciation, at least temporarily. The chosen were six Cabinet
Ministers at the Centre and six Chief Ministers: the Cabinet
Ministers were Morarji Desai * (Finance), Jagjivan Ram (Trans-
port and Communications), Lal Bahadur Shastri (Home), S. K.
Patil (Food and Agriculture), B. Gopala Reddy (Information and
Broadcasting), and K. L. Shrimali (Education); and the Chief
Ministers, K. Kamaraj (Madras), Biju Patnaik (Orissa), Bakshi
Ghulam Mohammed (Jammu and Kashmir), Binodanand Jha
(Bihar), C. B. Gupta (U.P.), and B. A. Mandloi (Madhya
Pradesh). Lest those who had escaped the hatchet should become
complacent, Nehru added: 'It is possible that some other sugges-
tions might have to be made by me at a somewhat later stage';
in fact, none was added.[21]

Once again press comment was mixed. The *Statesman* criticized 'the manner in which he [Nehru] had shuffled his cards.
. . . Mr. Nehru's remains an unsettling act, perpetrated in pur-
suance of principles undefined, at least unstated'; to that telling
remark it added a prescient observation about Shastri's earlier
resignation over a railway accident: 'this time the accident seems
calculated with the calculations remaining obscure'.[22] The
Hindustan Times welcomed the cabinet changes, though it called
for new blood in secondary posts,[23] while the *Hindu* offered a
gentle chiding, terming it 'an appropriate occasion more for a
re-examination of policies than for a mere reshuffle of personalities'.[24] Perhaps the bluntest comment came from the Ambala
Tribune: since the plan's purpose is to help assure victory in
the next general elections, 'where, then, is any renunciation of
love of power in anybody? The purge is preparatory to the
feast.'[25] At the other extreme was the *National Herald*, long
associated with Nehru, which paid the expected tribute: 'Altogether, it is a great day for the Congress and for the country.'[26]

* Hereafter referred to simply as 'Morarji', as he is generally called in India.

The 'Kamarajed men' were not selected by chance. Indeed, there is ample evidence that the multiple pressures which influence the making of Indian cabinets, at the Centre and in the States, operated in the reverse process of purge. Geographical equity is apparent: Morarji is from Gujarat, Jagjivan Ram from Bihar, Shastri from U.P., Patil from Maharashtra, Gopala Reddy from Andhra Pradesh, and Shrimali from Rajasthan; altogether, ten States were represented. Ideology played a major part, for Morarji and Patil were leaders of the Right, whose withdrawal tended to balance the earlier departure of Krishna Menon (1962) and K. D. Malaviya (1963). Among the others, additional specific reasons can be adduced.

Kamaraj genuinely wished to step down from government office in order to strengthen the Congress machine in the Madras countryside against the growing threat from the separatist Dravida Munnetra Kazhagam (DMK). Patnaik, too, wished to throw off the burden of daily State administration—for the larger, all-India stage; at the time he held a position of some importance in the 'Nehru Circle'. Gopala Reddy, a poor administrator and an ineffective minister, was the obvious scapegoat for Nehru's error in the Voice of America fiasco earlier that summer.[27] Shrimali's failure to make a mark in the vital sphere of education and his strong espousal of Hindi and vernacular languages had long been known—but Nehru's style had never been to dismiss colleagues.[28] Bakshi's standing in Kashmir, the Achilles' Heel of India's international image, was alarmingly low. The choice of Gupta, Jha, and Mandloi reveals the pressure of factionalism; their continued presence as Chief Ministers of the most faction-torn States in the Union was a barrier to the most formal reconciliation of competing Congress groups and a threat to Congress dominance in the Hindi hinterland. Jagjivan Ram was the ideal case for renunciation of power—he had been in the Union Cabinet since 1946. As for Shastri, it is known that his resignation was genuine; his willingness to withdraw was reported even before the Kamaraj Plan came before the Working Committee.[29] It may also be, as some surmised at the time, that his inclusion spared Nehru the possible charge of discrimination against Morarji.

The effects of the Kamaraj Plan on the succession were fundamental. The leading candidates, Morarji and Shastri, and a
lesser contestant, Jagjivan Ram, were deprived of direct power
and patronage; indeed, they were removed from that political
organ (the Cabinet) which would almost certainly furnish the
next Prime Minister; so, too, was Patil, a key figure in the ensuing struggle; all four were relegated to the party's enlarged
Central Parliamentary Board, in accordance with the stated aims
of the plan.[30] Moreover, Morarji's tactical advantage, as the
second-ranking member of the Cabinet, was eliminated; but for
the plan, he would have become Prime Minister on 27 May 1964
and would have been strategically placed in the battle of ' the six
days '; certainly there would have been a much higher probability
of his confirmation as Head of Government than was the case with
G. L. Nanda, who replaced Morarji as No. 2 in the Cabinet and
became the interim successor to Nehru for almost a fortnight.
A third consequence was to add Nanda to the group of aspirants
for Panditji's office; this was made logically possible by the
character of the Cabinet reshuffle on 29 August. Nanda moved
to the Home Ministry, with seniority after the Prime Minister;
T. T. Krishnamachari (T.T.K.), who had left the Finance
Ministry in 1958 under the cloud of the ' Mundhra Affair ',[31] now
returned to that key post as No. 3, and Sardar Swaran Singh took
over the Food and Agriculture portfolio.

Other implications of the plan were noted by some of India's
pundits. Krishan Bhatia remarked cynically that ' in all likeli-
hood [it] has only shifted the venue of the leaders' internal
struggle for supremacy from the Cabinet room to the Congress
office '.[32] Inder Malhotra correctly forecast new vigour and status
for the office of Congress President and the party High Command, than which ' nothing has been devalued in India so
drastically during the last decade . . .';[33] indeed, it signalled a
shift of power towards the Chief Ministers. Indirectly, K. Rangaswami asked ' whether the Kamaraj Plan has come as a boon to
revitalize the organization or has just blown the lid off a Pandora's Box ', revealing in an acute form the ills of factionalism,

corruption, opportunistic alliances, and the like.[34] Doubts about
a second round of resignations were expressed by 'Pragmatist'
because 'it will be some time before we have solved the problems
created by the first [one] '.[35] S. M. was more sanguine: 'What
has begun is an authentic process of catharsis which will result in
an all-round flexibility in the Congress approach. . . .'[36] But the
rawest nerve was touched by Nandan Kagal, who acknowledged
that 'there might be just a grain of truth' in the view 'that the
Prime Minister has chosen his successor' or at least that 'the
conditions . . . are being prepared '.[37] Rangaswami, too, referred
to this theme; even more important, he noted that Nehru had
vested the Working Committee with enormous authority regarding the succession—an authority which it was to assert—when he
told the AICC that if the Working Committee asked him to step
down from the Prime Ministership he would have no choice but
to comply! [38]

Most Congress leaders acclaimed the plan, though Mrs.
Gandhi, Nehru's daughter, inexplicably suspended judgement.[39]
The lone public dissent came from S. K. Patil, who declared on
two occasions that the plan was used to get rid of unwanted
ministers—though he himself had seconded the famous resolution! Later, he retracted somewhat, under pressure.[40] Even
Morarji, who suffered the most politically, termed the allegation of 'ulterior motives' 'unfortunate'.[41] A year later he
reiterated [42] that, initially, he did not think of the plan as inspired
by ill-will or dubious motives but that, on reflection—after the
battle for the succession—it seemed to him to have been motivated
not only to get rid of him but also to pave the way for Mrs.
Gandhi to the Prime Ministership; in fact, he added, Nehru was
trying to do for Indira in 1963 what his father, Motilal, had done
for him in 1929, passing on to him the highest office then open to
an Indian nationalist, the Congress presidency.

Almost exactly a year after the Kamaraj Plan, there was an
outburst of criticism, led by Morarji supporters, though he himself remained silent. Actually, it was a delayed reaction—from the
preceding AICC session in Bombay, on 16–17 May 1964, when a
non-official resolution urging the withdrawal of the plan had been
put forward but had not been discussed because of limited time.

Trikamlal J. Patel, a vocal Morarji advocate from Gujarat, had then based his case on Nehru's illness, the return of Shastri to the Cabinet, the failure to infuse the party with a new spirit of self-sacrifice, the need for a strong, firm administration, and the widespread discontent in the country.[43] The same arguments, suitably amended, were put forward at the Delhi AICC session in August 1964, backed by Man Singh, Babubhai Patel, and Ratilal Dave from Gujarat, Morarji's home State, and Banarsi Das from U.P., among others. With Nehru no longer present, the words were less restrained. The plan, said T. J. Patel, was a 'mischievous baby' with sinister motives, the real aim being to remove 'giants' (Morarji) from the government. Nehru was not spared, as the pent-up frustration of those who had lost the struggle for the succession burst forth. The Kamarajed ministers sat silently through the proceedings, as did the Congress Left, obviously enjoying the spectacle. Patil's attempted rebuttal was nullified by obvious self-interest. But Shastri, in a restrained defence of Nehru's motives—observers were shocked at how few of the late Prime Minister's colleagues responded to the vicious attack—revealed a little more about the original plan. He recalled that he himself had suggested to Nehru that Morarji need not be removed from the Cabinet—and that Nehru felt Morarji's stature would grow out of office.[44]

In the course of that debate one critic likened the twelve fallen leaders to the mythological *Navaratna* (nine jewels) churned out of the sea, and remarked: 'I would like to know where these twelve jewels are shining and what places they are adorning.' The picture was dismal indeed, apart from the 'de-Kamarajed' Union Ministers, Shastri and Patil, and Kamaraj himself. Morarji and Jagjivan Ram sat, and continue to sit, stonily in the Lok Sabha, side by side, and make public speeches, the former more actively; neither has done anything to strengthen the party machine. Nothing is heard of Gopala Reddy. And Dr. Shrimali has retreated to academe. Among the Chief Ministers, Patnaik continued to dominate Orissa politics from behind the scenes and later became the centre of a corruption storm in Parliament; Bakshi became ill and, under pressure, ultimately withdrew from Kashmiri politics; C. B. Gupta continued as faction leader in

U.P.; while Jha and Mandloi vanished into political oblivion. The Kamaraj Plan cannot be regarded as successful, in terms of its stated aims.

The plan was so significant for the succession to Nehru and beyond that one is compelled to explore some ambiguities, notably its origin and Nehru's motives. Nehru addressed himself to both of these points the day the Cabinet was re-constituted. He termed 'absurd and wrong' suggestions that the plan 'originated from me and was implemented through Mr. Kamaraj in order to remove those who were opposed to me. . . . Mr. Kamaraj had consulted me [in Hyderabad] and I had asked him to draw up a plan and put it before the AICC. It was good luck that the AICC accepted the plan with great acclamation.'[45] Kamaraj's version, a year later, is somewhat obscure. Although the plan had been named after him, he wrote, it was the Congress leadership, especially ' our great leader, Mr. Nehru ', who were largely responsible for its *evolution*.[46] There is some truth in these accounts. Nehru did not conceive the Kamaraj Plan—but neither did Kamaraj, it would appear; nor did Nehru *initially* view the plan as a hatchet—but it was so used by him, with devastating results.

The father of the idea was, almost certainly, Biju Patnaik, then Chief Minister of Orissa and a rising star on the Indian political scene—young (47), handsome, wealthy, ruthless, efficient, and ambitious. Patnaik claimed,[47] and others have confirmed, that he took the idea to Kamaraj, who was well-disposed for local reasons noted earlier. Patnaik discussed it with many persons, including Morarji and the Chief Ministers of Bengal, Bihar, and U.P., all of whom responded favourably. He then had a protracted discussion (three days) with Nehru, who was holidaying in Kashmir.[48] According to Patnaik, Nehru expressed doubt that Kamaraj was prepared to leave office, but he assured him that this was so. Nehru then met Kamaraj in Hyderabad and the plan was announced. A plausible reason for attaching it to the Madras Chief Minister is that Kamaraj commanded wider respect than Patnaik in the Congress and the country.

In its initial form, only Patnaik and Kamaraj were to leave office, according to the former; but something happened on the eve of the AICC session, on 24 August 1963, to transform it into a political hatchet. This view is confirmed by two pundits: Krishan Bhatia remarked at the time that the day before the session Nehru was thinking in terms of three or four leaders resigning, and the following day he passed a judgement affecting the political pattern of half the country.[49] And Nandan Kagal referred to 'the alarm and dismay with which Mr. Nehru's decisions have been received. . . . The boldness . . . is startling because it was unexpected.' [50]

What caused the change remains in the realm of speculation. It seems plausible, however, that Nehru, a consummate politician, suddenly realized the plan's potential, in a flash of genius. He could eliminate from the Cabinet two men, Morarji and Patil, whose ideology and personality he found distasteful. He could pave the way for another Untouchable representative to replace the otherwise immovable Jagjivan Ram. By adding Shastri to the list, he could avoid the charge of discrimination and, at the same time, nullify Morarji's advantage by virtue of seniority. More than that, he could send all potential successors to the wilderness and see which commanded the greatest support in the Congress and the country. And while he was about it, he could relieve pressures in three key States, U.P., Bihar and Madhya Pradesh, by reducing the influence of the faction in power; he could ease out Bakshi in Kashmir, for he had now become a liability; and in the Centre, he could dismiss Gopala Reddy, who had seriously embarrassed him over the Voice of America affair and, perhaps, infuse fresh blood into the Education Ministry. The plan would also bring to the fore a representative of the able and effective Chief Ministers, as well as a strong south Indian Congress leader of integrity, Kamaraj—to help cope with the delicate post-Nehru transition. In any event, this is precisely what happened. And by this complex decision Nehru had fully restored his political power, temporarily jarred by the China débâcle in the autumn of 1962. More than that, he had, in this writer's judgement, set down the rules for the 'battle of succession', to accord with his oft-expressed view—'let the People and the Party choose a successor; it is not my function'.

Soon after the Kamaraj Plan took effect the question arose in the minds of many—who would be the next Congress President, to assume office at the beginning of 1964? The massive purge, along with Nehru's declining health, had invested this post with a status and authority unknown since independence. And still concealed in the womb of time was the Prime Minister's critical illness a few months later, which would further enhance the prestige and power of the Congress President. This was the theme of the next phase of the struggle which, as one senior politician readily confirmed,[51] was really stage 2 of the Kamaraj Plan.

It began at a quiet gathering early in October 1963, in the pilgrim town of Tirupathi in Andhra Pradesh. Present were Kamaraj, Bengal's party boss, Atulya Ghosh,* the host State's Chief Minister, Sanjiva Reddy, and Nijalingappa, Chief Minister of Mysore. S. K. Patil kept in close touch by telephone. It was there, and then, that the 'Syndicate' was publicly born, a new, informal leadership bureau which was to play a vital role in the *management* of the succession to Nehru.[52] First choice of the Caucus † for party president was Shastri, but if he declined or Nehru was unreceptive—for any reason—Kamaraj would be asked to take the post; in any event, a contest was to be avoided. The real aim, however, was to keep Morarji from the presidency and thereby isolate him further from the centre of political power: the Syndicate was essentially a non-Hindi coalition—and Morarji was known for his firm and inflexible views, in particular on Hindi as the national language.[53] In more positive terms, the aim was to support the man who was least likely to divide and most likely to unite the party, so as to provide stable and effective leadership.

Atulya took the first soundings by issuing a statement to the Press, proposing Shastri as Congress President. Morarji, who keenly wanted the post, then approached Atulya and told him he would contest against Shastri—a preview of things to come—but that he would accept Atulya as President, according to the latter. It was at that time, too, that Shastri conveyed his reluctance to

---

* Referred to hereafter as 'Atulya', as he is generally known in India.
† The words Syndicate and Caucus are used interchangeably in this book.

Atulya, either because he was saving himself for an even more important position or because Nehru was keen to keep him completely mobile for any eventuality—or because Shastri wanted to avoid a contest with Morarji, at least at that stage.

The matter was complicated by the peripheral involvement of Atulya Ghosh. His Bombay City counterpart, S. K. Patil, told a Calcutta audience, in reply to a query as to why there had not been a Bengali Congress President since 1938, ' I will be very glad if a man like Mr. Ghosh became the next Congress President '; [54] Atulya was present but he remained silent because, as he related, he had already spoken while introducing Patil. The latter's ' casual remark ' seemed more pointed when he told a Bombay reception in honour of Atulya that the Bengali leader would become Congress President that year or the next, and ' the sooner the better for us . . .'.[55] Atulya replied that he was not a contestant and that the mantle should fall on one of the ' Kamarajed men '. On 7 October Atulya was reported out of the race, though he was pledged the support of both the Maharashtra and Bombay Pradesh Congress Committees (PCCs).[56]

It was doubtful that he was ever a serious candidate—although Atulya related an unknown incident to suggest the contrary: Nehru, he declared, had approached him at the Bengal Political Conference of the Congress in the spring of 1963 with a view to his becoming Congress President. He replied that he wanted time to consider because he felt that as long as Nehru was at the helm there would be no scope for him as President or as Minister—but he could not just say ' no ' to Panditji. He also acknowledged sharp differences with the Prime Minister over the years but added that ' in the last few years he was more inclined towards me '. The story seems fanciful, as far as Nehru's ' offer ' is concerned, because of Nehru's and, even more, Indira Gandhi's known distaste for Atulya's ' bossist ' methods and manner; and yet, not entirely fanciful, for Bengal Chief Minister P. C. Sen had written to Nehru suggesting Atulya for the presidency—and Nehru had replied, ' Atulya is one of our senior leaders. . . .' [57]

The selection of Kamaraj as Congress President illuminates the informal decision process at the highest level of Indian politics. As Atulya related it, and all but the nuances have been confirmed, he and Kamaraj spent most of 9 October together, just before the meeting of the Working Committee. Both asked whether the other had spoken to Nehru, in accordance with an earlier agreement that Kamaraj would first propose Shastri, Atulya would recommend Kamaraj if this were not feasible and, if necessary, Atulya would take the post: in any event, Morarji was being squeezed out; both replied in the negative. At the Working Committee, unknown to Kamaraj, Atulya, who was sitting close to Nehru, leaned over and told the Prime Minister that he did not want the post and asked whether Kamaraj was acceptable; Nehru replied in the affirmative. Then, just as the meeting was coming to a close, Atulya asked the Congress President to request the group to stay on for a few minutes because he wished to propose, informally, a name for the next Congress President. When he mentioned Kamaraj, the latter intervened; Atulya cut him short by saying, ' we are discussing you, have the decency to be quiet'. The proposal was approved. After the meeting Kamaraj reprimanded Atulya for not clearing it with Nehru, but Atulya assured him that this had been done—at the meeting.[58]   It is probably correct, as Sanjiva Reddy intimated,[59] that Nehru's real choice was Kamaraj—to see through the party reorganization flowing from the Kamaraj Plan. The Caucus arranged the selection, not only the initial Tirupathi decision and Atulya's move at the Working Committee, but also the fact that his proposal was backed in the Committee by Reddy, Patil, and Shastri. However, most parties have strong elements of hierarchy and authority wielded by a few; the test is how responsive and how responsible they are.

The question of whether the Syndicate was really indicating its candidate for Nehru's successor at Tirupathi is still open. Kamaraj denied this,[60] as did Reddy, though the latter implied that Shastri was their choice at that date; they did not declare it publicly so as not to offend Nehru, who was very sensitive on this issue. Certainly in the light of subsequent developments, Tirupathi and the selection of Congress President for 1964, including Shastri's decision to remain aloof, set the stage for the drama of succession eight months later. Both Morarji and Patnaik concurred.[61] The former, with only thinly-concealed bitterness, cited it as further evidence of his interpretation of the Kamaraj Plan; if it was really intended to use party leaders for organization work, then he, as the senior person, should have been made Congress President. Morarji added that Shastri declined ' because he knew I would contest and because he knew I would win '. The Orissa leader was even more blunt: the purpose of Tirupathi and its sequel was to plan the succession and, more specifically, to deny Morarji the prize.

The unanimous election of Kamaraj as Congress President was announced on 20 November, a few weeks after the AICC met in regular session at Jaipur. Most welcomed the choice. But there was one intriguing incident of dissent which shed further light on decision-making in Congress politics. S. N. Mishra protested at Jaipur against the *decision* of the Working Committee in favour of Kamaraj, arguing that this should not have taken place before the formal election. The then-President, Sanjivayya, replied that it was wrong to say the High Command had reached a decision: the matter had come up informally and unexpectedly, and the ' consensus ' was that Kamaraj would be the most suitable person; the 'consensus of opinion' in the Working Committee was not binding on the party, however.[62] In the tense atmosphere of the six days leading to the succession, the relationship of Working Committee to party, indeed to Government, was to be a major point of controversy, while ' consensus ' was formally elevated to the status of First Principle of Congress politics. The Congress after Nehru was particularly vulnerable and therefore particularly susceptible to this natural striving for consensus.

The Jaipur Session was preoccupied with a periodic ideological tussle over the degree of socialism to be embodied in the Party Programme. As frequently in the past, the Left scored a marginal verbal victory, but this was to be nullified two months later at Bhubaneswar.[63] The Kamaraj Plan was debated again, but no further lines of action were indicated. There was, however, one little-noted resolution calling on Prime Minister and Congress President to consult frequently, a symptom of the shift towards a more federal type of party and a sanction for an emergent pattern in the post-Nehru transition.[64]

By chance, this writer was interviewing the Prime Minister some days before the annual Congress Session. In reply to a question, he remarked, ' nothing important is going to happen at Bhubaneswar '. But on the opening day, 8 January 1964, Nehru suffered a serious stroke affecting his left side; all India held its breath, and the pace quickened in the struggle for the succession. It was during that last discussion, too, that India's leader revealed the most poignant expression of the change in his hitherto buoyant outlook and, perhaps, an instinctive knowledge that the end was not far off. Referring to my next visit, he said, in a slow, measured tone, ' August is a long time away '; and so it was.[65]

Nehru's illness at Bhubaneswar marks the opening of the third and last stage of the background to the drama of succession. The immediate effect was the emergence of an *ad hoc* duumvirate in the Union Cabinet for a fortnight. Around the bedside of the stricken Panditji, Home Minister Nanda and Finance Minister Krishnamachari attended to some matters normally handled by the Prime Minister; some who were present reported that even this ' transfer ' was not without tension. On the 11th, Nanda presided over a meeting of the Emergency Committee of the Cabinet—which both convened in Delhi. The two confirmed that they had been asked jointly to look after the Prime Minister's responsibilities during his illness—Nanda, those papers that went to Nehru as Prime Minister, and T. T. K. (Krishnamachari), those that went to him as External Affairs Minister; they would consult Nehru only when absolutely essential and would act jointly on all important matters; there would be frequent meetings of the Emergency Committee, consisting of the duumvirs, Defence Minister Chavan, and Food Minister Swaran Singh; Nanda, as senior Minister, was to chair meetings of the Cabinet and National Development Council.[66]

Delhi and all India—and much of the political world—now became obsessed with the question, ' after Nehru, who? '. An arch-enemy, Dr. Lohia, called for his resignation ' in the national interest, as well as the personal interest of the Prime Minister '.[67] The *Statesman* gently expressed the hope that, during his convalescence, he would give ' prolonged and earnest consideration ' to the task of lightening his burden.[68] One senior pundit echoed this sentiment in a concrete form : Mulgaokar urged Nehru to hand over the responsibility of co-ordination to Shastri, adding that he could avoid the impression of wanting to name him his successor by appointing him Minister without Portfolio rather than Deputy Prime Minister—which is exactly what Nehru did six days later.[69] Another pundit, Prem Bhatia, took the occasion to think aloud about ' Mr. Nehru's Illness and an If ' : if Nehru's illness had led to his withdrawal in August 1963, the Kamaraj Plan would not have been launched; hence, the Nanda–T. T. K. duumvirate would have been Morarji-Shastri, and Morarji would have been much closer to an acting Head of Government than Nanda; further, Jagjivan Ram and Patil would have been in the picture, and a process of polarization would have begun around Morarji and Shastri. Today, all four senior men are out of the Cabinet—in a time of crisis.[70]

There was much talk in the early days of Nehru's illness about Shastri's return to the Cabinet and Mrs. Gandhi's appointment as External Affairs Minister.[71] No moves were made to reduce Panditji's burden, however, until Kamaraj returned to Delhi from the South. Two days later there came a cryptic announcement that Shastri had become Minister without Portfolio—and Sanjivayya, an Untouchable, Minister for Labour and Employment.[72] Even then, Shastri's duties remained unspecified, until a vaguely-worded Presidential Order was issued—eleven days later : ' Shri Shastri will perform such functions in relation to the business of the Ministry of External Affairs, the Department of Atomic Energy and the Cabinet Secretariat as may be assigned to him by the Prime Minister from time to time '; [73] in short, he was to be Assistant *to* the Prime Minister; great care was taken not to elevate his status—he was ranked No. 4 in the Cabinet.

The decision to bring Shastri back to the Cabinet was a turning point on the road to succession. What pressures were at work? Prem Bhatia, who was exceedingly well-informed, wrote that the move ' was initiated long before Mr. Nehru was taken ill . . . [but] gathered strength in the past few days '; further, that Nehru's initial reaction was negative—it was too early to undo the Kamaraj Plan, and many would view it as an act of discrimination. Bhatia correctly anticipated that Nehru would await pressure in favour of Shastri's return and that Shastri would be even more important than in the past.[74]   On the question of timing, Atulya related that Nehru asked his opinion about making Shastri Deputy Prime Minister two months before Bhubaneswar, i.e., in November 1963; moreover, that Nehru sounded Nanda out, and the Home Minister was 'mum and glum', which is probably why Nehru never did so.   It was widely known that Nanda was not pleased about the appointment.

Closer to the mark, both on time and source of pressure, is Sanjiva Reddy's disclosure that the Caucus became profoundly concerned immediately after Nehru's stroke.   Soon after they put Nehru on the plane to Delhi, he, Kamaraj, and Shastri went to Madras; it was during that trip that they decided upon Shastri's return to the Cabinet.   Shastri saw President Radhakrishnan upon his return to Delhi on 14 January.   And many have confirmed that the President strongly supported the move; Nehru undoubtedly received this impression when he discussed it with the President on 21 January.   There was also the vital conversation between Nehru and Kamaraj on the 20th.   In recalling this episode, the Congress President related that it was Nehru who took the initiative, i.e., in saying he was thinking of bringing Shastri back, and he asked Kamaraj's view.   In any event, Kamaraj, out of respect, would allow the Prime Minister to convey his thoughts first.   What is certain is that Kamaraj approved fully.   Within the Cabinet, T. T. K. was perhaps the most vocal in support.   Thus, this crucial decision was a composite though not collective one, involving the Caucus through Kamaraj, the President, T. T. K., Nehru himself, and the passive approval of Mrs. Gandhi.   Countervailing pressure was exerted, within the Cabinet by Nanda and possibly others, and outside by the leaders of the Left, along with two of the principal 'Kamarajed men', Jagjivan Ram and Morarji.

The duumvirate of 8–22 January now became an uneasy triumvirate of Nanda, T. T. K., and Shastri, with an ill-defined division of responsibility under a dying charismatic leader.   A half-step away was Kamaraj, now frequently consulted and

informed—and behind him the still-shadowy but powerful
Caucus. One observer wrote: 'For the first time since independence, effective power . . . is being shared between the Head of
the Government and the Head of the Congress. The era of a
unifocal centre of power in New Delhi is coming to an end.' As
for the Cabinet, 'relations among the triumvirate are friendly,
but not entirely free from strain. . . . [There is] a fair amount
of give-and-take and consultation with one another . . . in twos.
. . . But the kind of arrangement he [Nehru] has made hardly
makes for the harmonious functioning of a team. . . . [And yet
it] is far better than has existed within the inner Cabinet
[Emergency Committee] during the last few years.'[75] So it
continued for the last four months of the Nehru era.

Apart from the triumvirs, a special role was played by Nehru's
daughter, Mrs. Gandhi. To some, she was the Mrs. (Woodrow)
Wilson of the Indian Government during that period. The
Prime Minister's schedule, his appointments, the papers to be
shown him—all came under her scrutiny and control. And,
while she may not have played a substantive role, with influence
on basic governmental decisions, she was an important element
in the power structure, by virtue of her unique access to the
Prime Minister, still the seat of ultimate decision.

The significance of Shastri's return to the Cabinet was not lost
on commentators, foreign and Indian. *The Times* (London)
wrote on the day of his appointment: 'The most likely candidate
[for the succession] is Mr. Lal Bahadur Shastri and another is
Mr. Gulzarilal Nanda. Both are undramatic personalities.'[76]
The Guardian welcomed Shastri's return 'for two reasons: first,
that the problem of the succession is at last being tackled, and
secondly, that Mr. Shastri is the man in view'.[77] The Washington press echoed the view that this was the first indication of
Nehru's choice of a political heir.[78]

Within India, the pundits concurred. Nandan Kagal
remarked that Bhubaneswar really solved the question, 'after
Nehru, who?'; by bringing Shastri back, Nehru was merely
responding to the Party's wishes. He did not blame Nehru for
the absence of a clearly-designated successor, though he acknowledged that it would have been better had one 'emerged'. In

that connection, he recalled that the logical candidate in the early 1950s had been Jaya Prakash Narayan—until he declined Nehru's invitation to join the Cabinet in 1953. He concluded with a plea to the Prime Minister to make ' clear provision for the unforeseeable future '.[79] Prem Bhatia wrote at the end of January: ' The succession issue is now commonly regarded as more or less settled . . .', but Shastri, shrewdly or modestly, does not assert it. ' Silent or aloud, his acceptance has all the marks of a *fait accompli* '—India was ' now entering the first phase of collective leadership'. Nehru did not name a Deputy Prime Minister, he added, because the succession had to sort itself out in a natural process of selection. In the crucial interim, the triumvirs would head the pyramid of decision-making at the Centre. Of the other two levels, the Cabinet had already ceased to be a body for important decisions; and even the Emergency Committee was not always involved; as for the Foreign Affairs Committee, it had virtually ceased to function.[80] The first biographer of Shastri [81] was also certain of the outcome: the Kamaraj Plan had ousted the Right, placed the Centre in complete control of the Cabinet, and had ' guaranteed the *gaddi* [crown] for Mr. Shastri. . . .' And the manner of Shastri's return marked him out as ' Mr. Nehru's chosen heir and successor. . . . [He] is being groomed for the Prime Ministership.' [82] Indeed, most careful observers of the Indian political scene marked Shastri out as the near-certain successor in January–February 1964. And yet the outcome, both in terms of person and stability, remained sufficiently in doubt to cause concern in India and abroad.

The last months were sad for Nehru and for India—a pall of gloom and an atmosphere of death hung over Delhi. Malhotra reported in mid-February that ' indecisiveness and drift . . . are more pronounced than ever. . . . The root cause . . . is the not-so-latent war of succession. . . .' Supporters of various candidates are magnifying the conflict and accentuating the tension. The ' rudderlessness of the Government ' is revealed by its ineptitude in Parliament.[83] A month later, he wrote that everyone in Delhi is ' appalled by the crippling malaise of inaction and inertia which has overtaken the Government and the leadership', the root cause being Nehru's ill-health. 'The shadow of the succession battle over Delhi grows continuously longer and darker.' Like others less well-disposed, he now advocated the Prime Minister's resignation while he was still able to preside over a smooth succession.[84]

In Parliament and the Press the voices of dissent became more audible. A. D. Mani, an Independent M.P. in the Rajya Sabha, reflected the feeling of many when he urged the appointment of a Deputy Prime Minister; the Jan Sangh leader Vajpayee concurred. Swatantra leader N. G. Ranga called for a full-time Minister of External Affairs.[85] The *Indian Express* echoed both themes,[86] while the *Amrita Bazar Patrika* (Calcutta) stressed the need for a minister who could speak authoritatively on behalf of the Prime Minister.[87] Rumours were everywhere and the Prime Minister's Secretariat felt it necessary to deny reports in the foreign press that Nehru had resigned.[88]

Panditji remained silent throughout the storm until 30 March 1964 when, an aged and weary figure, he spoke his mind before the Lok Sabha: 'The question [of appointing a Deputy Prime Minister] had not arisen before me yet.' Further—how pathetic it must have been to hear these words from the man of daemonic energy—'I think that I have recovered a great deal but am not yet fully fit.' Then came the measured compliment to Shastri: he referred to the 'heavy duties' of a Prime Minister, 'many of which are being discharged very efficiently' by his Minister without Portfolio; he was 'most grateful' for the 'useful functions' being performed, and 'we are working very well together'.[89]

Here was Nehru's final verdict on the vexed issue of a Deputy Head of Government and, indirectly, a successor:[90] he seemed determined to allow the selection process to take a natural course, confident in the maturity of India's political system and its ability to absorb his passing from the scene; in any event, his faith in democracy permitted no other way. There was also a shrewd, tactical appreciation of the danger inherent in designating a successor. 'If I nominated somebody', he remarked in April, 'that is the surest way of his not becoming Prime Minister. People would be jealous of him, dislike him.' In the same discussion, he said that it was unlikely Mrs. Gandhi would succeed him and that he was 'certainly not grooming her for anything'.[91] These words suggest that, at the least, Nehru's persistent refusal to appoint Shastri Deputy Prime Minister was partly due to his conviction that it would be the 'kiss of death'; they do not prove conclusively that Shastri was his chosen successor.

The Minister without Portfolio played an active, though quiet, role on many fronts, foreign and domestic, during this period of suspense. Immediately after returning to the Cabinet, he became involved in a periodically explosive situation concerning East Pakistan. He paid a visit to Kashmir at the end of January to supervise the solution of the holy relic ('Prophet's Hair') incident; and again in February, to reconcile the factions in the National Conference; in both tasks he was successful. And it was not lost on many that Home Minister Nanda was the logical emissary to Srinagar. Shastri made a major speech on international affairs in Parliament in February—and counselled against undue haste in the integration of Kashmir into India, advice that he himself ignored once in power.[92] He was outspokenly critical of Chou En-lai and China's policy towards India. He denied any discussion with American officials regarding the partition of Kashmir, warned the recently released Sheikh Abdullah not to preach secession, and ruled out an exchange of population with East Pakistan. Yet he stoutly defended Abdullah's release—in fact, he was instrumental in bringing it about—and supported the Kashmiri leader's proposed visit to Rawalpindi in May. He did not make an impression of vigour or decisiveness, perhaps because of his style—quiet understatement—or the continued presence of Nehru, or both.

Despite his modesty and humility, and his retiring public image, perhaps because of them, Shastri was unquestionably 'the people's choice' a few months before Nehru's death. Partial evidence was to be found in a public opinion survey on 'After Nehru, Who?' conducted in February and March 1964: Shastri's primacy was clearly established. Four closely-related questions were put to 2,010 persons (1,014 urban and 996 rural) in almost all States of the Union—by no means a representative sample because 80 per cent. of India's population lives in the countryside; the results, therefore, provided only an approximation.

First—'Have you heard or read of the recent illness of the Prime Minister?': the total in the affirmative was 74·4 per cent., comprising 91·1 per cent. of the urban respondents and 70·2 per cent. from the rural areas. Second—'Do you think that the Prime Minister's illness is such that he should immediately appoint a Deputy to assist him in his duties?': the total affirmative vote was 49·9 per cent., consisting of 62·6 urban and 46·6 rural replies. Third—'Do you think the person selected should be the one who is most likely to succeed Nehru as India's next Prime Minister?': 37·2 per cent. answered 'yes', 6·3 per cent. 'no' and 14·3 per cent. said it was not necessary; the remaining 42·2 per cent. gave a 'don't know' answer. Fourth, and most revealing—'Among the following, who do you think is best qualified to fill the role of the present deputy and the future Prime Minister?': the all-India breakdown was as follows:

	per cent.		per cent.
T. T. K.	4·9	Morarji	3·5
Nanda	4·0	Mrs. Gandhi	5·9
Shastri	26·9	Other	1·7
Kamaraj	7·8	Don't Know	44·3
Patil	1·0		

Shastri was the choice of 34·6 per cent. of the urban and 25 per cent. of the rural respondents who indicated a specific person. He ranked first in all States except Gujarat (Morarji's home State). And in the Hindi hinterland he had a towering plurality—Bihar 41·5 per cent., Madhya Pradesh 41·0 per cent., and U.P. 37·7 per cent.[93]

The results of this poll became widely known to India's political élite and attentive public through publication in the *Statesman* seventeen days before Nehru's death. It probably did not influence the final act in the struggle for the succession, though it strengthened the image of Shastri as the popular choice. And it may explain the victor's unruffled confidence during 'the six days' and later. Ten months after the contest, Nehru's successor declared,[94] without his usual modesty, that he never had any doubt about the outcome.

Nehru's last political appearance was at the AICC session in Bombay on 16–17 May. According to Mrs. Pandit, with whom he stayed during those two days—she was then Governor of Maharashtra—his health seemed markedly improved; his appetite had returned, and even a renewed zest for life.[95] Others have testified in a similar vein, including Professor P. C. Mahalonobis, his long-time economic adviser and member of the Planning Commission,[96] and Sheikh Abdullah, intimate friend and later celebrated political foe; the 'Lion of Kashmir' had held lengthy discussions with Panditji during recent weeks and recalled Nehru's mental alertness.[97]

The main topic at Bombay was Kashmir, and the Prime Minister gave some indication, at last, of a willingness to take the initiative in breaking the paralysing impasse. To the consternation of the nationalist Left, led by Krishna Menon, and the nationalist Right, led by Morarji, he warmly endorsed Abdullah's impending visit to President Ayub Khan of Pakistan.[98] Indeed, there were many who then felt, and some who still do, in Pakistan as well as India, that, but for Nehru's untimely death ten days later, an honourable solution would have been reached in 1964. By a tragic coincidence, news of a forthcoming meeting between Nehru and Ayub was announced in banner headlines in the Press of both countries on 27 May—the day Nehru died.

Nehru returned to Delhi on the 17th. The following evening, while strolling through the Moghul Gardens with President Radhakrishnan, he suddenly felt unwell, weak in the left limbs, as in January. The President feared another stroke. Doctors were summoned at once. They found no vital damage, rather, exhaustion, as a result of his visit to Bombay; their prescription was rest. Panditji yielded to the extent of postponing a press conference, which had been fixed for the 20th, to 9.30 on the morning of 22 May; the next day he went to Dehra Dun for a brief holiday.

The last meeting with the Press—his first since illness struck in January—was sad in two respects, in the recollection of those who attended: never had the time lag been so long between the end of a question and the beginning of an answer; and never had the breaks of silence during a reply been so frequent. He arrived ten minutes late but walked up to the dais unaided by attendants. He looked up at the clock on the wall, apologized, and slowly asked for questions. The highlight was an exchange with B. B. Saxena, who asked: ' Will it not be in the interest of good government and stability of the country that you solve this problem of succession in your lifetime? . . .' ' That is a leading question', replied the Prime Minister. ' It is on everybody's lips ', came the retort. ' They may be talking like that ', Nehru answered. And then, after a long pause, the now memorable words, ' my lifetime is not ending so very soon '. There was a hush among the usual cynical and hardened press corps, followed by a burst of applause.⁹⁹ Five days later Nehru was dead.

III

DRAMA

ONE of India's leading civil servants had occasion to see the Prime Minister shortly before he went to Dehra Dun: they were preparing for an unprecedented session of Parliament—beginning on 27 May—to enact an amendment to the Constitution. 'I had never found him more alert mentally, and more fatigued', recalled L. P. Singh. At his suggestion, the pending decision was put off for a few days.[1]

Published accounts of the last visit to Dehra Dun, a favourite resort, are scanty. Sri Prakasa, a childhood friend who later served as Governor of Madras and Bombay, related that he whiled away the hours with old friends and played with children, always his first love.[2] He returned to Delhi by helicopter on the evening of the 26th. Among those who met him at Palam Airport was Shastri, who learned that he was to accompany Panditji to the Commonwealth Prime Ministers' Conference in June. A month earlier, in reply to a question, Nehru had told the Upper House of Parliament: 'I do not think, as far as I know at present, I shall take any Minister with me';[3] now, Shastri was told to take some clothes suitable for London's summer weather.

After dinner, as was his habit, Nehru retired to his study, to dictate correspondence and notes on official papers which had accumulated in his absence. He was thus engaged at 9.30 p.m., when T. T. K. telephoned the Residence to inquire how the Prime Minister was feeling and what he was doing. As so often, especially in the last months, the Finance Minister had set out for 'Teen Murti'[4] but, at the last moment, he decided to telephone first; when asked whether he would be coming to see Panditji, he replied, to his lasting regret, that he would be along in the morning.[5]

Accounts of Nehru's last night vary in nuance but not in essence. He went to sleep around 11 p.m., with only a male attendant near by—at his insistence, doctors and nurses, who had kept a vigil around the clock at the height of his illness, had been withdrawn some time ago. He awoke around 2 a.m. in a restless state and was given a sedative. At 4 o'clock he awoke again, in greater pain, which was alleviated by further drugs. Then, at 6 in the morning, he complained of pain in the lower back and abdomen, and weakly added that he could not get off the bed. At last the doctors were summoned. They arrived at 6.45 to discover at once what some had feared—a ruptured aorta, which is invariably fatal. Mrs. Gandhi, present at the bedside of her stricken father, was told that it was a matter of hours. Senior members of the Cabinet, notably Nanda, T. T. K., and Shastri, were called to the Residence between 8 and 9 and told the grave news; in disbelief, they pressed the doctors for a word of hope, but in vain; the end was near.[6]

While Nehru lay dying—he was conscious for a fleeting moment when the doctors arrived and asked, 'what is the matter?', then slipped into a coma from which he never emerged —members of the Executive of the Congress Parliamentary Party were slowly making their way to Room 9 of Parliament House for the customary pre-session conclave. Nehru was expected to attend, as usual; he had told General Secretary Raghunath Singh the day before he went to Dehra Dun that he would be present and had approved the agenda. The meeting was fixed for 10 a.m. An hour earlier, Singh was told by Nanda at the Residence that Nehru was ill and would not be able to attend; it was decided to proceed with the meeting in his absence. At 10, Singh heard that Nehru was bleeding badly but did not tell his colleagues on the Executive, fearing they might become alarmed; the Minister for Parliamentary Affairs, Satya Narayan Sinha, confirmed the news. The meeting disbanded at 10.55.[7]

When Parliament convened at 11 o'clock, Nanda, in the Lok Sabha, and T. T. K., in the Rajya Sabha, rose to make public for the first time the gravity of Nehru's condition. The chambers emptied quickly, many to the lobbies or the Central Hall to ponder the uncertain future, some to the Residence to await further developments. Yet the House remained in session and, at 12, after the Question Period, debate began on the proposed 17th Constitution (Amendment) Bill concerning land holdings; there was little interest in the proceedings.

The official time of Nehru's death was 1.44 p.m., Indian

Standard Time. Members of Parliament, gathered in the Central Hall, were quietly told fifteen minutes later. The world was informed by All-India Radio on its regular news broadcast at 2 p.m. And at 2.19 Steel Minister Subramaniam returned to announce the Prime Minister's death before a stunned and sobbing House. Congress M.P.s, nearly 300 of them, proceeded to the Central Hall where Raghunath Singh told them: 'Panditji is dead, but we must not be perturbed. We should be aware of our duty and decide our course of action'—perhaps the first expression of the CPP's determination not to be ignored in the crucial decision soon to be made—though not consciously intended as such. 'For the moment,' Singh concluded, 'we should all go to the Prime Minister's house.' And they did so, proceeding on foot to the Residence, despite the intense heat of a Delhi summer day. It was now shortly after 3 o'clock. Within an hour, on the spacious lawns and in the house, talk of succession had begun, some desultory, some more serious. Many objected to this distasteful and indecent act of disrespect to India's leader. But human frailty, a long-suppressed and morbid concern about 'after Nehru, who?', and the personal stakes involved were quick to assert themselves.

In the meantime a crucial decision had been taken, unknown to the parliamentarians and the people, and to the world at large. At first informally, among the triumvirs, and then in the Emergency Committee of the Cabinet, convened at the Residence between 2 and 3 p.m., it was decided to recommend to the President that Nanda be appointed Prime Minister; Shastri took the initiative in this proposal. As Nanda later recalled, 'some of my colleagues met informally and decided that I should assume responsibility; then the decision was formally taken by the Emergency Committee; we all signed the recommendation'.[8]

There were some who criticized this procedure, as they were to deprecate the decisive role of the Working Committee four days later. Krishna Menon, a keen student of constitutional law, declared bluntly: 'It was unconstitutional. That is the worst thing that could have been done. Even for the President, theoretically, to exercise his extraordinary [emergency] powers would have been more constitutional, in my opinion. Or they should have called an emergency meeting of the [Parliamentary] Party or the Party Executive and there would have been no objection.'

Yet the choice of Nanda was logical and inescapable. As the President later related, he called in the Home Minister, the senior member of the Cabinet, at 4 o'clock and told him he would swear him in as acting Prime Minister—on one proviso, that he go back to his colleagues and have the Party elect a new Leader, who would then be installed as Prime Minister. Nanda agreed. Dr. Radhakrishnan recalled an Indian precedent, in this connection. He happened to be in Calcutta when Bengal's Chief Minister, Dr. B. C. Roy, died. The Governor, Miss Padmaja Naidu, sought his advice. ' Just swear in the senior-most member of the Cabinet ', he said, ' and ask the Congress Legislative Party to elect a new Leader.' ' That is what I did in Delhi.' And it is clear that the President arrived at this decision independently of the Emergency Committee's identical recommendation.[10] Thus ended the first formal act in the universal quest for an orderly succession.

While continuity in Government was thus being arranged, all eyes were riveted on ' Teen Murti '. Throughout the early hours of the afternoon a stream of visitors came to pay their last respects—Ministers, parliamentarians, politicians, and diplomats. Nehru's body remained in the upstairs bedroom, with Mrs. Gandhi, dressed in a pure white *sari*, seated on the floor beside her father, deep in grief. Outside, the multitudes of Delhi were gathering for a last *darshan* (visual communion) of Panditji. And downstairs, in the Residence and on the lawns, there were knots of people in conversation and commiseration. Nanda seemed overwhelmed by events. Shastri was quietly attending to sundry details. When a colleague approached to assure him that he was the choice of the country, he was reported to have said, ' yes, I know, but now it is for Nandaji to take over '—a comment which reveals much about his confident aloofness throughout the six days, the prevailing wind of opinion, and his initiative in the Emergency Committee. Yet an unseemly incident was brewing.

Morarji Desai had arrived at the Residence with his son around 2.30 and began to assert his administrative, some say

authoritarian, bent. 'Have you called the police?' he asked.
'Has the Army been informed?' They had indeed, long before
Nehru's death. As soon as the doctors had indicated the gravity
of his illness, senior civil servants had set in motion measures for
the funeral—the selection of a cremation ground, as close as
possible to Gandhi's *samadhi* (memorial ground) at Rajghat, the
movement of troops and police to line the route, etc. Nonetheless, Morarji made his presence felt. He ordered the construction
of an elevated wooden platform, on which the body was to rest.
When, after 5 o'clock, this had not yet been prepared, he told
Nanda to inform the restless crowd that there would be a delay
in the file-past; Nanda did so. He then issued instructions as to
where the platform should be placed. Dr. Sushila Nayar, the
Minister of Health, intervened to say that no one would be able
to see the body if it were done in that fashion—to which Morarji
replied, 'a decision has been taken, and so it will be'. Dr. Nayar
then retorted, 'who are you to give orders?', at which point
various people clustered around. The result was confusion.
Members of the family were distressed. There was a curious
ending to this tasteless bickering: the position in which the body
was ultimately placed was decided by the Secretary of the Press
Club, Raizada; he shifted the platform, asked one person to lie
down and others to go outside to see whether or not people could
see the body, and then sought, and received, T. T. K.'s approval.
The Army took over and organized the march-past, which
started around half-past seven. All through this incident Shastri
maintained a dignified aloofness.[11]

By that time people had gathered in their tens of thousands,
lined up a mile long. All through the night they came, to gaze
at their beloved Panditji, a man who was nourished by their
reverence and affection, who for seventeen years had led them
and taught them, cajoled and persuaded them, and had tried
desperately to take them into the modern age. It was not without
incident for, in the long wait, some had tried to climb the gates
and others had been trampled; but order was quickly restored.
There were various reactions among observers of the spectacle,
then and the next day, at the gigantic funeral. Some, notably
foreigners, were distressed by the appearance of light-heartedness,

even laughter, among persons in the crowd. Other people were visibly moved. Yet solemnity and order seemed lacking. There was the inevitable comparison with Gandhi's death sixteen years earlier. But Indians had been prepared for Nehru's passing—by the illness in January—and Gandhi had been struck down by one of his own countrymen, as Kennedy had been. And in the Hindu tradition, when death comes naturally to an old man who has lived a full and rewarding life, it is not an occasion for remorse. But with all that, people grieved, some quietly, some less so, all over India. Those who observed the faces of unknown Indians in the bazaars and streets of a myriad of towns and villages across the land reported a nation in gloom on the afternoon and evening of 27 May. All India mourned its charismatic leader.

Most of the principal actors in the succession drama were present in Delhi the day Nehru died: the President, the triumvirs —Nanda, T. T. K., and Shastri—Mrs. Gandhi, the other contestants—Morarji and Jagjivan Ram—some members of the Working Committee and some Cabinet Ministers; but not all. Kamaraj was in Madras when the news of Nehru's fatal illness reached the South. Atulya Ghosh was pausing at Bangalore airport, en route from Ootacumund to Madras, when Nijalingappa brought him the news and requested that Atulya telephone him from Delhi; when he reached Madras, the Congress President was at the airport; they raced to Delhi by Caravelle; ten minutes after they were airborne the news of Nehru's death came over the radio. They arrived at 4.40 p.m., shortly after Nanda had been sworn in as Prime Minister. On the ride from Palam to the Residence not a single word was exchanged. Atulya stayed in Nehru's bedroom half an hour and then went home.

A third member of the Caucus, S. K. Patil, was in London, on his way to the United States; he hurried home and reached Delhi on the morning of the 28th. So did Muslim leader Humayun Kabir, who was in Moscow negotiating an oil exploration agreement. Syndicate member Sanjiva Reddy, too, was away—in his village in Andhra, 200 miles from Kurnool. As he later recalled, he had no transport except a bullock cart! Fortunately, an officer appeared and drove him to Kurnool; when he entered the town, flags were already at half-mast.

He reached Delhi at about midnight and went briefly to the Residence.

The most remote was Defence Minister Chavan, then on a tour of the U.S. Air Force Academy in Colorado. He described the scene poignantly. It was midnight on 26 May; he was asleep at the Colorado Springs Hotel when the telephone rang; at first he thought it was a wrong number—'who would want to ring me at that hour there'—and he did not pick up the receiver; but it persisted, and he finally answered; the news came as a thunderbolt, from Philipps Talbot [12] in Washington. When asked his wish, he replied that he would like to return to India as soon as possible. Within an hour he was airborne, to join U.S. Secretary of State Dean Rusk's special flight to Delhi. They flew almost non-stop and arrived in mid-afternoon on the 28th, just in time to reach the cremation ground when the final ceremony was about to begin; but the crowds were so thick that they had to be taken from Palam by helicopter.[13] Less dramatically, they came from all over India, Chief Ministers and Presidents of the PCCs, Congress legislators in the States, and lesser party functionaries, some to witness the end of an era, others to be present at—and to influence—the beginning of a new one. By the night of the 27th the descent on Delhi was virtually complete.

Earlier that evening there were two broadcasts to the nation. President Radhakrishnan paid a moving tribute to Nehru, hailing him as one of the greatest figures of his generation, statesman, fighter for freedom, maker of modern India, 'a great emancipator of the human race'.[14] The new Prime Minister, Nanda, was less eloquent but more sentimental. More important, he provided clear evidence that he recognized his appointment as *de facto* Acting Prime Minister, though no such designation exists in the Constitution of India. 'I have been called upon by the President', he said, 'to step into the breach and undertake the duties of the Prime Minister until the Congress Party in Parliament elects a leader and the President invites him to form the Government.'[15] When Nanda was sworn in, all members of the Nehru Cabinet were asked to stay on. On the constitutional point of his designation, Krishna Menon again dissented: 'It would have been a better arrangement simply to call him "pro tem" or something of that kind; but somebody invented the constitutional theory, which is, in my own opinion, quite wrong, that there was an obligation to have a Prime Minister permanently.'

Kamaraj recounted that, to his knowledge and recollection, there were no *serious* discussions about the succession that day, in the Residence or elsewhere.[16] There was, however, much coming and going that evening. The Congress President talked with Nanda and Shastri—but not with Morarji—the dominant theme being, 'whatever we do must be done with unity and dignity'; this, indeed, was his motto throughout the 'six days'. There was also a quiet conversation between Morarji and a number of M.P.s, who invoked the Parliamentary Party's rights in the selection of its Leader. In that connection Atulya recalled that, at 10 in the evening, a few friends came to his house, reporting that canvassing for Morarji had already begun and asking him to put a stop to it. He related this to Kamaraj at 11.30; the Congress President agreed emphatically that the matter should not even be discussed until after the funeral. Chief Minister Naik of Maharashtra arrived an hour later and concurred. But nothing was done.

The most poignant eye-witness account of this instance of human frailty comes from Krishna Menon:

The moment his last breath was drawn, the issue arose. None of these people who professed loyalty to him, who come from his State, in whose interests he has sometimes disregarded people like me just to keep the peace, none of them . . . had the decency to keep their mouths shut until he was cremated. Around his body . . . were these people, sitting around discussing this matter, not discussing seriously —I am using the word 'discussing' as a euphemism.

In short, before the first day was over the contest was on.

The second day of the drama, Thursday 28 May, was devoted almost entirely to the funeral of Jawaharlal Nehru. That spectacle has been reported in such graphic detail in the Indian and world press that it need not be recounted at length here, especially since it did not influence the developing struggle—except to suspend activity for about twelve hours. There had, in fact, been

some talk about delaying the funeral a few days in order to
accommodate dignitaries from far-off lands who wished to
attend. Mrs. Gandhi talked with Morarji and K. D. Malaviya
about the arrangements soon after Nehru's death; their advice,
which she accepted, was to proceed within 24 hours because delay
might be taken amiss in predominantly Hindu India, with the
attendant danger of decomposition.[17] The original decision, as
announced in the press, was to have the cremation at 8 a.m. on
28 May; this was soon changed to the afternoon to allow foreign
visitors time to get to Delhi. Among those who arrived were
Lord Mountbatten, an intimate friend since Partition days, Sir
Alec Douglas-Home, Prime Minister of the U.K., First Deputy
Premier (later Prime Minister) Kosygin of the Soviet Union, and
Dean Rusk, representing the President of the United States.
Lesser notables from about fifty states also attended.

The cortège left 'Teen Murti' at noon and made its way
slowly through the streets of New and Old Delhi to the banks of
the holy Jamuna River, a distance of about five miles; it was
virtually the same route taken by Mahatma Gandhi on his last
journey in January 1948. The same dense crowds were there,
variously estimated at two to three million, ten to twenty deep
much of the way. Grief was less visible, but the huge throng
pressed forward to get a last glimpse of the man who had been
India's pre-eminent—many feared irreplaceable—leader since
independence. It took 8,000 special police and 6,000 troops to
keep order. The troops had been hastily summoned to Delhi by
the Chief of the Army Staff, General Chaudhuri, a move which
caused some concern, then and later.[18] And then, as the funeral
pyre was lit by Mrs. Gandhi's younger son, Sanjay, came a
familiar cry, 'Chacha Nehru, Zindabad' ('Long Live Uncle
Nehru ').[19]

The most disconcerting feature of the ceremony, to Nehru's
secular admirers, was the presence of Hindu monks at the elevated
cremation site, chanting Vedic hymns of a time-honoured tradition: it was an unashamed flouting of his expressed wish that
no religious rites attend his funeral. Nehru's words were
emphatic: 'I wish to declare with all earnestness that I do not
want any religious ceremonies performed for me after my death.

I do not believe in any such ceremonies, and to submit to them, even as a matter of form, would be hypocrisy and an attempt to delude ourselves and others.' [20]

Mrs. Gandhi was certainly aware of this provision in her father's will, but she chose, or was persuaded, to ignore his request. The most charitable interpretation is that the death of Nehru could not be regarded as a private affair, that the nation had taken over; and a nation steeped in religion would have been deeply offended by a disregard of tradition. But it may well be that Nehru the agnostic wanted to administer such a shock to his people as a parting gesture. In any event, if it were feared that this might cause civil commotion, his life-long commitment to secularism would have required the presence of representatives of all India's major religions. Some persons more learned than this writer in these matters remarked that it was not really an orthodox ceremony. And T. T. K., a colleague and friend of long standing, related that Nehru's agnosticism had become less and less pronounced in his last years, though he disliked ritual to the end; further, had he written his will after 1960, instead of in 1954, that provision might not have been there.[21] But Nehru had ample time to revise his will—and didn't. Moreover, the religious rites, orthodox or not, raised doubts about the depth of India's devotion to secular principles.[22]

The funeral ended around 4.30 p.m., but few of the key figures returned to their homes until 6.30 or 7, because of the dense crowds along the thoroughfares of New Delhi. Some, like Nanda and Shastri, returned even later because they stayed on to address a public gathering after the cremation. The new Prime Minister asked his colleague to join him on the return car journey and told him that he had heard from the Home Ministry intelligence network that Morarji's supporters were mobilizing men and money for the contest about to begin—a report corroborated by many knowledgeable observers at the time. According to Nanda, he also offered Shastri his support, having made a firm decision the previous day not to contest; he added that he had told Mrs. Gandhi and Kamaraj of this decision too.

This may be so, in the formal sense of not being a candidate. But some of Nanda's actions at the time led people to believe that he was not averse to continuing in the post of Prime Minister. First, according to unimpeachable sources, he asked the Congress President to be allowed to stay on as Head of Government for a few months, with the remark, ' if I am not satisfactory, then you can change '. Kamaraj apparently sought Dr. Radhakrishnan's advice and the President stressed that it must be done quickly, for if there were delay there would be time for intrigue. ' Bring me the name of a new leader within a week, and I will swear him in as Prime Minister ', he added; Kamaraj said he would do so—and did. Secondly, Nanda made another (many felt, inappropriate) announcement, on Thursday, declaring that he had taken charge of Nehru's portfolios, External Affairs and Atomic Energy, as well as retaining the Home Ministry, a strange act for a caretaker Head of Government. And thirdly, he made the tactless gesture of occupying the late leader's seat in the Lok Sabha at the special memorial service on Friday—while Panditji's ashes were still warm. All these acts, it was widely believed at the time, were designed to create the impression that he was Prime Minister in fact as well as in law.[23] Certainly they appeared to make superfluous the post of Minister without Portfolio.

The Congress President, too, was busily engaged on the evening of the 28th. He met three of his colleagues in the Caucus, Atulya, Patil, and Reddy, soon after the funeral. Later, he held discussions, by telephone or personally, with various Chief Ministers, Working Committee members, and Cabinet Ministers, among them Nanda, Shastri, T. T. K., Jagjivan Ram, Morarji Sukhadia of Rajasthan, Hanumanthaiya of Mysore, and Chavan. Perhaps the most crucial was the preliminary sounding of the Defence Minister, who was believed to control the Maharashtra bloc of 56 votes (in the Parliamentary Party) and whose views were uncertain.

The delicate mission was conducted by Reddy and Kamaraj's right-hand man, Congress General Secretary Rajagopalan, after Chavan had telephoned the Congress President. To their question of what he thought should be done and whom he supported, he replied: ' the world expects you to behave with dignity ', a mood which he detected in Washington during his pause en route

to Delhi and all along the flight home; in truth, the world was
holding its breath—expecting confusion but hoping for order and
dignity. Thus, ' we must do everything possible to reach a consensus, to achieve unanimity '; he could not commit himself to
anyone, he added, since his only commitment was to the goal of
unanimity. As to the method, he urged the convening of a
meeting of Working Committee members and Chief Ministers,
the two most important groups in the Party—the Parliamentary
Party was to follow their lead—with the Congress President
seeking the consensus; [24] this was the exact procedure which was
followed. Reddy has confirmed this account, with the added
remark that he interpreted Chavan's words to mean support for
the Caucus; it was really support for a federal consensual
decision. When Kamaraj telephoned later that night, Chavan
reiterated these themes. The Defence Minister was also being
courted by the other side: Morarji telephoned to say he would
like to see him, but Chavan put him off until the next morning.
In the meantime, Reddy moved on to see other, unspecified,
persons in the quest for votes.

Atulya Ghosh was also canvassing for Shastri—which explains,
in part, why the ultimate victor remained confidently aloof, then
and later. On the evening of the 28th ' several friends ' came to
the Bengal leader's home in New Delhi at 19 Canning Lane,
among them the Chief Ministers of Assam, Madhya Pradesh,
Mysore, and Rajasthan, and Reddy and Patil. In the afternoon,
Atulya, who had been unable to attend the funeral because of a
broken leg, whiled away the hours in the air-conditioned bedroom of Patnaik's luxurious home at 3 Aurangzeb Road. Patnaik,
who also did not attend, ' was obsessed for Morarji ' and tried to
discuss the subject, but Atulya refused. In one of those amusing
sidelights of an intra-Congress Party struggle, Atulya, Patil,
and Patnaik met every afternoon at the Orissa leader's home
to compare notes on the shifting fortunes of the respective
candidates.

In this search for support, Patnaik turned, among others, to
the Left. That evening he went to Malaviya's house. But as
there were about a dozen others present he did not speak openly.
Nonetheless, the former Oil Minister understood the gambit:

Patnaik counted on his opposition to Shastri because of the latter's role in Malaviya's ouster from the Cabinet a year earlier; the result was inconclusive.[25]

Another variable in the complex process emerged with Jagjivan Ram's visit to Malaviya the same evening. The Untouchable leader had already conveyed to Kamaraj his undisguised disdain for Shastri, to whom he considered himself a much superior candidate. Malaviya was left with the impression that Ram 'was inclined towards Morarji, but he was really pro-Jagjivan Ram'. Events bore him out two days later, when Jagjivan Ram openly announced his candidacy. But at that stage he was relatively inactive, as evidenced by his remark that 'very little happened' on the 28th.[26]

In the Morarji camp a major blunder was committed on the evening of the 28th, though it only became widely known the following morning. It seemed innocent enough, as the former Finance Minister later related the incident: 'Friends approached me and asked whether I would serve as Prime Minister; of course, I said I would.'[27] The snag was that it was leaked to the press. And the next day the story appeared in a rather different form: Morarji 'is the first one to throw his hat into the ring. He is believed to have told his associates that he is a candidate.'[28]

It is one thing to be known to be available for that high office; both Morarji and Shastri had long been so regarded. It is quite another to declare one's availability. And it is a fatal error, more so in India than in many other countries, to be believed to be making a bid for leadership; this is a violation of the concept and value of renunciation, so important in the Hindu view of things. And that was the impression created by the press report. This is the style in American presidential politics; but in India it is imperative to follow the maxim, 'let the office seek the man'—which is what Shastri did. There may be some substance in Morarji's bitter complaint that 'this was spread by Lal Bahadur's agents'. Nevertheless, after thirty-four years in Indian politics, seventeen of them as a Minister, and as an avowed follower of Gandhi's principle of renunciation, so recently reaffirmed in the Kamaraj Plan, Morarji displayed remarkable naïvety; he was to pay dearly for this lapse, for it enabled the Shastri camp to portray an image of a seeker after power. The impact was intangible and cannot be measured in terms of votes. It is unlikely that it was decisive, but it did have some effect in mid-stream.

Friday, 29 May, was probably decisive in the succession struggle. It was certainly the most hectic day, with closed-door consultations, group meetings, and whisper campaigns. The day began quietly enough, on a note of self-assurance: a *Statesman* leader commended the President's method of dealing with the interregnum—'this temporary breathing space contrived with exemplary democratic propriety'. Behind the scenes, however, various strands of a complex web were unfolding simultaneously, as pressure mounted on the key sources of power and influence within India's political system. One was the belated emergence of the CPP Executive, conscious of the danger that it might be ignored in the selection of its new Leader. Another was a much-publicized meeting of the Left at Malaviya's home. A third was the continued courting of Chavan and the Maharashtra bloc. A fourth involved Jagjivan Ram, reputed to control a group of Untouchable votes. Still another was a campaign on behalf of Mrs. Gandhi. And finally, there was the search for support among the State Chief Ministers and Presidents of the PCCs, for they wielded great influence with the parliamentarians through patronage and the control of election tickets; some M.P.s, of course, were put up for election in order to exile them from State politics and did not feel beholden to State leaders—they were associated with the dissident faction of the State Congress. It was a day of pressure-group politics *par excellence*.

The Parliamentary Party Executive had long been an insignificant forum for decision-making, a legacy of the Working Committee's pre-eminence in the nationalist movement, of the federal system, and of the comparative weakness of India's Parliament. But in the crisis of October–November 1962 it had taken the initiative for the first time and compelled a reluctant Prime Minister to dismiss Krishna Menon; both the Cabinet and the High Command had been no less keen to do so, but neither had dared even to attempt such an unprecedented act of pressure. That taste of power was not easily forgotten, especially now that lesser men were at the helm. Thus, when the Executive met on the morning of the 29th, some members asserted the right to select their new Leader. The thrust was blunted, temporarily, by the solemnity of the occasion, and the meeting adjourned until the following day after passing a fulsome condolence resolution.

Parliament met soon after to eulogize its foremost figure since independence. Nanda walked slowly to the Treasury Benches, stood with head bowed in front of Nehru's seat, wept, and then took his place as Prime Minister. The Working Committee had also planned a condolence session that day but postponed it until Saturday because of a public meeting to mourn Nehru's death, at which party leaders were to be present. Meanwhile the battle for succession went on.

The activities of the Left aroused much comment and contro- versy, far out of proportion to its real strength in the Party. Attention centred on a breakfast meeting at Malaviya's home and the seemingly strange report that it was about to throw its weight behind Morarji. Three eye-witness accounts of this con- clave are now available. R. K. Karanjia, editor of *Blitz*, recalled that fourteen persons were present, including Krishna Menon, 'who may not have known of its purpose'; Malaviya, he added, proposed that they back Morarji—in exchange for two seats in the Cabinet, presumably for himself and Menon, the two ousted Ministers of the Left.[29] Menon, as usual, was disdainful of the proceedings: 'Malaviya called a meeting at breakfast and, as happens in India, the greater part of the time was spent in arranging the breakfast!' In a more serious vein, 'the only contribution I made was to say that Parliament should decide. I felt even then that it was too early to discuss these matters, so I never even mentioned the Prime Minister's succession question at any time. Looking back on it, and if I knew what would have happened, I should not have gone to that breakfast. I went because Malaviya would have felt hurt.' As for the reports linking him with Morarji, 'I think it was largely American propaganda, to discredit me partly and to discredit Morarji Desai because the Americans at that time didn't want Morarji.

[Throughout that week] I never saw him and I never talked to him. On the day I am supposed to have sat at night with him intriguing, I had come back from the funeral, almost carried back; I had collapsed over there because of the heat and everything else, after the fire was set up.' [30]

Malaviya's version of the breakfast gathering and related themes also merits attention. He never intended nor implied to anyone, he said, that he would support Morarji. In fact, since he left the Cabinet in the summer of 1963 he had never had a political discussion with Morarji. His order of preference—which he conveyed to Kamaraj—was Mrs. Gandhi, Nanda, and Shastri, his sole criterion being who would contribute the most to Socialism. When he approached Nehru's daughter, she told him categorically that she was not a candidate. He then asked Nanda point-blank about his intentions. 'I am not a candidate,' was the reply, 'but if you make me Prime Minister I will accept.' In Malaviya's view, Nanda was eager to become Prime Minister, 'but he would not say so categorically'. Yet, after Mrs. Gandhi declined, Malaviya backed Nanda. However, 'if there was to be a contest between Shastri and Morarji I would have supported Shastri—and would have worked night and day for him'. But there was a contest between Shastri and Morarji—and there is no evidence that Malaviya was *engagé*.

About the breakfast meeting, Malaviya confirmed that Menon 'was like a spectator there'. Of his own role and attitude he offered an ingenious though not fully convincing account. There were, he said, about twenty-two Bihar Members of the Legislative Assembly (M.L.A.s) at his home, apart from the special guests. Like all politicians, they had their own personal and group interests to protect. And in the Bihar Congress, split into two almost equal factions, Morarji supported this group against Sahay, who was backed by Shastri and Atulya Ghosh; if Shastri became Prime Minister, with Atulya's aid, they might well lose their Assembly tickets. Thus they asked Malaviya at least not to disown newspaper reports of his support for Morarji. In short, while he had no intention of supporting Morarji, he could not openly alienate the Bihar group of his followers: he was, he said, caught in the web of Bihar factional politics.[31]

The account is not implausible, in the light of the pervasive character of factionalism in Indian politics and the interlocking connections of State and national Congress Party groups. One well-informed observer shed a little further light on this episode. Apparently, a Kashmir M.P., A. M. Tariq, threatened to expose Malaviya if he carried out the move in favour of Morarji, while Karanjia threatened to withdraw *Blitz's* support of the group. By mid-afternoon on Friday there was so much disagreement, compounded by Mrs. Gandhi's diffidence, that the Left was in disarray.

Not far from Malaviya's home at 2 Safdarjang Lane, a more crucial meeting was taking place: Morarji was making a bid for the Maharashtra bloc of 56 votes. Chavan, however, refused to commit himself, beyond saying that he would do what was right. The reason, he related later, was that he knew there would be a contest if he supported Morarji; in reply to a question, he remarked, 'no, Shastri would not have withdrawn'. 'I do not know what the outcome would have been, but there certainly would have been a contest'—and this he wished to avoid. Secondly, in his judgement, Shastri was the better person in India's circumstances.[32]

There was no other meeting between Chavan and Morarji during the battle for succession, so that the latter should have known he could not count on Maharashtra as early as Friday morning. But Morarji chose to interpret the words, 'what is right' as a pledge of support, as Sanjiva Reddy discovered when he spoke to Morarji immediately afterwards. This turned out to be wishful thinking but it was not without some foundation, for it was Morarji who had strongly and effectively recommended Chavan as his successor in the post of Chief Minister of Bombay in 1956. In a personal letter to Nehru he wrote: 'I have no hesitation in recommending Shri Y. B. Chavan. About his ability and intelligence there can be no doubt.' Moreover, his loyalty and discipline, said Morarji, had been amply demonstrated and he was the most acceptable Congress Maharashtrian leader to the Gujaratis.[33] When Morarji told Reddy of his expectation, the latter dissented; he added that the support of the former Chief Minister of U.P., C. B. Gupta, on whom Morarji counted, would not be forthcoming either; indeed, Gupta had left Delhi the previous night.[34]

There were probably other reasons for Chavan's attitude. When Patnaik spoke to him on Saturday afternoon, on Morarji's behalf, he acknowledged the former Finance Minister's great service to his career in 1956. But he doubted that he could carry the Maharashtra delegation because of deep-rooted Maharashtrian resentment over the behaviour of Morarji, a Gujarati, when he was Chief Minister of undivided Bombay, during the 1956 riots in Bombay City.[35] Moreover, Chavan's former lieutenant and his successor as Chief Minister of Maharashtra, Naik, had already made overtures to the Syndicate. Chavan probably felt that he had to fall into line lest he lost or weaken his political base—a further illustration of a cardinal fact about Indian politics, namely, that when a State leader moves to Delhi, he can no longer absolutely command the loyalty of his subordinates once his control over patronage has been transferred to other hands. Finally, Chavan's future as an all-India leader—he was only 51 and an obvious potential candidate for Prime Minister in the future—would not be enhanced by alienating the Caucus which, it was now clear, would secure victory for its candidate, Shastri. For these reasons, then, Chavan withheld his support from Morarji. But his decision was still unknown, at least unclear, even to the Morarji camp, on Friday the 29th.

M.P.s representing the bulk of the 60 million Untouchables or Depressed Castes have never been a cohesive faction within the Congress. Nevertheless, their most prominent member, Jagjivan Ram, could not be readily ignored; in a crisis, he could probably secure a majority of their votes, some 40 to 60, as well as a scattering outside his caste, especially from his home State of Bihar. Thus, despite his undisguised hostility to Shastri, he was courted by the Caucus, as well as by Morarji. The peripatetic Sanjiva Reddy came to see him that day and they went together to Kamaraj; Jagjivan Ram made clear his intention to contest if Shastri were a candidate. During the first three days of the succession struggle, however, the Untouchable leader made no overt move in this direction. On the contrary, he was closely identified with Morarji, with whom, he later acknowledged, he discussed the succession. Although he later denied, as 'interested propaganda', widespread reports of his alignment with Morarji and the latter's offer of the Deputy Prime Ministership for Untouchable support, there can be no doubt that this pragmatic partnership was taken as real and important in the assessment of the balance of forces on Friday. Even Jagjivan Ram admitted that he and Morarji had agreed that, in case of a contest, one would withdraw and support the other—and Morarji had no intention of withdrawing. Only when Morarji's campaign faltered badly did Jagjivan Ram make a move, on Saturday evening; and that was too late to be anything but a gesture of dissent.

Jagjivan Ram's contempt for Shastri was so marked—'any candidate would have been better than Shastri and anyone would have beaten him in a secret ballot in the Parliamentary Party'—that he took a most ingenious initiative on Friday: two emissaries were dispatched to secure a consensus in favour of Mrs. Gandhi and, Jagjivan Ram added, to expose Shastri's ambition, if he refused to step aside for her. To Morarji went D. P. Mishra, Chief Minister of Madhya Pradesh, and to Shastri and Atulya, Rajasthan's Chief Minister, Sukhadia. For Jagjivan Ram there was the comforting rationalization that this was in the 'national interest' because, like most members of the political élite, he believed that an open contest would be harmful. Mishra had the added incentive that, although known as a Morarji supporter personally, his State's M.P.s were not so inclined. Moreover, he was indebted to Nehru's daughter for restoring his political fortunes after twelve years in the backwoods.

Morarji's reply was firm: he refused to withdraw, saying in effect, 'I do want to be Prime Minister but my aim is not to keep Shastri out'; further, he expressed doubt that Mrs. Gandhi could 'run the country', noting her lack of administrative experience; 'that is not the way I play politics', he reportedly concluded. Shastri seemed more accommodating: 'If she is the unanimous choice of the Party, I will be the first to nominate her.' Atulya, as usual, was more blunt: 'Why should Shastri stand down; what sins has he committed?'[36]

Did Mrs. Gandhi play an active role in this gambit? Almost

certainly not, in the opinion of all persons consulted. Was she
aware of Ram's scheme? Almost certainly yes, according to
many, including family members. Would she have accepted a
' draft ', had Morarji co-operated? There is no evidence either
way. It is true that she was in a state of near-shock during those
days and had not entirely recovered even months afterwards. It
is also true that, as she later indicated,[37] she would have preferred
a long spell of privacy to attend to her father's papers and other
memorial activities. But she did accept a Cabinet post less than
two weeks after her father's death—and was not compelled to do
so. And she does have strong views about the paths India should
follow in domestic and foreign affairs. Nor is the Prime
Ministership a post one easily declines. She was saved the agony
of making a difficult decision, but probably would have found it
impossible to reject a ' call ' by the party élite; and there is the
interesting report, unconfirmed, that a leftist M.P., Khudilkar,
asked her on Monday 1 June why she had turned down the
Prime Ministership; to this she reportedly said that no one had
offered it to her![38] Ram has added the view that she knew
about the emissaries but ' was not very keen about the post—and
was very doubtful that either Morarji or Shastri would withdraw '.

There remains the intriguing question of whether she would
have been offered the Prime Ministership had Morarji agreed to
step down. Some felt that Morarji's veto was decisive, that the
' draft Indira ' movement would otherwise have skyrocketed.
Ram, among others, disagreed, noting that, even if Morarji had
co-operated, the Syndicate would not have permitted Shastri to
withdraw. Support for the latter view comes from Patnaik, who
recalled that on Friday afternoon, when Morarji's prospects were
ebbing, he proposed Mrs. Gandhi as a compromise choice to
Atulya and Reddy—during their daily get-together at his home.
' They became ashen-white, accused me of concealing this
aim all along, and refused outright.' When Patnaik added
that, earlier in the day, he had told Shastri Mrs. Gandhi might
be a candidate, and that he had seemed well disposed, ' they
became livid and threatened to support Morarji, rather than
accept Indira '. The reason, he added, was that they were
smarting under her manner since her father's illness in January.

They may also have had legitimate doubts about her administrative and political competence. While it is true that Patil and Reddy, however powerful in their State and region, did not control the Party as a whole or even the Caucus, let alone the Working Committee, they were not alone among the professionals in their attitude to Indira. The source of her strength was a *mélange*—the Left, probably Nanda, Jagjivan Ram (after Morarji's hopes faded), a disparate number of admirers of Panditji and of herself, and an intangible search for continuity among those who feared change of any kind. But the people and the Party clearly favoured Shastri, and the Caucus was their managing agent.

Powerful State pressures also asserted themselves on Friday. Almost all State contingents of M.P.s met separately, with the Chief Minister, the President of the PCC, and other party functionaries, to assure the protection of their interests in the outcome, with respect to patronage, representation in the Cabinet, etc. But to the contestants the principal focus of lobbying was the State leaders, both for their support at the high élite level, notably in the Working Committee meeting soon to be held, and, if necessary, at the Parliamentary Party level, if the issue were forced to a vote. Kamaraj saw at least ten Chief Ministers on Friday, possibly more, along with key members of the Caucus and other, uncommitted, persons, like T.T.K. The trend of opinion on that day, he later recalled, was clearly in favour of Shastri; and, in so far as possible, he tried not to intrude his own views during these discussions—it is well known that he is a man of few words at all times—except to reiterate the need for dignity and unanimity; his goal was to avoid a contest. In that connection, one of the Chief Ministers, Balvantray Mehta of Gujarat, reportedly made the novel suggestion of a formalized duumvirate of Morarji and Shastri, similar to the informal duumvirate of Nehru and Patel;[39] it remained unclear who would be Prime Minister, for Mehta had a dual loyalty—to Morarji as a Gujarati and to Shastri as President of the Servants of the People Society; such, among others, are the criteria for political choice and action in the Congress.[40]

Atulya Ghosh was no less busy that day. All Chief Ministers except four—those of Gujarat, Punjab, Orissa, and U.P.—

spoke to him or he to them on Friday, and all conveyed the impression of favouring Shastri. All agreed on the need to maintain dignity, and many were apprehensive that Shastri would not accept the ' call '. As to why they came to see him, a mere State leader from Bengal, he remarked: ' They are my friends of long standing, and friends meet in distress; we could discuss the question openly and objectively.' No wonder Atulya was (and is) regarded as one of the most powerful men in India. On that day, too, Patnaik came to his home to press Morarji's cause. He tried to argue in terms of votes and a contest, but Atulya was adamant. In his view India could not afford a competitive vote at that juncture; in the future, perhaps, there could be a contest, but the difference between Nehru and any successor was so great that the gap could only be narrowed, and then no more than partially, by unanimity. They agreed to disagree.[41] Apart from Patnaik, others lobbying for Morarji included Narayan Singh, B. B. Mishra, and Mrs. T. Sinha; they turned to the Chief Ministers in earnest when it became apparent that the CPP would not be the forum of decision; but by then the real preference for Shastri had been asserted.

Saturday, the 30th, may be described as a day of rearguard action by the Morarjiites and discreet consolidation by the Shastri camp, with a last, frenzied initiative from the Left. The delayed Working Committee meeting was held in the morning but it confined itself to a condolence resolution; it adjourned until the next day, presumably to give Kamaraj more time to hammer out a consensus.

A group of leftists also met in the morning and declared their neutrality between the two leading contestants; they would support Nanda, they said, if the High Command were so inclined. As a follow-through, two M.P.s (Bhagwat Jha Azad and S. R. S. Deshmukh) and others on the Left met Kamaraj and reportedly suggested that, if unanimity were unattainable, Nanda should continue in office or Mrs. Gandhi should be persuaded to accept the leadership; the Congress President was not impressed. In any case, Nehru's daughter had reportedly declined further pressure

for a 'draft', this time by Madhya Pradesh leaders, and, significantly, told a group of parliamentarians that she was against a
change in the Prime Ministership at that time.[42] Krishna Menon,
for his part, emphatically denied that he was supporting 'either
Mr. Desai or anybody'.[43]

The (erratic) strategy of the Left was now clear: first, the
alliance with Morarji, not only to restore their political fortunes
but also ideologically based on the not unknown affinity of
nationalist Left and nationalist Right; then, support for Mrs.
Gandhi, symbol of the continuity of Nehruism and, in her own
right, akin to their policies—possibly also malleable to their
wishes. She, knowing that political strength lay with Shastri, and
emotionally ill-prepared to wage a contest at that time anyway,
declined to stand and joined the Left in backing Nanda for the
Prime Ministership. The rationale was not implausible—to
break the Shastri-Morarji impasse and thereby achieve the much-
prized unanimity. But Kamaraj and the Caucus would not
co-operate; their aim was no less clear—and they had the power
to win.

The CPP Executive resumed its adjourned deliberations in the
afternoon—a scheduled meeting in the morning had been postponed. There were some who pressed the Morarji line that, if
an election were held, the Working Committee should remain
aloof. Others supported the continuation of Nanda in office.
But ultimately a three-point consensus was reached: an early
election, just after the end of the current session of Parliament,
on 5 or 8 June, so that the formation of a new Government
would be free from the stress of a daily sitting; secondly, an
overwhelming emphasis on unanimity, with an expression of
appreciation of Kamaraj's efforts in this direction; and, finally,
the fixing of the date of election of a new Leader by the CPP in
consultation with the Congress President; a Deputy Leader, K. C.
Reddy, was authorized to meet Kamaraj for this purpose. By
this decision the CPP Executive yielded in the abortive power
tussle with the Working Committee; it realized that power lay
with the High Command and the Chief Ministers. Kamaraj had
alienated some of the parliamentary leaders by a seeming disdain
for their status but he mollified their sensitivity, with the aid of

Patil, by inviting two members of the Executive to the crucial Working Committee meeting the next day. Yet they were only two out of forty-two persons, and the great decision was to be taken by the organizational wing of the Party; the challenge was rebuffed.

Not all were prepared to accept this defeat, however. Later that day, four of Morarji's supporters on the CPP Executive, led by Ravindra Varma,[44] sent (and publicized) aggressive letters to the Congress President saying that they would not tolerate his, i.e., the High Command's, interference with a free vote in the CPP.[45] By evening the defiant ones had retracted their futile gesture, but evidence of acute tension was now out in the open. This was not solely, or even primarily, an assertion of the parliamentary wing of the Party; rather, it was a desperate effort by the Morarji camp to stem the growing pressure for unanimity —which meant a Syndicate-dominated Working Committee consensus in favour of Shastri. The only hope for a Morarji victory—which he and his supporters acutely realized—was a secret ballot among the 537 Congress M.P.s; only thus could they possibly offset, at least in part, the State party machines, most of which were in the Shastri camp. The Morarjiites were strengthened in this strategy by the knowledge that, three years earlier, had Nehru allowed the election of a Deputy Leader to be decided by a secret ballot—in fact, he depreciated the contest and the status of the post by insisting on two Deputy Leaders—Morarji would probably have secured a majority; perhaps even a year earlier he would have received a clear mandate; but now, after the Kamaraj Plan, and on the morrow of Nehru's death, the balance of forces within the Parliamentary Party had shifted markedly to his disadvantage. But only in this forum was there an element of uncertainty and, therefore, a possible path to victory.

Unknown at the time was a quiet gathering of Muslim M.P.s at the residence of the Minister of Petroleum and Chemicals, Humayun Kabir. Like most other interest groups in the Congress, they met to evaluate the likely consequences of a Morarji or Shastri victory for the security and welfare of their community. No decision was reached, in the sense of advocating all Muslim M.P.s to vote as a bloc if there were an election in the CPP. But there was a consensus, a realistic one, that Morarji would be much less sympathetic to Muslim aspirations and fears but would be more effective in putting down communal disturbances, a not uncommon residue of Partition days. The episode had no influence on the outcome of the struggle but it reveals the play of interest groups—of all types, communal as well as occupational—in the Indian political system.

The mood of India's political élite on Saturday afternoon, 30 May, was reflected in Jagjivan Ram's explanation of why the CPP Executive agreed to consult, really to accept the direction of, the Congress President in fixing the date for the election of a new Leader: 'You must not forget that the nation had suffered a great tragedy. The overriding consideration was to avoid conflict, not to fight on petty issues—which this was. The nation would not forgive persons who pressed that issue to a contest. At no time was the tragedy of Nehru's death far from people's minds.' As to the query, why abdicate responsibility to the Congress President, 'ultimately the Party organization is supreme; we recognized this'. More accurately, the federal system was supreme—and Kamaraj was its spokesman.

In the evening, Jagjivan Ram finally made his move. A group of Untouchable politicians, mostly members of the Working Committee of the Depressed Classes League, met at Ram's home, passed a condolence resolution and urged him to proclaim himself a candidate; Ram yielded. Two reports noted the presence of eighteen persons; [46] Ram himself recalled thirty or forty; in any event, two Union Deputy Ministers were there, D. Mannchan Dass and B. S. Murthy, along with the former Congress President and incumbent Labour Minister, Sanjivayya. The case was simple—and unconvincing—namely, that Ram, as the person with the longest service as a Minister, from 1946 to 1963, should succeed by virtue of seniority and administrative experience. There was no formal resolution, said Ram; and he agreed to step aside if unanimity could be reached; he did so the next morning. Nevertheless, Ram's gesture on Saturday evening was of some consequence for, at a time when Morarji's hoped-for support was vanishing on many fronts, the Untouchable leader reduced his strength by at least 20 more votes, possibly up to 60.

The writing was on the wall, therefore, when Morarji met Kamaraj for an hour in the evening; one report said that he was reluctant to do so and that he agreed only after the Congress President sent word that he was coming to see him.[47]   Afterwards, Kamaraj told pressmen that he hoped the ultimate choice would be unanimous and that the Working Committee would probably settle it the next morning.   Morarji was still not ready to concede; he declared that he would not shy away from a contest ' if people find me fit for the job '; ' everyone ', he added, was trying to bring about a unanimous choice.[48]

Before the day was out Shastri's triumph was assured, though some foreign observers at the time perceived a trend to Morarji late on Friday night and in the early hours of Saturday.   One diplomat went so far as to say, ' he came remarkably close to getting a majority of the votes '.   Morarji himself claimed a majority of 100 in the CPP—until the ' defections of three persons whom I had helped to their present position ', Chavan (Maharashtra), Mishra (Madhya Pradesh), and Sinha (Bihar); that (through the votes they controlled) reduced his majority to 10, he said, which was precarious and easily upset.   He fully realized these acts of ' betrayal ' only on Saturday afternoon and evening, though Chavan, the most important of the three, had conveyed his thoughts to him on *Friday morning*.   In any event, he said, the Syndicate overcame his initial majority of 100 by what he termed ' the bossist technique of a consensus '.[49]

In perspective, this seems a total misreading of the balance of forces on Friday and Saturday.   In the all-important Working Committee the breakdown was 11 to 5, with 3 uncommitted: backing Shastri were Kamaraj, Patil, Atulya, Reddy, Nijalingappa, i.e., the Caucus, along with Chavan, Ram Subhag Singh, Sadiq Ali, the two General Secretaries, Rajagopalan and Manaen, and Shastri himself; Morarji had the support of Patnaik, Jagjivan Ram, Sanjivayya, and Sukhadia; while Nanda, Mrs. Gandhi, and Fakhruddin Ali Ahmed were uncertain.   Morarji probably had a slight majority in the CPP Executive, 16 to 14.   But among the 537 Congress M.P.s in the Lok Sabha and Rajya Sabha, a free vote almost certainly would have favoured Shastri. It may well be that, in mid-afternoon on Friday, his clear majority was only about 30, but the hard core of Morarji's support was never more than 150, probably less, concentrated in four States—Gujarat (25), Orissa (20), Punjab (21), and Rajasthan (20). Of these, he had about 70 votes; and to these must be added half of the two populous Hindi States, Bihar (57) and Uttar Pradesh (82), perhaps another 70, with a scattering among the other States.

Even the most generous estimate known to this writer showed Morarji 79 votes short of a majority on Saturday morning, at the alleged height of his strength: [50]

Congress Parliamentary Party

	Lok Sabha	Rajya Sabha	Total	Shastri	Morarji
Andhra	33	13	46	38	8
Assam	9	7	16	13	3
Bengal	22	11	33	28	5
Bihar	42	15	57	27	30
Gujarat	15	10	25	3	22
Kerala	7	5	12	5	7
Madhya Pradesh	26	10	36	18	18
Madras	31	12	43	40	3
Maharashtra	41	15	56	41	15
Mysore	25	9	34	20	14
Orissa	14	6	20	3	17
Punjab	13	8	21	5	16
Rajasthan	13	7	20	6	14
Uttar Pradesh	60	22	82	35	47
Other *	23	13	36	26	10
Total	374	163	537	308	229

* Himachal Pradesh, Jammu and Kashmir, Manipur, Tripura and appointees.

At best, this view of Morarji's support is right in detail but wrong in spirit, for the Caucus was determined to block him and had the power to do so. No wonder that Patnaik, never one to abandon a battle prematurely, advised Morarji to concede late on *Friday*; once it was known that Morarji would not step aside for Mrs. Gandhi, the outcome was virtually certain. As Sanjiva Reddy remarked, the problem thereafter was how to avoid a

contest, for this was deemed bad for the country and the Party.
By Saturday night—a day earlier, according to Caucus members
Atulya and Reddy—the struggle for the succession began to move
from the stage of pressure-group politics to decision. But many
of the actors, notably Morarji and Jagjivan Ram, still refused to
recognize the fact of certain defeat at that point. The drama was
to continue another two days.

Sunday, the 31st of May, was the day of decision. It was
also the day of triumph for the Caucus, especially for Kamaraj,
the stolid, seemingly phlegmatic, but astute and efficient manager
of the orderly succession to Nehru. The day was important for
other reasons, too. The Congress élite displayed maturity and
sophistication of a high order. The political system revealed
resilience and strength in the greatest internal challenge to its
stability and continuity since independence. The rules of the
game in the dominant party of a one-plus party system adhering
to the democratic ethic were laid bare. So were the mechanism
and process of decision on momentous issues of Indian politics.
And, related to that, a new institution emerged in the power
configuration of the Union.

The oligarchs assembled at 8.30 in the morning for what
turned out to be the most significant meeting of the High
Command since 14–15 June 1947, when the Working Committee
approved the Mountbatten Plan of Partition.[51] Present for the
historic occasion were forty-two persons—the nineteen regular
members of the Working Committee, thirteen Chief Ministers
(two others, Nijalingappa and Sukhadia, were on the Committee),
two representatives of the CPP—Deputy Leader K. C. Reddy and
Chief Whip Satya Narayan Sinha—and eight 'invitees', including Krishna Menon and the former party President, U. N.
Dhebar, and senior Cabinet Members, notably T. T. K., Subramaniam, and Swaran Singh. Everyone present, except Mrs.
Gandhi, spoke.

The discussion, which lasted all morning, centred on two
questions: whether or not unanimity was essential; and whether
or not the Working Committee was competent to advise (instruct)

the CPP on the election of a new Leader. Kamaraj led off with an appeal for unity and solidarity, and an early election. In the ensuing debate most echoed these sentiments. Almost all pressed for unanimity, while acknowledging that a contest was a normal part of democratic procedure. On the vexed issue of the propriety of the Working Committee taking the lead—the nub of the power struggle between the organizational and parliamentary wings of the Party and, more important, the key to certain victory for Shastri or possible triumph for Morarji—the battle was joined. The overwhelming majority of oligarchs who spoke asserted the right of the Committee, as the supreme executive, to guide the Parliamentary Party. In that connection, one Chief Minister noted that it was the Working Committee which had accepted Partition, but this was before an independent Parliament and new Constitution had given a special status to the majority party in the House. In reply to a query, Rajagopalan revealed that the Working Committee advises the CPP on the election of the President and Vice-President of India.[52]

There were some voices of dissent, however. Pratap Singh Kairon, 'strong man' of the Punjab, suggested that Kamaraj conduct a secret poll of all Congress M.P.s without restricting their choice, select the one with a majority, and then 'elect' him unanimously. This pro-Morarji gambit was rejected as unworkable, perhaps because of a natural reluctance to take *any* chances about the outcome. Another person, apparently Patnaik's hand-picked successor as Chief Minister of Orissa, Biren Mitra, suggested obliquely that the CPP should have the freedom to make an unfettered choice. As one commentator remarked, the atmosphere was 'too uncongenial to air his views more explicitly'.[53] Patnaik himself, along with Balvantray Mehta of Gujarat, agreed to unanimity and consensus but urged that it be sought and achieved without rancour or victimization. Apart from this conspicuous minority, however, the prevalent view was that expressed in a *Hindu* editorial that morning: 'the Parliamentary Party should abide by the decision with discipline and unanimity' and 'the choice will brook no delay'.

At a certain point in the discussion Kamaraj announced, quite correctly, that there appeared to be agreement on unanimity and

Working Committee leadership in the election process; how then to proceed? In the somewhat confused exchange that followed, the consensus technique was born. Its origin, both as to persons and time, is subject to different memories and interpretation. At least five versions are now available. Some attribute it to Kamaraj, after consulting Working Committee members before the meeting.[54] According to Jagjivan Ram, it was Dr. Ram Subhag Singh who put the proposal that the President seek a consensus, but the scheme was hatched by the Caucus, he claimed, on the night of 30 May, when the danger of a formal election still loomed large. Nanda recalled that Atulya Ghosh moved a resolution to that effect. Reddy suggested that there was no need to go beyond the Working Committee consensus—the élite view. Closest to the truth, perhaps, is that ' it emerged spontaneously from the prolonged discussion '; such is the recollection of Atulya, Chavan, and Menon; the leader of the Left put it this way: ' Whether he [Kamaraj] said that after somebody else said it or . . . . In the Working Committee there is such disorderliness, do you see; anyway, it emerged, shall we say, and he pronounced it.'[55]

All these comments relate to the *procedure* for ascertaining a consensus—by the President—not the substantive idea of consensus or unanimity, which was very much in the air during the preceding four days. Yet even the time of origin and the purpose of the technique is a point of disagreement and controversy. Ram claimed that it was devised the night before the Working Committee meeting, to ensure Shastri's selection. Morarji termed it a ' trick ' to overcome his substantial majority in the CPP. Kamaraj himself, and other members of the Syndicate, date it to the morning of the meeting, as a natural by-product of the idea of unanimity; certainly they deny the conspiracy thesis. Yet these questions of *who, how,* and *when,* concerning the consensus, are secondary to *what* it entailed and the logical consequences therefrom.

Before the meeting was over, the enlarged Working Committee, which was henceforth to be the Grand Council of the Republic, authorized its President to ascertain the opinion of Congressmen as to who should succeed Nehru and to tender his

advice to the CPP. Kamaraj was requested to consult Chief
Ministers, Working Committee members, office bearers of the
CPP, and 'such other Congress M.P.s as he may desire to
meet'.[56] This was, indeed, almost *carte blanche* discretion to one
man to determine the succession—through consultation and
advice—and the person concerned was known to prefer one of
the candidates. No names had been mentioned at the meeting,
but with this decision the cards were stacked in favour of Shastri,
despite Kamaraj's much respected impartiality.

Everyone knew that this marked the irreversible turn in the
road, though Shastri assured the public that evening that the
Congress would tackle the task of selecting a successor 'with
honesty and integrity'.[57] The *Times of India* used the apt
caption the following morning, 'Shastri's Election as Leader
Certain', with the remark that, while the CPP would still have
the final choice, 'the consensus approach will leave little room
for any serious contest'. The *Indian Express* did the same—
'Shastri All But Prime Minister'. And the *Hindustan Times*
correctly observed that the Working Committee decision assured
a unanimous choice because all the candidates were present when
the consensus procedure was adopted. The defeated candidates
were bitter. Jagjivan Ram related later, 'then we knew we
were outmanœuvred'. Morarji went home after the meeting and reportedly said, referring to the Caucus, 'they have
manœuvred it'. Chavan agreed, but there was no rancour:
'The consensus at the Working Committee meeting decided the
succession; it decided everything.' Only Nanda hedged about
the finality of that event. 'It provided the direction,' he said,
'though not an absolutely certain outcome.' This seems more
like wishful thinking, but Nanda expressed well the near-
universal rationale for the consensus idea: 'We were all conscious that the world's eyes were upon us, and we did not want
to display too open a fight.'[58] And as for a consensus arrived at
by the Working Committee, the *Times of India* anticipated the
chorus of justification during the next week by observing that it
would produce a genuine national consensus since the States have
a legitimate stake in the all-India leader. 'Far from being
undemocratic or dangerous, it is a practical approach which even

Mr. Nehru suggested during his lifetime ', it wrote, invoking the sanction of the charismatic leader.[59]

As a person avowedly disinterested in the outcome—' quite bluntly, cynically, what is the difference between tweedle-dum and tweedle-dee so far as I am concerned '—Krishna Menon's account of the Working Committee meeting adds insight and flavour : [60]

The first time I opened my mouth about the succession was when we met in the Working Committee. I have no doubt that these elders or whatever you call them had already made up their minds, do you see. And the first thing that was decided, or rather put out, in that atmosphere—it was all a kind of Amy McPherson business— was that we should have a unanimous selection. [Then the reference to how it ' emerged '.] In the course of that discussion I said a unanimous choice is obviously a right choice, but we should not say that it is absolutely necessary to regard a contest for the leadership as undemocratic. Whether that led to the inference that I wanted some-body, I can't tell you, but I was purely theoretical and I brought no emotion into it. I left it like that; and nobody objected to it. Then, I think, Morarji, in that meeting, took some very foolish steps. First of all, he said that whoever else would withdraw, he wouldn't.

The next stage of the meeting was—no names were mentioned by anybody at that meeting—it was left to the Congress President to discover what the Party wanted. It might have been more or less a formality. I said that the only thing left was the method by which Kamaraj would report or come to a decision as to what the Party thought. Nothing was said that he might not call a party meeting or a party executive meeting, and so on.

Meanwhile the Congress Parliamentary Party decided that they were not to be by-passed. That was steamrollered here [Working Committee] with the remark, ' who were they . . . after all, they have no one of stature as we people have '. Though, mind you, there were a couple of people in the Congress Parliamentary Party at that time who would have kicked up a shindig, but they [CPP Executive as a whole] didn't want to because they were all afraid of who would come to power, and the man who came, if you were against him, there would be difficulty here. So it [Working Committee meeting] ended in this way.

Soon after the meeting ended, the three General Secretaries of the CPP, Raghunath Singh, Bibuthi Mishra, and Pajhazan, called on the Congress President. In accordance with his wishes, they fixed a meeting of the Parliamentary Party for Tuesday 2 June, at 9 a.m., in the Central Hall of Parliament; since there was no Party Leader, Kamaraj was asked to preside. Within minutes thereafter Congressmen began to descend on his home, for the Party President had let it be known that he would be prepared to see anyone who had a view to express. He was as good as his word.

During the rest of Sunday and Monday, the period allotted for the mammoth one-man poll, Kamaraj met about 200 M.P.s, individually and in groups, as well as members of the 'Grand Council of the Republic' and others; in a period of four hours on Sunday, he talked with about 100. This led some to remark that the poll must have been perfunctory, and in a sense it was. Kamaraj knows no Hindi and does not feel entirely at ease in English, so that the exchange must have been very brief indeed. Some caricatured it thus: 'Shastri, yes or no', the President would say; or, even more cruelly, 'I like Shastri; whom do you like?' It was natural, and even prudent in these circumstances, for the rank-and-file to fall into line. As Menon put it, characteristically, 'when the Congress President calls you, unless you are a fool like me, you more or less express his opinion'. Menon himself told him, at noon on Sunday, that 'the right thing to do is to allow Nandaji to carry on, on the definite understanding that it's an interim arrangement, and we don't want to make a permanent choice to split the party; mind you, this was all in the context of two candidates'. By 3 o'clock there was no doubt that Morarji was beaten. Those who observed the Morarji camp during the poll detected the mood of defeat. Some of his supporters pressed him to carry the battle to the floor of the CPP meeting. But he knew the 'rules of the game' too well and refused.

Only Nanda, the self-declared non-candidate, had any illusions at that point. According to him, Kamaraj was 'puzzled, because a large number of persons wanted to continue the status quo'—the Menon formula. Moreover, at some time during the poll, he said, Kamaraj and Atulya came to him and asked if he was a contestant. He reiterated that he was not—but implied that he was prepared to serve as a compromise choice by telling them that they could count on him for whatever seemed 'the appropriate decision '.[61] Kamaraj had no doubts.

The denouement was now approaching. On Monday evening, the Congress President conveyed his reading of the Party's choice to the five candidates, active or passive—Shastri, Morarji, Jagjivan Ram, Nanda, and Mrs. Gandhi. When asked what Kamaraj had said to him, Morarji told pressmen, ' he does not speak much; he just said, " Lal Bahadur Shastri " '.[62] About his own reaction, he said: ' Unless you feel happy in difficult circumstances, you will never be happy. That is my philosophy of life.' [63] But to Kamaraj, he later revealed, he expressed his real feelings about the selection process: he considered that Kamaraj should not have sought the consensus, since he was one of the partisans. Kamaraj denied this and claimed to have been neutral, but Morarji did not believe him and warned him, if he continued ' to run the Party's affairs this way ', to ' beware of 1967 ' (the next general election).[64]

Nonetheless, one of the rules of Congress behaviour at the élite level is to accept defeat and close ranks, though there have been exceptions.[65] Morarji withdrew and offered to nominate Shastri before the Convention; Kamaraj agreed. But Nanda, ever conscious of his status as Prime Minister, even if only *ad interim*, insisted on the honour; Morarji yielded once more. Later that evening, Shastri called on Morarji; nothing is known of their fifteen-minute conversation.

There is one final reported episode at the close of the drama which bears notice. Some members of the Caucus were concerned lest Shastri decline the call to office. According to Atulya Ghosh, Kamaraj told him on two occasions during those tense days that he could not get Shastri's consent. Then, on Monday night, 1 June, after a visit to Nehru's cremation site, Shastri went to the Residence and suggested to Mrs. Gandhi that she become Prime Minister. Atulya became agitated when he heard this and hurried to Shastri's home. There, in a ninety-minute meeting, he said, he finally persuaded Shastri to accept and clinched the argument by urging him not to ' resist the call from your own people '.[66]

It may well be that Shastri withheld his consent from the Congress President, that he visited Mrs. Gandhi and, in some form, ' offered ' her the post of her father's successor, and that Atulya had a lengthy conversation with Shastri that evening. But the incident, as related, seems fanciful. In withholding consent, Nehru's successor was merely avoiding the trap that ensnared Morarji early in the battle—' let the office come to the man '. If he ' offered ' the post to Mrs. Gandhi, it could only have been an empty gesture, for Shastri knew better than anyone that such an ' offer ' was beyond his power. And as for the claim that he had to be persuaded, he later declared that this was non-sense; he had no hesitation in assuming the post, because he knew that he was the choice of the people and the Party. He acknowledged, however, that, ' if someone else had come forward [presumably as Party choice], I would have stepped aside '. Finally, ' I did say to one or two people that, if they came forward, I would withdraw '.[67]

There remained the constitutional formalities. These were conducted with decorum and propriety on Tuesday 2 June, which one writer hailed as an historic occasion, dramatic, dignified, solemn, and at times touching.[68] Another termed it the most moving scene since the ' tryst with destiny ' on 14–15 August 1947.[69]

The Central Hall of Parliament was full at 9 a.m., when the meeting came to order. Raghunath Singh of the CPP Executive, supported by Ram Subhag Singh of the Working Committee, urged Kamaraj to take the chair. The Congress President led off with a tribute to the illustrious Panditji and spoke briefly about his consensus-seeking procedure—but he did not announce the results; this he left to the defeated candidates, further evidence of his consummate skill throughout the drama. Prime Minister Nanda then proposed Shastri as Party Leader. Morarji seconded the motion, and it was carried by a standing ovation.

At that point the press was permitted to observe the proceedings. Key figures affirmed their loyalty to Nehru's successor—Nanda, Morarji, Jagjivan Ram, and the Deputy Leader of the CPP, K. C. Reddy. Then Kamaraj spoke again about the tasks ahead. As if to remind the victor of the decision process, he declared that no one would be able to fill the void left by Nehru's death and that the Congress would have to function on the basis of ' collective responsibility, collective leadership, and collective approach '. The unanimous election, he concluded, was a fitting but humble tribute to Nehru.

The diminutive and gentle Shastriji then thanked his colleagues for love and affection and read a prepared statement. He spoke with poise throughout, except when referring to Mrs. Gandhi bearing with fortitude the tragedy that had befallen the nation; to emphasize continuity, he added that he looked forward to her ' continued association with us '. He was thankful to Nanda and Ram, expressed ' my most sincere thanks to Mr. Morarji Desai '; he heaped praise on Panditji's daughter and remarked that he was ' extremely grateful ' to Kamaraj. The wounds were being healed publicly, if superficially. As to policy, Shastri declared himself the continuator of Nehru: ' Socialism is our objective. Our policy has already been defined and enunciated. What is essential is its proper and quicker implementation.' [70]

It was Kamaraj, however, who held the centre of the stage during the closing act of the drama. All speakers paid effusive compliments to his tactful and unifying direction of the decision process, notably S. K. Patil, in an unscheduled vote of thanks to the Congress President. Menon, among others, was annoyed: ' I asked Kamaraj, " what is the idea ", and he said, " I cannot stop him coming up, I never asked him to ". He [Patil] wanted to appear; he is a very good tactician that way; Kamaraj would not repudiate him. This was the end of that meeting.' As for the mood in the Convention, ' there was a certain amount of resentment that the Party was being overlooked, the Parliamentary Party; but the Parliamentary Party itself is a caucus; so while there were about a hundred people who felt that way, it was a finished question '.[71] Indeed it was.

Seven hours after his unanimous election as Leader of the CPP, Shastri called on the President and was invited to form a government. Nanda, who had tendered his resignation a little earlier in the day, was asked to stay on as head of a caretaker government until Shastri was sworn in. It was another week before that took place, but the succession to Nehru, perhaps the most impressive achievement of the Indian political system, was now an accomplished fact.

The outcome of the struggle and the manner of its achievement were widely acclaimed in India and abroad. Menon and the Left, Morarji and the Right, Nanda, Jagjivan Ram, perhaps Mrs. Gandhi as well, were disappointed, but the overwhelming reaction was approval—and relief. This was amply reflected in the Press. The *Indian Express*, even before the Convention, wrote: ' Good sense has prevailed after a brief controversy. . . . The democratic procedure has not suffered. . . . Even Mr. Kamaraj could not have possibly imposed on the Parliamentary Party a candidate who was not known to have the overwhelming support of the electorate.' [72] The *Statesman* remarked proudly: ' Events have proved even better than hopes '; what was now needed was the avoidance of bitterness and the formation of a Cabinet on the basis of merit; further, Shastri should not burden himself with any specific portfolio.[73] The advice was not heeded: there was little change in the Cabinet—indeed, only two new faces: Mrs. Gandhi became Minister of Information and Broadcasting, and Sanjiva Reddy, Minister of Steel and Mines; S. K. Patil was de-Kamarajed and given the Railways portfolio; Shastri himself took over Nehru's special care, External Affairs.[74]

The *Times of India* commended the choice and observed that the Congress had shown ' unity of purpose which will stand it in good stead in the years to come '. Nehru would have been pleased and the gloomy prophets were confounded, it proudly declared. And echoing the Congress President's sentiments, ' as Prime Minister, he [Shastri] will be no more than first among equals '; the principle of collective leadership would obtain.[75] The *Express* echoed these sentiments on the morrow of the CPP

Convention: 'The disciplined manner [of election] . . . does it credit. . . . It would have rejoiced Jawaharlal.' And while Shastri would not be another Nehru, he has great strength; his task would be to carry India 'on the road and along the signposts which Jawaharlal built'. Preoccupation with continuity was most evident in the *Patriot*, self-appointed guardian of the Nehru tradition: 'The people . . . hope that he will never stray from the path marked out for him and his colleagues by his great master'; to this end it advocated the inclusion of Menon, Malaviya, and Mrs. Gandhi in the Cabinet.[76] And the leading daily in south India, the *Hindu*, wrote, with uncharacteristic candour: 'On the choice . . . there can be no two opinions . . . [Shastri] is eminently fitted to promote this collective leadership.'[77]

Among the pundits, two comments will suffice. B. G. Verghese summed it up in these words: 'He was nominated with dignity and elected with grace. The choice is not unexpected. Mr. Shastri was probably Nehru's unnamed nominee too. . . . The Congress has made a wise and fortunate choice.'[78] In Prem Bhatia's view, 'it was no small achievement . . . to have brought about a smooth settlement within five days of the Prime Minister's cremation. Things could have been much worse.'[79] President Radhakrishnan was later reported to have said that he was not too happy with the consensus technique because some persons felt they should have had the right to exercise a secret ballot. However, he accepted it because he knew that, even if a secret ballot had been held in the Parliamentary Party, the result would have been the same; Shastri would have received more than 300 votes, and Morarji 150. In short, the forms of constitutional democracy were rigorously maintained, party sentiment was accurately gauged, and the popular choice was selected, all without shattering the unity of the Congress élite or the tranquillity of the realm. It was an occasion for legitimate pride.

IV

PROCESS

SEGMENTS of the decision process which led to 'the making of a Prime Minister' have already been analysed. Among them were the impact of the Kamaraj Plan, the Tirupathi meeting and the selection of Kamaraj as Congress President, and the formation of a *de facto* triumvirate after Nehru's illness as Bhubaneswar. These developments, in perspective, comprise three preliminary phases of the process leading to the succession, whether by design or by natural evolution.

We have seen how the 'Great Purge' reshuffled the cards in the deck of Congress leadership and Cabinet status, to the detriment of Morarji and Jagjivan Ram, and to the benefit of Nanda. The latter became thereby the logical, in fact the necessary, successor, even if for an interim period only. More significant, had Morarji retained the No. 2 rank in the Cabinet he would have been sworn in as Prime Minister on 27 May; and it would have been exceedingly difficult, if not impossible, to dislodge him. We have also seen how the assumption of the Party presidency by Kamaraj placed the Caucus in a strategic position to influence, one might say to shape, the succession, certainly to manage it in an orderly fashion. Whether the succession was in the minds of those who gathered at Tirupathi is a moot point; Kamaraj denied it, but Reddy and Atulya acknowledged that it entered their calculations about the presidency. It is difficult to believe otherwise, for Nehru's illness in 1962, at the age of 72, had made the political élite uncomfortably aware that the challenge of a peaceful, well-managed transfer of power would not be long in coming; and the subsequent behaviour of the Caucus, as well as their oft-displayed shrewdness, support this interpretation. Notable in this regard was their unconcealed eagerness to bring about Shastri's return to the Cabinet. Indeed, every week of his membership in the Cabinet triumvirate enhanced his prospects of victory, while the competing candidates, now the 'have nots', observed with controlled anger from afar. So much for the setting or background to the decision.

A multiplicity of themes have emerged from the empirical inquiry into the six-day process of succession. The first was Morarji's haste in declaring his availability for the office of Prime Minister, in violation of a cardinal rule of the political system. More important were the contrasting strategies of the Shastri and Morarji camps, the former relying heavily on the organizational wing of the Party and quiet lobbying, the latter seeking support in the Parliamentary Party and pressing the case for an unfettered secret election by the CPP—and pursuing these aims with conspicuous vigour. Closely related, yet an autonomous variable in the process, was the abortive struggle between the CPP executive and the Working Committee, representing the two long-competing wings of the Party, for the right to play the decisive role.

We have also explored the strategy of the Left, moving in haste from an alignment with Morarji to the more comfortable position of supporting Mrs. Gandhi and then Nanda, all in an effort to block Shastri's path. Even more opportunistic was the strategy of Jagjivan Ram, first in backing his former rival, Morarji, then in throwing his weight behind Mrs. Gandhi, and, finally, proclaiming himself a candidate. There was, too, Nanda's contradictory behaviour, a seeming disinterest in the post, which only thinly concealed an eagerness for the prize. If there was any strategy at all, it was in creating the appearance of an active Head of Government and, secondly, offering to serve as a compromise in order to break the impasse and maintain Party unity. Only Mrs. Gandhi's role remains somewhat obscured by the personal tragedy and the utterly passive nature of her involvement in the process, apart from indicating her support for the continuation of the interim arrangements, i.e., Nanda as Prime Minister. Was that out of conviction, ideological or other—or was it, as some suggested, part of her own strategy to succeed her father a few months later?

The inquiry also revealed the operation of basic forces in the Indian polity. One is Regionalism, as expressed in the composition of the Caucus: it was a coalition of South, East, and

West, the non-Hindi-speaking coastal regions of India. Another, closely related, may be termed State Autonomism and Parochialism. There were various forms in which this was manifested. Most important was the pivotal position of the State party machine in the all-India configuration of power. As regards the succession, its impact was twofold: first, the individual role of Chief Ministers in shaping the decision of the Grand Council of the Republic, as invitees to the enlarged Working Committee meeting on 31 May; and secondly, the influence of State chiefs deriving from their known control over blocs of votes in the CPP. State loyalty as a criterion of political action was apparent in at least two major developments: Maharashtra's antipathy to Morarji for the events of 1956 which, apart from any other consideration, would have denied this large bloc to the Gujarati leader; and the reported revolt of members of C. B. Gupta's faction in U.P., rejecting his support for Morarji against a 'local son', Shastri. The latter may not have been in their faction, but the historic primacy of U.P. in the Congress, as well as in the Union Government, with all the patronage and pride that this entailed—all this, they thought mistakenly, would be better safeguarded with Shastri than Morarji, an outsider.

Factionalism is a third basic force in India's political system, at all levels. Closely linked to this is the interpenetration of personal and group rivalries in State and Union politics. Illustrative was the split in the Bihar Congress, the Sahay faction backing Shastri, and the Jha faction, Morarji; so too in U.P., with Gupta supporting Morarji, and Tripathi backing Shastri; and in Madhya Pradesh as well. A curious result of this linkage between the two levels of politics, as noted earlier, was the dilemma confronting Malaviya, a self-conscious leftist, under pressure from left-wing M.L.A.s in Bihar, whose faction in the State Party is befriended by Morarji.

The interplay of differentiated and specific interest groups in the struggle for the succession was a notable feature of the process. There were institutional interest groups at work, such as the Working Committee, the CPP Executive, and the PCC leadership. There were also associational interest groups, more or less well-organized for political activity: the caste type (Untouchables, supporting Jagjivan Ram); communal (Muslims); M.P.s from each State, who met as a distinct interest group; and factional groups within the State Congress leadership and their extensions to the State parliamentarians. Occupational interest groups, labour or entrepreneur, do not appear to have played a role in the process as such, though moneyed interests, especially in Bombay and Gujarat, reportedly invested substantial sums in the outcome. The outstanding non-associational interest group in the process, in fact the newest in the political system, was the Caucus or Syndicate, really a committee of Chief Ministers and their allies at the Centre. Another was the ideological Left. And the press and pundits acted throughout as a cohesive interest group in the background, and during 'the six days', supporting Shastri as the most suitable man to succeed Nehru.

There are other facets of the process which merit attention. One is the attitude of Pandit Nehru to the succession and the related issue of his preference, if any. Another concerns the reasons for the choice of Shastri, among the politicians and the populace. A third is the explanation of Morarji's behaviour, especially his withdrawal. There is also the intriguing question of the Army's role in the brief interregnum. More important is the part played by the Syndicate in the decision. One must examine as well the reasons for a tranquil succession. And, finally, there is the issue of constitutionality.

The attitude of India's charismatic leader to the perennial question, 'after Nehru, who?', was steadfast to the end: he resisted all pressures to name a successor or even—to the consternation of many—to train a group to ensure the continuity of his policies. Those who bore him animus merely trotted out the familiar, 'après moi, le déluge'. But the reasons were much deeper, as one would expect from a character as complex as Nehru. First was a genuine belief in the democratic ethic. Secondly, and closely linked to this, was his profound faith in the ability of India's political system to meet the test of an orderly succession. Not only was it not his task to arrange continuity; the attempt to do so might cause irreparable harm to the fabric of constitutional democracy—and this was a cherished value in his vision of India. No less germane was a tendency to denigrate the role of a future leader, the product of two strands in his make-up: the Marxist residue in his philosophy led him to attribute change and progress primarily to the 'masses', not the élite; and his own experience gave him the comforting assurance that he had laid the foundations for modernity and secularism; these he considered irrevocable. This became apparent as early as 1956, when he remarked about the future:

All this trains, educates people, makes them think in a particular way and drives all of them forward in a particular direction. Now, some of them [successors] may stop the pace, not going in that direction, or they may make it faster. But I don't think it is possible in the future for the mass of the people to be taken away, far away, from their moorings.[1]

There was still another reason for his unwillingness to designate a successor, perhaps deriving from the experience of Eden and Butler in 1957. As noted earlier, he declared just a month before his death that to nominate someone would be the surest way of his not becoming Prime Minister, for it would arouse jealousy and envy.[2]

Events justified Nehru's assessment and his calculated risk. But did he not inwardly have a favourite and did he not take steps to ease his path to the succession? Evidence is inconclusive on this point, and views are sharply divided among those who were close to him. Mrs. Pandit was emphatic in asserting that her brother did not regard—let alone designate—Shastri as his successor. T. T. K. was equally convinced to the contrary and cited the Kamaraj Plan and Shastri's return to the Cabinet in support of this contention. Kamaraj concurred and added that he interpreted the latter act as a clear indication of Nehru's choice of Shastri—indeed, that Panditji was paving the way for the man who ultimately triumphed in the struggle.[3]

There were two other gestures in favour of Shastri. Nehru dispatched him to Srinagar to ease the tension in Kashmir arising from the 'Prophet's Hair' incident at the end of 1963, though Nanda was the logical emissary as Home Minister; he also encouraged Shastri's policy of conciliation and supported him on the release of Sheikh Abdullah. More telling, perhaps, was the Prime Minister's last-minute decision to take Shastri to the Commonwealth Conference, noted earlier. One may also cite two negative actions in this connection: Nehru's intervention in 1961, preventing the certain election of Morarji as Deputy Leader of the Parliamentary Party, regarded by most at the time as a stepping-stone to the succession; and the removal of Morarji from the Cabinet in August 1963; Shastri, too, was removed, but he soon returned.

Yet all this merely proves that he preferred Shastri to Morarji; it is not sufficient evidence for the T. T. K.–Kamaraj view, expressed *after* Shastri became Prime Minister. Was there, perhaps, someone else whom Panditji would have chosen, if he had had the power and inclination to do so? The only other person who was the subject of serious speculation was his daughter. Once again, there are conflicting views. Nehru himself had denied any intention to groom Mrs. Gandhi for the Prime Ministership, as indicated above. Mrs. Pandit suggested that he thought of her as a member of the Cabinet but no more and revealed that he was upset by Mrs. Gandhi's reported remark in Hong Kong shortly before his death that, if offered the post of Prime Minister, she would accept. The Finance Minister was even more emphatic, adding that Nehru had told him it would be improper for him to pre-arrange her role in public affairs in any sense. This seems the most authentic expression of Nehru's attitude, though there are some who strongly dissented.

Morarji was one, but as an interested party his 'evidence' must be treated with caution. He referred to the elimination of all other competitors through the Kamaraj Plan and cited two uncorroborated 'facts': that Nehru tried to secure Mrs. Gandhi's election as Congress President in the autumn of 1963; and that members of the Caucus informed him that they were trying to deny the succession to her.[4] Patnaik shared this view and based it on two other developments. One was Nehru's appointment of his daughter as Chairman of the high-powered National Citizens' Council during the Emergency of October–November 1962. The other was a plan to bring her into the Cabinet as Foreign Minister in January 1964. If the latter was his intention, it never came to fruition. And as regards the former, Patnaik claimed that Nehru, in reply to his suggestion that she become Foreign Minister, said: 'You don't understand. In the Citizens' Council she can establish a national image with all the people who rule India.' This, too, is an interested appraisal.[5] One further item in the case was mentioned, however, by a know-ledgeable senior Congressman, namely that Nehru brushed aside Pandit Pant's objection to making her Congress President in 1959 —on the grounds that she was young and could assume the post later—and even rescinded the selection of Nijalingappa, Chief Minister of Mysore, to make way for her.[6]

Only the Nehru Papers may be able to cast definitive light on Nehru's intentions and preferences. For the present, one can attempt no more than intuitive speculation. There can be little doubt that Panditji was eager to prevent Morarji from succeeding him; by the early 1960s, at any rate, he found Morarji's autho-ritarian temperament, his ideology, and his stubborn addiction to traditional fads utterly distasteful—though in the early days he relied heavily on Morarji for advice on a wide range of issues, political and personal. Indeed, as early as 1953, Nehru had invited Morarji to join the Union Cabinet: 'The burden of work has been very heavy on me' (since Gopalaswami Ayyangar's death), he wrote. 'It was bad enough before. So naturally I have been thinking of someone or more than one coming here and sharing it with me. Your name and Pantji's [Pandit Pant] came to my mind. I feel we must strengthen the Centre.'[7] Morarji declined at the time, fearing the consequences in Bom-bay, which might have had a chain reaction in the country at large.[8] He finally accepted in 1956, at the height of the Reorganization of States.

Throughout the fifties, in fact, Nehru showed respect, even affection, for Morarji. Two examples will suffice. In 1952, in the midst of a sharp exchange with S. K. Patil over a contro-versial sales tax bill in Bombay, Nehru wrote to Morarji that he had no doubt whatever about his impartiality: 'The odd thing is that sometimes real impartiality is not appreciated.'[9] Four years later he wrote '. . . may I add to it [a telegram] and say how much I have admired your calm steadfastness of purpose in the

face of attack and difficulty. . . . In the middle of this turmoil
you have stood out without losing your temper or allowing your-
self to be swept away. Please remember that you have all our
friendship and admiration. . . .'[10] Admittedly this was a birthday greeting, and Morarji was being challenged by the advocates
of a separate Maharashtra—but it went far beyond mere courtesy
in tone. After Morarji came to Delhi, however, the relationship
changed. With years of close contact came disenchantment,
especially with Morarji's inflexibility on matters extending from
prohibition to Hindi as the official language. Nehru never lost
his respect for his administrative talents but, one may surmise,
he became increasingly concerned that Morarji's brittleness could
cause grave damage to the unity of India, then, as always, in a
perilous and incomplete state. The South, in particular, was
alarmed by Morarji's insistence on Hindi, and Nehru must have
known that a large section of public opinion would bitterly
oppose his policies. Hence his obstacles to Morarji's succession,
in 1961 and 1963.

In Shastri's case, there were no such qualms. He was not as
forceful and decisive as Morarji, but that was an asset in a country
as large and complex as India, especially in a leader who would
lack Nehru's charisma. Moreover, he had shown organizational
ability in a number of governmental and party posts, in U.P.
and the Centre. But most of all, he had made no enemies
and was an accomplished conciliator, as revealed in the Assam
language crisis of 1962 and in Kashmir. Shastri also had the
merit of greater ideological affinity, or so it appeared to Nehru.
For these reasons, then, Panditji probably regarded him as the
most suitable person to succeed him. Yet he would not pre-empt
the legitimate function of the Party—and the people to be
governed. Leaving the decision to the Congress not only
accorded with his political faith; it also had the advantage of
testing Shastri's genuine popularity with the political élite. Hence
part of the rationale for including him among the 'Kamarajed
men'. He assisted him by bringing him back to the Cabinet—
but he did not assure his succession. His attitude was almost
certainly, 'I think that Shastri is the best candidate', or rather,
'the country is safest under Shastri, but let the Party decide'.

Nehru's thoughts on Mrs. Gandhi and the succession remain obscure. He may have had the temptation of a father to see his daughter in a prominent position of responsibility. But he had a strong aversion to the idea of a dynasty—which he knew, in any case, would have been widely resented. Stated differently, he must have known the mood of the Congress élite well enough to realize that they would not accept her as his *immediate* successor.

While Nehru's views on his successor remain open to question, those of Shastri's peers do not. They discerned five distinct assets in his political and personal make-up: first, he comes from the Hindi heartland and, at that time, it was inconceivable that anyone from a non-Hindi-speaking area could be Prime Minister; secondly, his political reputation is unblemished and he has no known enemies; thirdly, he has had vast administrative and organizational experience, having held an array of elective positions in Party and Government, from that of Secretary of the Allahabad Congress Committee to Union Home Minister; fourthly, he is a centrist by ideological conviction and temperament, a conciliator and a man with an open mind, who would not split the Congress or the country; and, finally, he combines the qualities of ability and genuine humility with a natural ambition effectively concealed by gentility.

Conversations with members of the Caucus indicated that these reasons loomed large in their preference for Shastri. Kamaraj put it this way: 'He listens to everyone's views, does not impose his own, and is guided by the consensus of his colleagues', i.e., his fourth asset; some critics, like Patnaik, referred to this as his pliability and to their consequent expectation that Shastri would be 'their man'. Kamaraj added that 'India is a vast country with diverse languages and cultures, and opinion seemed to be strongly in favour of Shastri'. Atulya Ghosh, as usual, was more expansive and cited five reasons for his choice: Shastri is respectful of the Opposition and will consider their views dispassionately—a necessary condition of democracy, he added; he knows his own limitations, 'a quality that most of us lack '; ' he knows India very well '; ' for all practical purposes he ran the Congress election campaigns in 1952, 1957, and 1962 '; and, finally, ' he is the only person who approaches all-India stature, for he is known to Congress workers all over the country '.

Sanjiva Reddy, by contrast, stressed Morarji's shortcomings: ' He is too brittle and rigid; he thinks that he alone knows the right path; that was the only reason we opposed him for the Prime Ministership.' Although he did not mention it, there may also have been a feeling of resentment, conscious or otherwise, due to Morarji's opposition to the formation of a separate State of Andhra in 1953. In a letter to Nehru, Morarji had expressed his views with characteristic candour: ' It would have been better ', he wrote, ' if the main resolution of the Congress on linguistic provinces had been held in abeyance for ten years '; further, the creation of Andhra would affect the Telugu areas of Hyderabad: ' This may in turn set in motion political forces which it would be difficult to control or satisfy '; and then the warning, ' I strongly feel that the course that you propose to take will be highly disastrous. . . .' [11] The contents of this letter were not known to Reddy, but Morarji was incapable of concealing his real views from his colleagues. And it seems not unlikely that the Congress leadership in Andhra did not forget—or forgive.

In the case of S. K. Patil, the distaste for Morarji was more personal, the result of prolonged rivalry in Bombay politics: the former was undisputed master of the Bombay City Congress machine since pre-independence days, while Morarji was the ' strong man ' of the Bombay State Government from 1946 to 1956, first as Home Minister and then as Chief Minister. Typical, perhaps, was a bitter clash in 1952 over a Government-proposed multi-point sales tax Bill. Patil resorted to various tactics to oppose and embarrass the Government of Bombay. One of them was a direct challenge to the parliamentary wing of the Party (Morarji), as revealed in a blunt correspondence with the Chief Minister. If the imposition of new taxes is the sole responsibility of the Administration, wrote Patil, the Congress is free to judge the proposals: ' The support of the Congress [when it] . . . has not been previously consulted cannot be simply automatic or taken for granted.'[12] Morarji replied by reading him a lesson on how budgets are prepared in India's governmental system: 'No budget can ever be prepared in this manner. . . . [As for the Union budget] even the Working Committee is not consulted and rightly so.' And then the personal element: 'The tone of your letter has pained me very much.'[13] Patil continued to press for delay and at one point remarked: 'These might appear harsh words.'[14] Morarji sent a reasoned reply—there were no other sources of revenue, the taxes are essential, etc.— and a barb calculated to wound: 'I . . . can assure you that your harsh words will not create any ill will in me';[15] it is doubtful that this Gandhian dictum had any effect.

Nehru himself became involved in the controversy, as Congress President; his support for Morarji was unqualified. In one letter to Patil he wrote: 'I have read this speech [on the sales tax Bill] with amazement.'[16] In another, he chided Patil for trying to undermine the authority and prestige of the Bombay Government through speeches and interviews.[17] Patil responded with an emotional denial of any political ambitions and a reference to his dilemma in the 1951–2 elections—to go to Parliament, because of 'your persistent dislike of me', or to go to the State legislature, which would have created friction with Morarji.[18] Nehru denied 'persistent dislike', though he admitted that negative reports from Bombay had influenced him. And he, too, lectured Patil on constitutional government: in the U.K. system, 'the Prime Minister or the Chief Minister has a very special position'.[19]

Patil undoubtedly altered his views on the proper relations between the governmental and organizational wings of the Party after he joined the Union Cabinet. But in the earlier years he took a very strong line. Thus, as the conflict continued in 1953 —it lasted eight months—Patil proposed that 'if we fail to agree, we shall invoke the advice of the Prime Minister' (he really meant the Congress President).[20] Morarji refused and proposed a solution of disputes by voting in a joint conference, to which Patil replied: 'it would reduce the Congress organization to a secondary position where . . . it must be prepared to accept the verdict of the administration'.[21] Patil then boycotted the

proposed meeting.   And Morarji made known his view to
Nehru: 'there cannot be a super cabinet'.[22]   Nehru agreed.

Apart from the Patil-Morarji relationship, this three-way
correspondence highlights a perennial trait in Indian politics,
especially at the State level—the conflict between the two wings
of the Congress for control over policy.   It has made of the
Congress a two-party system in most States, a competition
between 'haves' and 'have-nots' in the framework where
ideology is of no consequence.   The lesser parties then perform
as third parties in formalized two-party systems elsewhere, as in
the United Kingdom and Canada.   But in the context of the
succession, it reveals a personal component in the attitude of
Patil to Morarji.

One cannot be certain as to what triggered the crystallization
of the Caucus and the growth of anti-Morarji sentiment.   A
likely explanation, however, was a revealing incident in the Lok
Sabha in the spring of 1963; the topic under discussion was the
Finance Minister's (Morarji's) proposal for a Compulsory Deposit
Scheme.   On that occasion Morarji laid bare in a dramatic form
his gravest political weakness—a marked tendency to authoritarianism.   He did so by propounding the disturbing doctrine
that, even if Parliament unanimously asked him to do something,
he would not yield if he felt the consensus of the House were
wrong.   In perspective, there can be little doubt of grave consternation among many members of the Congress élite, some of whom
began to think in terms of what later became the Kamaraj Plan.

The objective consequences of that debate were such as to
merit further exploration.   Opposition to the Bill mounted on
26 April 1963 and was shared by M.P.s of most parties: the two
principal themes were that it would add to the peasant's burden,
and that it was really in the nature of a forced loan, not a tax,
and thus *ultra vires*.   Among those who spoke were Swatantra
leader Ranga, the voluble and effective H. V. Kamath of the
PSP (Praja Socialist Party), and three Congress stalwarts, Mahavir
Tyagi, A. P. Jain, and S. R. S. Deshmukh; all asked the Speaker
to summon the Attorney-General to explain the constitutional
pros and cons to the House.   The Speaker noted that, under
the Constitution, only the Government, which employs him, can

direct the Attorney-General to report to the House. He then
sought Morarji's opinion, prefacing his request with the remark
that most members of the House wanted him to appear. The
Finance Minister was brittle and haughty: 'I have the greatest
respect for the honourable members of the House, for the House
and, if it can be greater, for you [the Speaker]. But that does
not mean that I should accept every desire *even if it is unanimous*. There are some things where one has to do one's duty.
... The Attorney-General is an officer of the Government. ...
There is no provision in the Constitution whereby the House
can call him (and there is no point in doing so).' It was a strange
doctrine to be heard in the House.

Kamath persisted and reminded the Speaker of his earlier
reference to Article 88 of the Constitution, which gives the
Attorney-General the 'right' to speak to Parliament. The
Speaker then asked Communist leader Hiren Mukherjee for his
view. '... certainly it stands to reason', he said, 'that the
independent services of the Attorney-General, which are available
under the Constitution to Parliament, should be requisitioned.'
Morarji retorted by reading out *part* of Article 76, specifying that
the Attorney-General perform such legal duties as may be
assigned to him by the President (Government); hence, said the
Finance Minister, the Attorney-General has no independence.
Others argued that the rest of Article 76, stating that he is also
required to discharge functions conferred on him by the Constitution, read in conjunction with Article 88, would give the
House discretion to summon him.

The Speaker was in a quandary because there was no precedent
but he felt a primary responsibility to express the will of the
House. He criticized the Finance Minister for his disrespect to
Parliament. And Morarji, rigid to the end, compounded the
blunder by leaving no one in doubt about his attitude: 'I am
very sorry. I am either misunderstood, or I have expressed
myself wrongly. ... I have only said that I cannot fall in with
the desire myself [to summon the Attorney-General]. ... Even
if the House is unanimous, if it is outside the Constitution, it is
my right and duty to say that I do not agree with it.' This
'defence of the Constitution' may have been good constitutional

law, though many would question even that; but it was a crass contempt for the House. Even the Speaker was annoyed: '. . . I would just put it again to the Finance Minister that if it is a responsible government, and this government is responsible to this House, then it should not be said that even if the House is unanimous, the government would not do it.' He then agreed, with some hesitation, that if the House so wished, the invitation to the Attorney-General might be sent.

A flurry of points of order followed. And then Morarji, visibly agitated, made a revealing slip: 'After all, I am told today that I cannot pass, I cannot enact this law because it is not within the constitution. . . .' There was a stormy interruption, with Communist leader Dange taunting him: 'How can he use such words, "I cannot pass"? Who is he to pass it? The whole House has to pass it. . . .' This time Morarji apologized: '. . . all honourable members make mistakes like that for which you cannot hold them to ransom. . . .' Some were willing to forgive, though clearly the vast majority of the House was opposed to Morarji on the substantive matter. More important, they would not easily forget his disdain for the will of Parliament.[23] Taken in conjunction with his tendency to authoritarianism, this display of unbending rigidity may well have created the spectre of possible dictatorship in the minds of many, notably the middle-of-the-road leaders of the Party. Certainly, with Morarji at the helm, their role as colleagues, in the Cabinet and the Working Committee, would be depreciated; even the role of Parliament would suffer on the anvil of 'strong' government. Certainly, too, the time sequence suggests a connection—the Lok Sabha incident in April 1963, the Kamaraj Plan four months later, and the formation of the pro-Shastri Caucus less than two months after that. The causes of the pro-Shastri attitude in the majority of Congress leaders lie deeper, but the Compulsory Deposit Scheme debate very probably served as a catalyst.[24]

The expectations of the Caucus and others who supported Shastri were conveyed in candid interviews some months after the succession. There was concern—in some cases, fear—that Morarji in power would be a one-man government, and that democracy and Indian unity, and their own influence, would be sacrificed to the gods of 'duty' and 'the right path'. By contrast, there was confidence that Shastri, in appearance and manner a gentle and decent person, would be a benign leader; that he would keep the governmental machine going without serious upset; that, as a small man, he would genuinely strive for collective leadership; that he would take into account public opinion; that he would rely on expert advice; that he would be 'practical', and that as a result India and the Congress would be better off under his stewardship.

The intellectual élite shared this assessment, by and large, though some doubted Shastri's capacity for national leadership. So did the attentive public, the five million Indians whose interest in politics extends beyond the periodic election campaigns and who help to shape policy through opinion and responsive pressure; to them as well as to the élites of India, Shastri was the 'safest' among the possible successors to Nehru. And in this they echoed the sentiment of the large, amorphous, usually inarticulate mass public, according to the limited evidence of its preference.[25] As B. G. Verghese remarked: 'Mr. Shastri represents the highest common factor in terms of party political support and national unity. His is the middle way. . . . [He] emerges as another focus of reconciliation within the ruling party as much as in the nation. . . .'[26] Like Nehru before him, though in a different sense, he was the acceptable link among diverse strands of Indian society: he was a northerner and Hindi-speaker but was not anathema to the South because he did not propose the imposition of Hindi; he was secular in outlook (though less so than Nehru) but acceptable to religiously oriented Hindus; he was modern, compared to most Indian politicians, but respectful to and respected by traditionalists; and, in ideology, he was a centrist with a pragmatic approach, responding to the pulls of Left and Right, public sector and private sector, but not committed wholly to either.

We have already identified the roles of the key actors in the process: Kamaraj, the astute kingmaker; Shastri, the retiring king-in-the-making; Morarji, the proud, eager candidate; Nanda, the aspiring non-contestant; Jagjivan Ram, the frustrated politician; Mrs. Gandhi, the grief-stricken recipient of attention; and the President, guardian of constitutional continuity and conscious of history in the making. Others, like Atulya, Patil, Reddy, and Patnaik, were the key lobbyists in the contest, with Chavan and the Chief Ministers the main objects of their courting; and Menon was the interested onlooker. There remains the question of Morarji's behaviour. His initial error was undoubtedly due to over-confidence, stimulated by his supporters. More important, why did he withdraw rather than force a vote in the CPP on the 2nd of June? Morarji himself offered two reasons: first, that India's image in the world and concern about 'after Nehru, what?', often expressed to him abroad, made it seem better to avoid an 'unseemly fight'; and secondly, to maintain the unity of the Congress, for only the Congress could bring progress to India, until other parties were solidly formed.[27] There is no reason to doubt these motives, for Morarji was, more than anything else, a man of principle with a strong sense of discipline and commitment to the Party. Gandhian training and thirty-four years of service made any other course unthinkable. There may also have been the awareness—or calculation—that Shastri's succession might be short-lived and that an opportunity would soon arise; to split the Party now, and lose, would mark the end of his political career, whereas a dignified retreat could only enhance his national stature. As with so many, then, principle and self-interest probably guided his actions.

A marginal but intriguing aspect of the succession was the role of the Army. The facts about its involvement are precise and beyond doubt; the intentions, if any, obscure and controversial. On the day of Nehru's death, General Chaudhuri, Chief of the Army Staff, ordered the movement of 6,000 troops into Delhi, and they were conspicuously present on 28 May, the day of the funeral. Two weeks later, Defence Minister Chavan called Chaudhuri in for an explanation. There were no further developments in this episode, but the Indian capital, notorious for rumours and political gossip, was not without speculation, then and later. Many accepted the official explanation that three brigades were brought in to assist the police in lining the funeral route and in maintaining order. There were some, however, including persons at the highest level of government, who were concerned about a possible military *coup* in the interregnum. No one spoke of this publicly, nor was it reported in the press. But the fact of concern has been confirmed to this writer by many knowledgeable Indians and foreigners, among them a senior member of Cabinet, high-ranking civil servants, diplomats, and pundits.

Concern was natural in a developing and recently-emerged independent state in Afro-Asia: the military had seized power in more than half a dozen such countries, and India was facing the crisis of the passing of its charismatic leader. Most pointed was the case of neighbouring Pakistan, with the same colonial experience, political system, and tradition of civilian control over the armed forces. Not only had Ayub taken power in 1958; according to virtually all observers, he had brought stability and progress after a decade of misrule and stagnation. Now, with Nehru gone and the future uncertain, and the economy in grave trouble, would the Army in India attempt to emulate the Pakistan precedent? The persistent speculation of decline 'after Nehru' only accentuated the concern among sections of the political and intellectual élites.

Yet the fact of concern does not prove intent. On the contrary, there is no evidence whatever of any serious thought or plans to attempt a takeover—though some individual officers may have toyed with the idea. General Chaudhuri's account of the 'incident' seems convincing. He was at Ootacamund in the south when Nehru died. He returned to Delhi immediately and asked the local commander whether sufficient troops were on hand to manage the funeral arrangements. The answer was affirmative, but Chaudhuri soon discovered otherwise—and he was in a good position to assess the situation because he had been in charge of Gandhi's mammoth funeral sixteen years before. The decision to bring in 6,000 troops from the Western Command was taken by him personally, after consulting the Cabinet

Secretary and Home Secretary; the Defence Minister and Defence
Secretary, he emphasized, were both away, and the politicians
seemed preoccupied and overwhelmed by events.   He informed
the President after he acted, and the reply in effect was, 'do
whatever you think necessary'.   As for the claim that police
reinforcements were brought in to counter a possible Army move,
this, he said, was a figment of imagination; and, in any event,
the police were no match for his troops. What made his account
of a simple and sensible act of administrative necessity even more
persuasive was his unsolicited reference to Chavan's 'summons'
a fortnight after the event; the delay was due to the fact that
Chaudhuri had suffered a heat stroke on the day of the funeral.
The Defence Minister's attitude was in no sense critical, he
remarked.   And then, with absolute assurance, he said: 'I
would do it again if confronted with the same problem.' [28]

One must conclude, in the absence of further evidence, that
civilian concern was unwarranted.   Nor should it be inferred
that fear of an Army *coup* was widespread in the Establishment;
indeed, it was concentrated in the Central Bureau of Intelligence,
a branch of the Home Ministry. And, in that connection, an
element of personal and institutional rivalry may shed light on
the 'tempest in a teapot'.   Malik, the Director of the CBI, had
resented Chaudhuri's accusations of serious errors in its assessment of Chinese strength and troop movements in the autumn of
1962—the CBI was in charge of both civil and military intelligence operations; in the opinion of many, this was a return
thrust to undermine the position of the Army and Chaudhuri
personally. It failed on both counts.

The Caucus has already been dissected in great detail.   It
remains to point up its distinctive functions in the orderly succession to Nehru.   The term 'managing agent' comes readily to
mind, not only because of its historic association with India but
also because it aptly conveys the dual role of the Syndicate.   One
was to serve as the coalescing agent for diverse interest groups
which viewed Shastri as the most effective protector and trans-
mission belt for their specific interests—regional and State,

.nstitutional and organizational, ideological and electoral. The other was to channel these complementary interests into a concentrated thrust and to manage the mechanics of a tranquil election—through the device of consensus.

It would be erroneous to attribute Shastri's election to the Caucus. As the victorious candidate remarked later,[29] ' even if these gentlemen had done nothing, a large majority, at least 80 per cent., of the Congress Parliamentary Party, would have voted for me. I knew that. I did not speak to anyone about it; I sensed this support.' This assessment may underrate the contribution of the Caucus and exaggerate his majority—but it is basically correct. In the last analysis, the outcome was determined by peaceful competition among various interest groups. The decisive factor was the clear majority for Shastri in the three key institutional groups, the Working Committee, the State party machines, and the CPP, superimposed on the relatively inarticulate but known choice of Shastri by the mass public. The role of the Caucus was to give political form to that real national preference. But it was also more, namely, to prevent the competition from becoming disorderly, with dire danger to the unity of the country and the Party, and to the stability of the political system.

The essence of the Syndicate's role as managing agent emerges most clearly, perhaps, from a metaphor. The succession to Nehru may be likened to a vault with a complex combination: a two-thirds majority in the Working Committee plus support of the Chief Ministers of the four southern States, Bengal and Maharashtra plus sizeable factional backing in U.P., Bihar and Madhya Pradesh plus a mood of fear of extremism and authoritarianism in the CPP and the public at large plus a compulsion for orderly change amidst continuity. Only Shastri fitted that combination in 1964, and the Caucus knew its ingredients. Stated slightly differently, Shastri was the key to an orderly succession, and the Syndicate deftly unlocked the door.[30] It was a notable feat of political mechanics. And, in that connection, it is noteworthy that four of the men responsible for the smooth succession—Kamaraj, Atulya, Reddy, and Shastri—had never travelled outside the sub-continent. Yet they responded quickly and effectively to the rules of a democratic system. Like the vast majority of India's political élite, their experience inside the Congress over many years had been sufficient to teach them this style of politics. The Congress Party had served as the primary instrument of acculturation to democracy in India.

Those who criticized the consensus technique and pressed for election by the CPP alone erred on two counts. They forgot—or chose to ignore—the fundamental character of the Congress. And secondly, they mistook procedure for substance, failing to see the real consensus behind the electoral device. The Congress is not just—some would say, not primarily—the Parliamentary Party. Rather, it is an amalgam of the AICC and the Working Committee, the party organizations in the States, the non-governmental leaders, and the CPP. The last are really delegates of the Congress to Parliament, as well as being representatives of their constituencies. Consultation among all these groups was appropriate, necessary, and sound: appropriate, because it was in accordance with the structure and custom of the Congress; necessary, because a broad-based acceptance was a precondition to healthy relations between the Centre and the States; and sound, because all major interest groups were given a sense of participation. There were still other elements in the rationale of consensus. It prevented a public display of factional strife in the Congress at the Centre—it was already alarmingly frequent in most of the States. It helped to still the fear of disorder after Nehru. And, finally, it halted a potential split between the organizational and governmental wings of the Party at the highest level.

The ultimate justification for election (or selection) by consensus lies elsewhere, however. The choice of Shastri reflected the 'national mood'. Even if the contest had been formally decided by the Parliamentary Party, the result would have been the same. This is so not only because the same forces which managed the election through consensus would have operated through the CPP, but, more important, because those forces expressed the genuine preference of the Indian people. There is, indeed, a deeper meaning to the consensus, objectively perceived: through Shastri, India was indicating its desire for the continuation of the main features of Nehru's policy—Democracy, Secularism, Planning, and Non-Alignment, though marginal changes were not ruled out; Shastri was the person who best symbolized these values and goals.

Perhaps the most striking characteristic of the succession was its smoothness. On the surface, this may be explained by Kamaraj's skilful direction of the enterprise and the Caucus's sense of purpose. But there are more basic factors to be noted. First, decision by consensus is not new to the Congress tradition; in fact, it is an established part of the ' Congress system '. Voting is virtually unknown to the proceedings of the Working Committee, and while a formal ballot is taken at AICC meetings, the result is invariably unanimous for the record—after divergent views have been aired. Secondly, the appearance of unanimity, smoothly reached, is an admirable instrument for the perpetuation of Congress power. There was, too, a deep concern about external opinion and a genuine desire to demonstrate maturity in handling a potential crisis. But most important is the pragmatic outlook of almost all members of the Congress élite. It is true that Morarji is identified with the Right, Shastri with the Centre, and Mrs. Gandhi and Nanda with the Left. But these labels are ill-suited to Congress politicians. All are formally committed to Socialism, yet they mean different things, and few understand the term or its implications. Morarji as Prime Minister might be more favourable to the private sector and Mrs. Gandhi to the public sector, but neither would deviate radically from present policy. And the ideological component in their behaviour is minimal. They are adaptable to the powerful currents carried by India's interest groups; none is highly motivated ideologically. As Prime Minister Shastri later reflected, ' there are no ideological differences between the factions, they are all personal; therefore, there are no compelling factors to lead to an open split '.[31] Thus, it was relatively easy to close ranks once the man with a clear majority was known. In this particular process, the actors, the managers, and the electorate (CPP) were conspicuously free from the divisive force of ideology. In the largest sense, a great polyglot party flushed out its groups, who contested maturely for the prize of office; it was a good omen for the future stability of India.

As for the issue of constitutionality, the forms were meticulously maintained. Within two hours of Nehru's death, the President swore in the ranking member of Cabinet as Prime Minister. On 2 June the Congress Parliamentary Party elected a new Leader, and the same day he was invited to form a government. This was duly sworn in on the 9th. Constitutional propriety was maintained throughout. Moreover, the procedure of election and the involvement of the Congress President were in order. Congress M.P.s are nominated by the Central Parliamentary Board, itself appointed by the Working Committee. A Congress President tendering advice to his own nominees as to the choice of their leader in Parliament does not violate the letter or the spirit of the democratic process. Indeed, the consensus procedure in India in 1964 combined the former U.K. Tory method of consensus among party leaders, as recently revealed in the succession to Eden (1957) and to Macmillan (1964), with the Labour Party's method of election by the Parliamentary Party. Nor was it inferior in sophistication to its British counterparts.

V

IMPACT

The death of Nehru made inevitable a change in the power pyramid of all-India politics: the ' age of charisma ' was about to give way to an era of ' collective leadership '. The succession catalyzed the change and charted its course. And Shastri was astute enough to realize this. In any event, his political style was markedly different from that of Panditji.

Lal Bahadur's approach to politics may be termed ' low posture ' yet subtle, quiet yet decisive: it is the product of three decades in the jungle of U.P. politics. There, in the Hindi heartland, where factionalism and casteism reign supreme, he acquired those qualities which make him almost unique in the Congress élite—a man virtually without political enemies. Whether at the district level or in Lucknow, where he served as Parliamentary Secretary to Pandit Pant and, later, as Minister of Home Affairs and Transport in the State Government, he moved deftly and lightly, always self-effacing and soft-spoken. Yet in many circles he was known as an extremely tough, even ruthless, positive manipulator of his own group, and a man as able to press his own interests as any other U.P. politician. Then, as General Secretary of the Congress in 1951–2 he demonstrated organizational ability of a high order, marshalling the Party's resources during the first general election.

He entered the Union Cabinet and moved steadily up the ladder, from Transport and Railways (1952) to Industry and Commerce (1957) and, upon the death of Pant in 1960, to the prestigious and powerful Home Ministry. The one notable event in a competent but hitherto undistinguished record occurred in December 1956, when he resigned from the Cabinet after a serious railway accident. This act of Gandhian renunciation brought him popular and Party esteem. And when he repeated this self-less gesture in the summer of 1963, by offering to resign even before the Kamaraj Plan was crystallized, his reputation for integrity and service reached its peak. By that time, too, he had demonstrated to the nation his extraordinary talent for conciliation, through the 'Shastri formula' for linguistic co-existence in the strife-torn Cachar District of Assam.[1] He repeated this triumph in the aftermath of the 'Prophet's Hair' incident in Kashmir at the beginning of 1964.[2] The contrast with Morarji's inflexibility had a profound effect on his colleagues, as noted earlier.

It was this combination of qualities—humility, patience, respect for conflicting viewpoints, sensitivity to powerful emotional currents, along with subtlety and quiet firmness—that Shastri brought to the awesome task of succeeding Jawaharlal Nehru.[3] As he himself remarked, with persuasive simplicity, his guiding principle was the persistent search for consensus: 'If I can carry everyone along with me, that is much better. Even those who disagree must feel that their views are listened to.' And, without apology, he added: 'This approach may delay decisions a little, but that does not bother me at all. It is a price worth paying.'[4] Somewhat earlier, he told university students in Allahabad that he had recently solved two difficult Kashmir problems 'with humanity and firmness'; further, that while Ministers should take policy decisions, they should leave it to administrators to implement them.[5] No wonder that he won the respect of both warring politicians and status-conscious civil servants, as well as the public at large. Indeed, some who worked closely with him in the Home Ministry testified to his talent for harmony with his professional advisers, without the sacrifice of firmness in decision. He was to continue that *rapport* at the summit of government.

To say that Nehru possessed the magic power of charisma and that Shastri did not is only to point up the most striking contrast in their style and in the decision process before and after the succession. These differences need to be explored more deeply. One way is to compare the working of Cabinet under the two Prime Ministers. Another is to dissect the changes in the power pyramid at the all-India level of politics. A third is to probe the relations between the party hierarchy and the government at the Centre. A fourth is to examine the changes, in substance and spirit, in the relationship of Union and State Governments. And finally, one must assess the impact of the succession on the balance of influence exerted by non-party and non-governmental pressure groups in the Indian polity. In this manner, the short-term effects of the succession can be systematically uncovered.

Nehru served as Prime Minister for seventeen years. With the exceptions of Patel, Azad, Menon, and Pant, there was not only the contrast between the pre-eminent leader and his lesser colleagues, but also the difference in generations. Panditji was already a national figure when most of his Cabinet members were still at school or beginning their apprenticeship in politics; even Morarji was an unknown civil servant in Gujarat when he presided over the historic Lahore session of the Congress in 1929. But Nehru was more than that to his associates. He was Gandhi's political heir, hero of the masses, India's spokesman to the world, symbol of a renascent people, and the last of the giants of the nationalist movement; he was the incomparable Jawaharlal, and he could do no wrong. It was this intangible but universally acknowledged status that shaped the attitude of Cabinet colleagues almost to the end of his life.

A few persons, who inwardly opposed some of Nehru's policies, likened the Cabinet at the height of his power and vigour to a *darbar*. There was no real discussion, they recalled; the Prime Minister would simply refer to the Agenda, pronounce his point of view, and so it was done. Others, including civil servants who observed the proceedings, termed this portrait of a docile Cabinet a myth—and the expression of a sense of frustration and subordination; they testified to frequent spirited discussions, with the Prime Minister registering the consensus. Certainly in the economic sphere he was guided by his Finance Minister; such is the testimony of Morarji, even after the bitter-ness of the succession struggle; indeed, he asserted that Nehru ' never interfered with my domain; whatever advice I tendered on a financial issue, he accepted '. It was the same with T. T. Krishnamachari (T.T.K.)—and finance occupied the dominant position in Cabinet decisions. As for the budget, said Morarji, British practice was followed: the Finance Minister drafted it and consulted only Nehru and Pant, the Home Minister; the

Cabinet was taken into confidence only two hours before the budget speech was delivered to Parliament. And even in the powerful Economic Affairs Committee of the Cabinet, where there was more substantive discussion, the primacy of the Finance Minister was acknowledged by all; his views generally carried.[6] If Nehru was given *carte blanche* in foreign policy, it was, after all, his portfolio; more than that, they knew little about it and felt it was in competent hands, at least until the last year and a half.

The most perceptive account of the Indian Cabinet ' from the inside '—certainly the most comprehensive—was provided by Krishna Menon some months after the succession. The spirit and process, as well as the structure of Cabinet under Nehru, were explained in a candid memoir, from which the following extracts are taken: [7]

On Nehru's attitude to Cabinet colleagues:

He treated them with respect, certainly, but he knew he could decide what he wanted. That is to say, he would carry the persons concerned—either they would shrug their shoulders or else they would not know—or they would persuade him. In his best days he was quite amenable to argument. He was not a person who sought consultation, but you could ' force ' consultation upon him.

On the technique of securing Cabinet approval:

When I wanted to get something done, and I knew there would be difficulties, I would speak to the Prime Minister beforehand and he carried the burden; that was his job. He would conciliate the Finance Minister. Sometimes he might speak to the Home Minister or another Minister because he might feel, and say, ' I don't want to do it, it looks as though the Defence Minister wants this, and I spoke to him . . . so here it's come up, let's agree on this.' And in each case he, usually at the end of a Cabinet meeting, mentioned it.

On the process of discussion:

The Prime Minister on the one hand and Ministers who are in general forceful—they carry their points, or rather, they will have a greater effect. The Prime Minister usually gravitates towards the man who is running the job; this is the natural condition of things; but if something is against the declared constitutional policy, you could not but bring it up. But even before that the late Prime Minister would see what was in it.

Cabinet meetings take a long time sometimes, usually because there is no orderly discussion, [but] big cross-talks. In my opinion, cross-talk always suppresses the man who has something to say.

[As to whether the discussion was focussed] No. The Prime Minister would turn around and say, 'what do you say about it?'—he would go around the table on a question of that kind. Sometimes he would make it very obvious that he was asking somebody, sometimes he would not be obvious at all; that is the tact of a Prime Minister; that is his privilege. There is no particular kind of sanctity about these meetings. They are like any other committee.

Anyone could talk; there was no senior or junior Minister in that sense. I know one junior Minister who always talked about anything under the sun! I know another Minister of State who used to talk on every subject. You put up with it; and then someone would say, 'we would like to hear someone else' or something like that. It was just like in any other meeting. But then, of course, it's the Indian approach.

On the process of decision:

Now the process of decision is: there are a certain number of items on the agenda; these are matters which either require a formal sanction, in the sense that Government orders have to be issued, or it may be some matter about which there has been some general desire to see that the thing is kept in restraint, and therefore it's better for it to come before Cabinet as a kind of check; for example, the sending of delegations abroad.

In the meeting of Cabinet, the way of recording these things is not for somebody to move a resolution that has to be written down. The discussion takes place and ultimately, whatever decision was made, whatever its form [earlier, he had remarked, 'even if it goes to Cabinet, Cabinet never takes a vote'], the Prime Minister, who is Chairman of the Cabinet, mentioned it to the Cabinet Secretary on the side. Practically, he dictates it and the Cabinet Secretary takes it down. In other words, so long as he [Nehru] was Chairman of the Cabinet—I don't know how it works now—there was no question of the phrasing being left to civil servants; if it were, it would be their decision; so he dictated it. On the one hand, it showed that they were brief and they were the essentials, and they were regularized. This was the normal procedure, with all its variations.

That is what went into the minutes. So, since he was the dictating man, he was more or less summing up the discussion. So that, at any time, if it were referred to, it would be what he had dictated. He had a great deal of tact in that way, though he was not a conjurer or anything. He was more methodical than people like me—he could always make notes—but still he was not methodical in the usually understood sense.

On Cabinet discussion of foreign policy:

[Other members of Cabinet would discuss foreign policy issues.] They would say something and then the Prime Minister would more or less educate them—' we cannot do that because that would have this effect . . .'. On the majority of questions they were in agreement with him, and if something else was said he would explain it. He would never say that this was none of your business. [Was he a patient educator?] Partly, yes: sometimes impatient and sometimes patient.

On prominent persons in Nehru's Cabinets:

Azad: He actually spoke very little and not too often.

Pant: He didn't speak very much either—because they would have discussed with the Prime Minister beforehand—unless it's a question on which he is asked to speak; sometimes Panditji would say to him, ' will you please explain this to them '.

There were one or two people who talked a great deal. I don't think they had a great effect.

I hardly spoke on defence in Cabinet. There was a Defence Committee meeting separately. In many cases it was the Prime Minister's responsibility.

On the composition of earlier Cabinets and its consequences:

Perhaps it would be wrong to call them composite Cabinets, but they certainly contained persons who were not Congress Party members, or even if they were they were very new entrants [people like Ambedkar, S. P. Mookerjee, and John Matthai].

While every Indian has a kind of regard and awe for the Prime Minister [Nehru], they [non-Congress ministers] had no particular affiliations in that way; he could not take liberties with them in the same way that he could with others, although his personality counted with every one of them. Those Cabinets, therefore, may be regarded as more formal; and it's even probable that, on ticklish questions, the people closer to the Prime Minister might have thought things out so that they faced the whole Cabinet with a—I don't say with a made-up mind, not in the same way as a sub-committee, but they would not have added to the confusion by differences among themselves. Or it may be that Patel or someone else might have gone to speak to some of these people and say, ' these are our difficulties, these are our problems ', and to bring about as much harmony as possible. I have no direct knowledge [of that period] but I imagine that was how it would have worked. That is my inference, and it's not just an academic inference.

On an experiment in informal Cabinet meetings and Nehru's exalted status:

Cabinet meets any time it likes. But the Prime Minister was a comparatively orderly person and he tried to make the Cabinet meet on a fixed day, although it didn't often work. Sometimes he found there was not sufficient give and take among members; and at one time, I very well remember, after joining the Government [1956], it was suggested that each member of Cabinet should ask the whole Cabinet to tea once a week, and that was done. But then that also became, in the Indian way, not just a tea, but a feast! And so the whole thing collapsed after a time because it became a kind of ritual; it didn't have the same purpose.

The Prime Minister would go around and sit down and speak to people and move from seat to seat and things of that character. But somehow or other, on account of his big personality, on account of the fact that people trusted his wisdom or his ultimate judgement, debate in the Western understood sense did not take place. But that doesn't mean there were no exchanges or that there was prevention of initiative.

On the Prime Minister's relationship to his colleagues:

There are very few occasions when there have been sharp cleavages of opinion or expression—there have been questions, largely turning on a person who has some personal fixations and so on—I mean occasions in my recollection, where in a Cabinet or a Cabinet Committee propositions have been put up by the Prime Minister himself, where some of his senior colleagues, having arrived at a different view by extraneous circumstances, have not agreed with it, and the thing had to be put off. If there was a difference with one of his senior colleagues, it would not be brought to the Cabinet. The late Prime Minister had sufficient common sense and sufficient sense of propriety to solve it beforehand or tell his colleagues, 'I am very sorry but this matter has to be like this'; and he could either resign or otherwise. I cannot remember any instances where in the Indian Cabinet people resigned on principle. Having resigned for other reasons, they would invoke principle.

There are people who said, 'I was not consulted'—responsible members used to say that; but why should one carry in one's head what was not necessary, especially when you knew that that would be the decision even if you were there! And then, even if the matter were over, you could go to the Prime Minister about it. There was no case that I know of where things were not modified, corrected, looked into, and so on. Secondly, sometimes he would say, 'yes, it could have been so, I am afraid the decision has been taken ', in which case other persons would not press him.

On the Defence Committee and Menon as Defence Minister:

I had no case of the Defence Committee where proposals before it had to be postponed. And it took years to get a decision in some committees.

On the Economic Affairs Committee:

Certainly in the later days it did not have much impact on Government because economic affairs were largely considered, if you can say ' considered ', by the Finance Minister, the Economic Affairs Committee and by the Planning Commission, by public discussion and so on. In the early days, I believe, it did function very much more.

On the quality of Indian Cabinets:

As time went on, in my opinion, people with less and less experience and lower and lower stature became members of the Cabinet. I mean, in the old days, the Prime Minister, Maulana Azad, Patel— these were three giants from the point of view of the national movement. There have been in Cabinet also two or three people who took a very international outlook, who would be able to take their place in almost any Cabinet in the world. Equally there have been people who are just parish politicians, who are very efficient in a limited kind of way. There were some about whom there may not be two of the same opinion; these are usual in any Government.

On the Cabinet in Nehru's last years:

The greater part of the business which is discussed in Cabinet is often not on an agenda. Now, with the late Prime Minister, increasingly it was becoming so, unfortunately, that each Minister was governing his own department and he got his agreement with the Finance Minister if he wanted money or, generally, got the Prime Minister to agree, and the Prime Minister would have to carry the burden; that is how it was.

An assessment of Nehru's Cabinets until 1958 has been provided by this writer elsewhere.[8] Suffice it here to recall the key figures. From 1947 to 1950 Sardar Patel occupied a unique position, as Deputy Prime Minister and *de facto* duumvir with Panditji in a super-Cabinet. For the next two years Nehru relied heavily on the administrative talent of Gopalaswami Ayyangar,

and for two years thereafter on the dynamic Rafi Kidwai, a
U.P. comrade since the late twenties. Pandit Pant did not quite
replace Patel during his sojourn in Delhi as Home Minister
(1954–60) but he was Nehru's indispensable aide in Parliament,
Cabinet, and Party affairs, with *carte blanche* in domestic
matters, though he consulted Panditji regularly, of course.
Throughout the first decade, too, Maulana Azad held a special
place in the inner Cabinet circle, though, as Menon revealed,
neither he nor Pant spoke often *in* the Cabinet; there was no need
to, for they would be consulted in advance. Apart from Pant
and Azad, two other key men were T.T.K. and Krishna Menon,
the two modern intellectuals in the Cabinet, with whom Nehru
felt most at ease. Thus Pant and Azad, Hindu and Muslim
traditionalists, and T.T.K. and Menon, modern secularists, stood
closest to Nehru in that period. And important in his own right
was Morarji Desai, who emerged as a major figure from 1958,
when he took over the Finance Ministry from a temporarily
discredited T.T.K.

With the death of Azad in 1958, Pant became the undisputed
No. 2 in the Cabinet, as Deputy Leader of the Congress Parliamentary Party and *de facto* Deputy Prime Minister. Two years
later, when Pant died, Morarji became the most likely candidate
for the succession, though his influence on Nehru was vastly less
than that of Pant. It was at that time that Nehru first intervened
to weaken Morarji's status in the CPP, in the abortive election of
Deputy Leader. Menon, of course, remained, as friend and
intellectual stimulant—not only in foreign affairs—but his influence had always derived from a special personal bond and
Nehru's respect for his incisive and provocative mind. By that
time, too, Lal Bahadur Shastri had begun to make a mark as
Home Minister and loyal aide, troubleshooter and conciliator
par excellence. On the eve of the third general election, then,
the three men of consequence among Nehru's Cabinet colleagues
were Menon, Morarji, and Shastri.

The year 1962 brought critical changes, however. First,
T.T.K. returned to the Cabinet after a lapse of four years,
clipping the wings, in part, of the ascending and aspiring
Morarji. Later in the year, with the Sino-Indian border war,

came Menon's departure.   And, coincident in time, Nehru's spirit was shattered by Chinese perfidy and military defeat: the sure touch of leadership gave way to uncertainty and the groping for new underpinnings to policy, at least until March–April 1963 when, to his relief, no one in Parliament asked for his resignation, though criticism was severe.   With the purge of August–September 1963 (Kamaraj Plan), Nehru's primacy was fully re-established, perhaps stronger than ever, until he was felled by a stroke the following January.

There can be no doubt that Nehru felt a much stronger affinity to T. T. Krishnamachari than to Morarji, both as Finance Minister and as confidant.   Nor is there any doubt that both were keen rivals for the Finance portfolio.   Morarji has related, for the first time, that when C. D. Deshmukh resigned as Finance Minister in August 1956, because of disagreement with Nehru over the reorganization of Bombay State, the Prime Minister offered him the portfolio.   Morarji replied that he could not leave Bombay until 1 November, the scheduled date for States' Reorganization.   Nehru was acting Finance Minister—though he knew nothing about it!   He then informed Morarji that he was giving T.T.K. temporary charge of the Ministry, to which Morarji raised no objection.   Thus, when he came to Delhi, he found T.T.K. securely ensconced in Finance.   He had to settle for Industry and Commerce.[9]   Two years later, Morarji took over the post.

T.T.K. has also revealed an interesting tale of his return to the Cabinet in 1962 and Nehru's alleged intentions.   Just before the general election, he recalled, when Nehru had suffered from a kidney ailment, he came to visit Panditji in Delhi.   The Prime Minister strongly urged him to stand for the Lok Sabha with a view to rejoining the Cabinet.   T.T.K. was reluctant, noting that, in any case, Morarji was lodged in Finance.   Nehru reportedly replied that he wanted T.T.K. with him and that, after all, Morarji might be defeated.   T.T.K. returned to his home in Madras, where letters from Nehru pressed the case for his return.   He yielded and won a seat in Parliament.   When he saw Nehru again, the Prime Minister regretted not being able to give him Finance, but offered him any other ministry and asked him to designate the post he wished.   The upshot was the novel

Ministry of Economic and Defence Co-ordination. More reveal-
ing of Nehru's intentions, T.T.K. was made Chairman of the
Cabinet Economic Affairs Committee, a post traditionally held
by the Finance Minister.[10]   Later, when the hatchet struck
Morarji, T.T.K. returned to Finance, and his Co-ordination
Ministry was abolished.

Some who sat in Cabinet at the time of the Chinese invasion
recall that, with Menon gone and Nehru reeling from the blow,
three men became increasingly vocal in the discussions—T.T.K.,
Morarji, and S. K. Patil. When the last two were ' Kamarajed ',
T.T.K. became the most effective and influential member of
Cabinet, though he was outranked by Nanda, who had replaced
Shastri as Home Minister. Of some interest is the fact that, in
all the memoirs of Cabinet Ministers over the years, not once was
Shastri mentioned as a prominent participant in Cabinet deliberations—though he exerted influence quietly and informally.
During those last months of 1963, Nehru, as Prime Minister,
was often peevish in Cabinet, ' which he had never been before ',
recalled one member; ' he drove himself to do things which he
should not have done '. After his stroke, he simply did not
function.[11] And in those final months, Cabinet was dominated
by a duumvirate of Nanda and T.T.K., with Shastri added to
make an informal triumvirate after a fortnight. So it remained
until Nehru's death.

No less important than the shifting configuration of Cabinet
members was the flourishing of a new institution which virtually
replaced the Cabinet in the last eighteen months as the supreme
decision-making body in the Government of India: this was the
Emergency Committee of the Cabinet. It was an *ad hoc* committee, created by the Prime Minister in the dark days of October
1962. Its membership fluctuated at his discretion. But of its
influence there can be no doubt. It met almost daily, sometimes
more often, between late October 1962 and January 1963. Thereafter it met less frequently, but at least a few times weekly, to
consider any issue of importance. It was, in truth, an ' Inner
Cabinet ', comparable to the War Cabinet in the U.K. during
the Second World War. Inevitably, Cabinet declined further
in importance, almost rubber-stamping Emergency Committee

decisions, and a new category of minister emerged, the Emergency Committee member, who was privy to, and consulted about, many more affairs of State than his lesser colleagues. The initial membership comprised Morarji, Shastri, T.T.K., and Chavan, apart from the Prime Minister. After the Kamaraj Plan, Nanda and Swaran Singh replaced the two ousted ministers. Such was its composition when Nehru died and the Committee met to recommend that the President appoint Nanda as interim Prime Minister.

In the 'making of a Cabinet', Shastri revealed his political style at the very outset of his tenure as Prime Minister: the process was cautious, undramatic, and unimaginative. Indeed, continuity was its most striking characteristic. All thirteen senior ministers on the Nehru team were retained, as were the fifteen Ministers of State and all but two of the twenty Deputy Ministers. The only notable changes were the addition of three members to the Cabinet, Mrs. Gandhi, S. K. Patil, and Sanjiva Reddy, and the reshuffling of portfolios, in a display of irrational pragmatism. As many observed at the time, Mrs. Gandhi was really the replacement for her father, and Patil had long been a minister, so that Reddy was the only new face. His appointment led to the comment of a 'pay-off', for it came only six months after an adverse judgement on his behaviour by the Andhra High Court, which had led to his resignation as Chief Minister.

Changes in portfolio lacked rhyme or reason—except as a response to individual pressure on the Prime Minister. Thus, the energetic Subramaniam, who had displayed initiative and efficiency in the Ministry of Steel, Mines and Heavy Engineering, was moved to Food and Agriculture—partly, so it seemed, to make way for Reddy, and partly to extricate Swaran Singh from that portfolio, which has long been the 'graveyard of all-India politicians'. The charitable view was that Shastri wished to bring dynamism into the pivotal area of food production, but some recalled that Swaran Singh was a favourite of the new Prime Minister. Not only was his new portfolio, Industry, enhanced by the restoration of the Department of Technical Development and the transfer of Heavy Engineering to its jurisdiction, but subsequent events affecting the Sikh

representative in the Cabinet also supported that interpretation.
And as for Subramaniam, the severe food crisis of 1964-5 would
have undoubtedly led to political oblivion for someone less able.
Other changes lacked a rational basis. Two examples will suffice.
The veteran Chief Whip, Satya Narayan Sinha, declined the offer
of the Ministry of Civil Aviation and so was given the Ministry
of Communications, as a supplement to Parliamentary Affairs!
The Law Minister, Ashoka Sen, was 'compensated' with the
Department of Social Security.[12]

One angry pundit expressed dismay at such 'marriages of
inconvenience' with a clever metaphor: some 'Ministries and
departments are treated like so many pieces of cloth in an absent-
minded tailor's shop; they are cut and recut, sewn together and
torn asunder, and often stitched into garments without any
regard whatever to texture, colour-scheme or even measure-
ment'.[13]   More subdued but with an unconcealed disappointment,
moderated only by a sense of stable continuity, was the *Statesman's* reaction, typical of the Delhi press: 'Mr. Shastri has
chosen a Cabinet which is like himself. It inspires confidence
but no excited comment, leans in no particular direction too
conspicuously and can be counted upon, if any group can be, to
combine the pragmatism of a mixed economy with a socialistic
preference. In politics, too, domestic and foreign, it will distin-
guish itself more by the stability it will promote than by striking
out for new frontiers . . . the end result is a bland homo-
geneity though it was not pre-planned.'[14] Yet this was
precisely what the decision process indicated about the country's
preference.

Blandness referred to the striking omission of Morarji and
Jagjivan Ram. The latter's exclusion from the Cabinet was not a
source of concern and, in any event, was expected. There were
some, however, among them members of the Caucus, who
wished to extend the consensus to Cabinet-making; perhaps, too,
they felt that Morarji could be dangerous in resentful opposition.
In any event, Shastri made the gesture by inviting him to join
the Cabinet, on the evening of 8 June. As so often in Indian
politics, the reconciliation was thwarted by an impasse over
status. Morarji felt that the No. 2 rank which he enjoyed in

Nehru's Cabinet ought to be restored.   But in the interim Nanda
had succeeded to that rank and had even served as Prime
Minister; it would have been embarrassing to downgrade him.
Shastri offered him the No. 3 rank, but the proud Morarji
declared that it was 'not consistent with my self-respect and
dignity'; no specific portfolio was mentioned, though the obvious
choice was an enlarged Ministry of Commerce and Industry.
Yet the outcome probably suited both men—Shastri because of
concern that Morarji might overshadow him or undermine his
authority from within, Morarji because of a conviction, or hope,
that the new Government would soon falter, and because of
injured pride.[15]

Throughout the 'Shastri Transition'* there were only two
other changes in the Union Cabinet, both the product of nature.
Within six weeks of the succession, Swaran Singh took over the
Ministry of External Affairs from a Prime Minister weakened by
another heart attack.[16]   And H. C. Dasappa, who replaced
Swaran Singh as Minister of Industry, died later in 1964.   For
the rest, the Council of Ministers, at all three levels, has remained
intact.   What accounts for Shastri's diffidence—some termed it
an error or lost opportunity—in regard to his predecessor's team?
Two factors were probably at work: first, that in the immediate
aftermath of Nehru's death, everything associated with him was
considered sacred; and secondly, the new Prime Minister was
unsure of his political strength at the outset and was not prepared
to weaken the glow of a tranquil succession.   At a later stage,
drastic changes, even if he were so inclined, would be unsettling
in a period of grave internal and external pressures.   And it may
be that the working of Cabinet during the transition was to his
satisfaction.

An assessment of Cabinet, in India as elsewhere, must be
tentative and qualified: no minutes are published, and deliberations remain shrouded in secrecy.   It is possible, however, to
compare the Indian Cabinet before and after the succession in
general terms—with the aid of reflections of half a dozen persons

---

* The phrase 'Shastri Transition' as used throughout this study is a
  synonym for Shastri's first year in office as Prime Minister (June 1964–
  June 1965).

who have served under both Nehru and Shastri.[17]   There are
striking contrasts and continuities.

The fundamental change, it appears, is a more relaxed
atmosphere and greater freedom in discussion—the result, no
doubt, of the absence of charisma and the gap of the generations
noted earlier.   The spirited exchange of ideas was not unknown
in Nehru's Cabinet, as Menon and others have testified; but
under Shastri it is the norm.   Nor is it confined to the few senior
Ministers; all members of Cabinet participate actively in the
debate on a wide range of issues.   In short, the Cabinet as an
institution has come to life.   A corollary, but sufficiently important to be regarded as a distinctive difference in itself, is that
decisions now represent a much more genuine consensus than
before.   This is partly due to Shastri's guiding principle in
decision-making and partly to the prolonged, some say excessive,
deliberations.   Relatively speaking, decisions in the past often
appeared to be imposed from above, i.e., faith in Nehru's wisdom
obtained, and Cabinet colleagues were reluctant to challenge him.

A third contrast is the attitude of the Prime Minister to his
associates: Nehru was not averse to keeping his Ministers in the
dark, while Shastri does not.   More specifically, Nehru often
called meetings with officials, sometimes at the junior level,
without informing their political chiefs.   Shastri is the complete
reverse; he, too, meets with officials—at the Secretary level—but
he invariably sends a copy of the minutes to the Ministers concerned.   Indeed, Shastri is reluctant to make decisions; he seems
always to be hoping that they will 'emerge' from patient and
endless discussion, especially as regards the solution of complex
problems; the crises over food and language, which dominated
the Shastri transition, are outstanding examples and will be
explored at length later.   Still another basic change is the restoration of the Cabinet's primacy and the relative decline in status
of its Emergency Committee.   That body remains a decision
organ in foreign affairs, for example during the serious conflict
over the Rann of Kutch in 1965, but it meets less frequently than
in the past, and, except in the midst of a major crisis, less
frequently than the Cabinet itself.   Finally, there is the intangible
of Shastri's infinite patience which gives the impression of

indecision—within the Cabinet as well as to the country at large. In the opinion of some Ministers it also leads to a waste of valuable time, but to Shastri it is the legitimate price for consensus.

It would be incorrect, however, to infer from this that Shastri allows himself to be guided by his colleagues. With all his humility and patience, there is a fibre of political toughness. Moreover, the Prime Minister knows that he was the choice of the Party and the country, and while he does not flaunt this basis of power he asserts it when necessary. There are many illustrations of this quality during the first year of Shastri's tenure as Prime Minister. To begin with, he formed the Cabinet himself; the presence of Caucus member Atulya Ghosh outside his office at 1.30 a.m. on 9 June was misunderstood—his only function was to hand over the list from a tired Shastri to waiting reporters.

Shastri's decisiveness was also evident in the subtle denial of the External Affairs portfolio to Mrs. Gandhi. All were agreed that he felt the need to have her support and even participation in his Cabinet. As subsequent events proved, however, he was unwilling to place her in charge of India's foreign policy. Whether she was offered this post and declined, as some believed, is unclear; she may, indeed, have been given *carte blanche* to choose a portfolio for the sake of form, so as not to alienate Nehru's daughter on the morrow of the succession. If so, it may well have happened that an informal emissary persuaded her that it would be unwise to accept, either because External Affairs would be too strenuous and/or because there would be sniping in Parliament at dynastic continuity, which her sensitivity could not easily bear. All this is speculation, but two facts stand out. Shastri took the portfolio himself and, when illness compelled him to lighten his burden, he did not give the post to Mrs. Gandhi, despite the urging and expectations of some colleagues. He chose Swaran Singh instead. And his timing of the appointment provides a second striking example of autonomy in decision-making. T.T.K. and Mrs. Gandhi were in London at the Commonwealth Prime Ministers' Conference. Nanda was away. And even Kamaraj was not consulted, to his chagrin; like many others, he read about it in the newspaper. The choice,

as later developments showed, was designed to give the Prime
Minister a free hand in the conduct of foreign affairs. When
one of his colleagues expressed some reservations about the
appointment, he gently remarked, ' this is the prerogative of the
Prime Minister '.

Another instance of firmness, related to the above, occurred
when Pratap Singh Kairon was compelled to resign as Chief
Minister of the Punjab. The Congress President urged that
Swaran Singh be released from the Union Cabinet, but Shastri
was adamant; he was keeping him for External Affairs. Later
in the year there were two particularly delicate tests of Shastri's
capacity for decision. One concerned Nagaland; the other Sheikh
Abdullah. Various members of the Cabinet opposed the extension
of a cease-fire with the Naga underground movement; one openly
advocated the arrest of Jaya Prakash Narayan, the expulsion of
the Reverend Michael Scott, and the reprimanding of Chief
Minister Chaliha of Assam, the three members of the ' Peace
Mission '. Shastri listened patiently and then made the decision
to continue the cease-fire and the negotiations. Similarly, when
the Kashmir leader applied for a passport to go abroad, ostensibly
to make the pilgrimage to Mecca but, as it turned out, to seek
support for an independent Kashmir as well, only two members
of the Cabinet were favourably disposed; some senior Ministers
objected vigorously. The Prime Minister listened quietly and
then said, ' I think that a passport should be granted and I have
asked Swaran Singh to do so.' If these accounts are accurate, and
there is no reason to disbelieve them, the appearance of vacillation
is belied by the evidence. But the style of Shastri is very
different from that of his predecessor.

There are also continuities in the Indian Cabinet, both in
structure and function. Procedure regarding Cabinet meetings
is unchanged: any Ministry that wishes to place an issue before
Cabinet submits a paper to the Cabinet Secretariat, which circu-
lates it to all members; the Cabinet Secretariat prepares
the agenda and serves as clearing agent, recording body, and
guardian of Cabinet decisions and minutes; senior ministers (members of the Cabinet) attend meetings by right, while Ministers
of State are present only when a topic affecting their direct

jurisdiction is on the agenda; the Cabinet Secretary and one or more aides are always present throughout the proceedings; Secretaries of Ministries may attend at the discretion of their Ministers but will usually withdraw after the issue of concern to them has been discussed.

As in Nehru's day, too, Cabinet meets at least once a week for 1½ to 3 or 4 hours; under Shastri, meetings are much longer and more frequent; they are called at the discretion of the Prime Minister. Decisions continue to be by consensus; there is never a vote. In the post-succession period, however, decisions are not infrequently postponed to a further meeting because of Shastri's penchant for a full consensus on all issues—wherever possible. Even the informal weekly meeting of Cabinet at different homes has been restored; no officials are present, and discussion extends over a wide range of controversial issues. Indeed, according to some members, the Wednesday afternoon 'tea' gathering has become the real arena of decision; formal Cabinet meetings often merely give statutory approval to decisions reached there. But most of the time in formal Cabinet sittings is devoted to free and frank discussion; as in Nehru's day, items on the agenda are usually settled within half an hour.

Many other features of Cabinet remain unchanged, and Krishna Menon's view of the Nehru Cabinet 'from the inside' remains valid. Thus, on the Prime Minister's relationship to his colleagues:[18]

In a Cabinet the Prime Minister is not an overlord. He is *primus inter pares*, that is the usual conception. He is the chief among equals, but still he is the chief, do you see; and he is among equals, which means that it depends on how many equals are with him and how many equals are not. And secondly, being with equals, he can talk to them that way.

The fact that a matter is not referred to Cabinet cannot for outside purposes be regarded as depriving it of sanctity because, if the Prime Minister didn't refer a matter to Cabinet, it is his own decision, and his own funeral if anything goes wrong.

So, too, for the special position of the Finance Minister and the reasons for it:

Because everybody wants money! The Finance Minister here also has other powers, in economic affairs, exchange control, etc. In a controlled economy like ours there are so many checks and balances, and the general inability of Members of Parliament to appreciate financial questions—all these things come into it. And Finance Ministers, whether they are able or not, have been assertive men very often.

It is reasonable to assume that T.T.K., Finance Minister under Shastri as well as Nehru, continues to hold a special position. The formal functions of a Cabinet meeting are also unchanged:

There are certain matters upon which the Services should have decisions. There are certain matters upon which the Prime Minister himself may want a discussion. And there are certain matters which a member of the Party may bring up, in regard to some State decision on food, on all kinds of matters.

There are matters which Cabinet might refer to a committee. Then the decision of that committee would have to come before Cabinet. But if it's one of the Standing Committees, then, whether it comes from there [to Cabinet] or not depends upon the Prime Minister.

The committee system of Cabinet also remains the same, though the relative importance of committees has changed; yet that, too, is a pre-succession development. The most important structural innovation of Nehru's last years, the Emergency Committee of the Cabinet, remains pre-eminent in foreign and security matters, virtually replacing the Defence Committee and the Foreign Affairs Committee as the key organ of deliberation and decision in this sphere. Thus, Menon's description of the Defence Committee is now accurate for the Emergency Committee:

The Defence Committee of Cabinet is a Cabinet itself; that is to say, it is not the whole of the Cabinet, but the Defence Committee of Cabinet functions as the Cabinet—decisions taken by the Defence Committee are tantamount to decisions taken in the Cabinet, unless, of course, the Prime Minister, who is there, should say that this is a matter which should be referred to our colleagues.

As for other committees:

[They] are sub-committees of the Cabinet. The Economic Committee of the Cabinet doesn't make any decisions; matters are referred to it or they can even take up something and study it if they want to, and then it comes to the Cabinet, theoretically. The Foreign Affairs Committee is also in that position but it is more like the Defence

Committee of Cabinet and less like the other committees. It is merely a matter of practice. The Foreign Affairs Committee consists of members whom the Prime Minister nominates.

Finally, on the principle of collective responsibility, Menon's remarks bear notice:

Whether in England or here, the term 'collective responsibility' covers many sins and also excludes many virtues. Collective responsibility as such doesn't exist today. It's not even that for the sins of one Ministry the whole Cabinet would resign; if it were so, the resignation of certain members would not have taken place! Collective responsibility regarding decisions on actions which concerned a Department [Ministry] don't necessarily come before Cabinet. They would come there if the Prime Minister thought it was necessary or if the Minister thought it was necessary; and no doubt any member could raise it. But you must appreciate the fact that, while in certain circumstances, through the consent of the Prime Minister, one Minister may call for the papers of another Ministry, this is not usually done. First of all, each man has his own troubles. Secondly, he doesn't want to antagonize his colleagues or create difficulties. So collective responsibility, in the sense that a decision once made is everybody's, is very largely a myth, certainly in the Indian Cabinet. Even today, one Cabinet member speaks almost like a Swatantra Party man, another member speaks very much more with the emphasis of Gandhi's philosophy, a third one speaks, perhaps, with a socialist point of view, and so on.

Whether this portrait of 'collective responsibility' is accurate for the Shastri transition is unclear. The only open breach within the ranks of Cabinet occurred in January 1965, when Food Minister Subramaniam and the Minister of State for Oil and Mines, Alagesan, dramatically resigned over the Government's language policy; they were persuaded to return by the Prime Minister; and, in any event, their behaviour was perfectly consistent with the principle.[19] As for differences in outlook among Cabinet Ministers, this is normal and not incompatible with collective responsibility. What is certain, however, is the enhanced status and influence of the Cabinet as an institution. Thus, in commenting on Home Minister Nanda's ill-fated anti-corruption campaign, through the unofficial *Sadachar Samiti*, one pundit noted:

What Mr. Nanda unwittingly forgot was the collective assertiveness of the Cabinet. This is a change from the days of the late Prime

Minister which no member of the Cabinet can afford to ignore.
Ministers today have not only a sense of responsibility but a feel of
power.   Had the *sadachar* proposal been adopted as a Cabinet
decision, Mr. Nanda could have at least hoped for reluctant defence
in the face of opposition outside the Government.   But . . . all he
got was a shrug of the shoulders from colleagues. . . .   This is a
metamorphosis in the Cabinet's personality which should surprise no
one.   The change in outlook was inherent in the emergence of the
new leadership.[26]

Structurally viewed, the Council of Ministers under Shastri—
as under Nehru in the last years—consists of four concentric
circles radiating from the Prime Ministerial core: Emergency
Committee of the Cabinet (6); Cabinet (16); Ministers of State
(15); and Deputy Ministers (20); the last two can be ignored in
terms of the decision process on policy matters.   In the Emergency Committee, apart from the Prime Minister himself, are
the Ministers of Home Affairs, Finance, Information and Broadcasting, External Affairs, and Defence—in that order of Cabinet
rank; noteworthy is the omission of the Railways Minister and
the Minister of Law and Communications, both of whom outrank
the Defence Minister.   Indeed, the ranking system in the Indian
Cabinet lacks any consistent rational criterion, apart from Nanda
(Home) and Krishnamachari (Finance), the Prime Minister's
fellow triumvirs in the months preceding the succession.   Neither
Mrs. Gandhi nor Sanjiva Reddy had ever served in the Cabinet
until June 1964, yet they rank fourth and ninth respectively; and
one is in the Emergency Committee or Inner Cabinet, while the
other is not.   Moreover, the Minister of Information and Broadcasting never had Cabinet rank until Mrs. Gandhi assumed the
portfolio.   Ranking of members of Cabinet is not only uniquely
Indian; it appears to be based on a composite of the incumbent's
political importance in the Party and seniority, as intuitively
perceived by the Prime Minister.   Otherwise, the precedence of
Information and Broadcasting over External Affairs and Defence
would appear to be mere whim.   And even then, it is difficult to fathom the placing of Patil and Reddy, the two most
important Party leaders in the Cabinet apart from Shastri, so
far down the list, with both excluded from the Emergency
Committee.

One effect of ranking is to blur the distinction between Prime Minister and all other Ministers. Another is to replace the traditional Cabinet concept of ' first among equals ' with a sliding scale of status. And a third, through the Emergency Committee, is to make some members of Cabinet more equal than others! Yet formal status is not a measure of influence or involvement in the decision process. According to those ' on the inside ', Swaran Singh was, in the early months, the closest to Shastri in the Cabinet. The people who matter in the broad spectrum of Cabinet deliberations are T.T.K. and Nanda and, when he intervenes, Patil. Mrs. Gandhi speaks rarely in Cabinet, as in Parliament, and has not made a mark in either. There are others who participate actively, and ably, like Education Minister Chagla and Petroleum and Chemicals Minister Kabir, but they lack a political base or seniority or both. Defence Minister Chavan speaks little in the Cabinet but exerts considerable influence in decisions. At the other extreme is Rehabilitation Minister Tyagi, whom Nehru would often silence; Shastri, by contrast, uses him as a sounding board for the views of the average Congressman in the Hindi-speaking area. As befits a Cabinet of relative equals, all members take a greater initiative in affairs concerning their own Ministry.

An ideological classification is subject to the overriding fact that the Shastri Cabinet is essentially centrist in outlook. It is possible, however, to discern rightist and leftist orientations. One of the principal conservative spokesmen in the Nehru Cabinet, Morarji, is gone; but S. K. Patil remains as the articulate champion of the private sector and, in foreign affairs, attachment to the West. Less outspoken, and perhaps less committed in principle, is Sanjiva Reddy, his colleague in the Caucus. And though not openly identified with the Right, Subramaniam has, in private conversation, expressed ideas which are reminiscent of nineteenth-century *laissez-faire* economics. The forthright advocates of socialism in the Nehru Cabinet, Menon and Malaviya, are also gone. Nanda remains, but his commitment appears to many to be less principled. Mrs. Gandhi shares her father's outlook; indeed, she is probably further to the Left. But like Nehru from the 1930s onwards, she will tread carefully lest an overt commitment isolate her from the Centre. Labour Minister Sanjivayya has the strongest emotional attachment to socialism. And Chavan, a likely candidate for the post-succession succession, is the most sophisticated, though uncommitted, leftist in the Cabinet. The Prime Minister himself symbolizes the dominant trend in the Party and Government, conservative in spirit and outlook, yet pragmatic and aware of India's need for the ' middle way '.

The breakdown along a traditionalist–modernist spectrum differs, with modernism in the ascendancy: T.T.K., Mrs. Gandhi, Patil, Sen, Kabir, and Chagla are the leading modernizers in Cabinet; Tyagi and Minister for Parliamentary Affairs Sinha are socially reactionary, while the others would fall along various points of the spectrum. Nanda, for example, tends to obscurantism, while Shastri is much more attuned to Indian tradition, in culture and society, than his predecessor or many of his colleagues.

Not all States are represented in Cabinet proper, but all regions have at least one spokesman for their interests. So too with the principal communities. There are four Ministers from the South—T.T.K. and Subramaniam (Madras), and Reddy and Sanjivayya (Andhra). There are two from each of the flanks—Kabir and Sen (Bengal) and Chavan and Patil (Maharashtra). Swaran Singh is from the Punjab, Nanda from Gujarat. And four represent the Hindi hinterland—Shastri, Mrs. Gandhi, and Tyagi, from U.P., and Sinha from Bihar. Chagla is from Bombay City, but neither he nor T.T.K., Patil or Mrs. Gandhi is a State representative in any sense except that of place of origin or residence. As for the communities, Hindus of necessity predominate. But there are two Muslims, Chagla and Kabir, a Sikh, Swaran Singh, and an Untouchable, Sanjivayya. In all respects, then, the Shastri Cabinet, like its predecessors, represents the main strands of Indian society and Congress politics.

Changes in the working of Cabinet under Shastri were part of a larger process initiated by the succession—the redistribution of power at the all-India level of politics. There were only two institutional innovations, the Prime Minister's Secretariat and the 'Grand Council of the Republic'. But these, along with the interplay of pressures in the existing fabric of decision-making, pointed to a striking shift in the pyramid of power at the Centre. This became evident not only within the Government itself but also in the relations between Party and Government hierarchies.

The creation of the Prime Minister's Secretariat, in July 1964, seemed inconsequential at first; indeed, on the surface it was a mere administrative device to ease the burden on Nehru's ailing successor. Yet it reflected something deeper in the Shastri transition, the re-emergence of the Civil Service as a powerful pressure group on policy. To some it was reminiscent of ICS primacy in the days of the British *Raj*, but events proved this an incorrect analogy; nonetheless, it marked the accretion of influence by the traditional ' steel frame ' of Indian Government.

The origins of the new Secretariat may be traced to Shastri's reliance—some say, dependence—on the advice of civil servants during his tenure as Home Minister and even earlier. Whether this was due to lack of self-confidence or a well-conceived division of function is a matter of interpretation—probably both were involved; in any event, it was a marked trait of his style, another contrast with his predecessor who used the administrative skills of his professional aides but firmly maintained their subordinate role. The idea was first broached to a senior member of the ICS soon after he assumed the Prime Ministership; he was apparently thinking of a personal staff with two co-equal Secretaries, L. K. Jha for economic affairs and L. P. Singh for administration; there would also be deputies for external and home affairs, and other spheres of government. Nanda, however, was unwilling to release Singh, then Special Secretary in his Ministry and soon to be promoted to Home Secretary. Moreover, Jha insisted that efficiency required a small staff with a clear chain of command; and, not unnaturally perhaps, he was unwilling to share status and power at the summit. In the end, Jha's views triumphed, after protracted debate, and he emerged as the sole Secretary to the Prime Minister. Lesser officials, including three Joint Secretaries, were gradually transferred to the new staff; some of them, it was noted, related to Shastri by caste or region—a not unusual custom in Indian public life. But as Jha urged throughout, it remained a compact group, partly because he did not want to become a prisoner of a large staff, and partly because of lack of space in the Ministry of External Affairs wing of South Block, where the new Secretariat was strategically housed. To some who observed the battle over its formation—it was not a smooth process free of conflicting interests in the bureaucracy—the conscious model was Kennedy's White House staff, with L. K. Jha cast in the role of McGeorge Bundy. Jha himself disclaimed the intention to emulate the American pattern, on the grounds that it was 'impracticable'. This is correct, in a sense, for the cabinet system of government in India does not lend itself to the concentration of power in the manner of the U.S. presidency. Nevertheless, the Secretary to the Prime Minister rapidly emerged as the most influential civil servant of the Shastri transition.

The rationale of the new Secretariat and its formal functions were explained by Jha in a candid and revealing interview a few months after his appointment.[21] Two factors were cited for its creation: the difference in manner of work (style) and decision-making of the two Prime Ministers; and the fact that Nehru held a specific portfolio while Shastri does not. These were elaborated in a persuasive line of argument. Whenever a proposal was put to Nehru, outside the sphere of external affairs, he would answer promptly, ' yes, I agree ' or ' no, I have doubts ', and he would pass the matter on to the appropriate Ministry for detailed consideration; later, when this issue came before Cabinet he would put his mind to it; and, not infrequently, at that late stage Nehru would reject the proposal, with the result that the effort in preparing material would be wasted. By unconcealed inference, the new Secretariat was designed to prevent this ' inefficient ' way of conducting Government business, by keeping the Prime Minister advised throughout. Stated somewhat differently, Jha remarked that Nehru took decisions quickly and Shastri acts slowly.

Some disagree with this portrait of Nehru's inefficiency, but there can be no doubt that he had a multiple staff: a personal secretariat, headed by a Principal Private Secretary, to assist him with routine papers; a Secretary-General of External Affairs; a Private Secretary (Planning) to maintain liaison with the Planning Commission, and others. And yet he lacked an integrated staff to co-ordinate his varied activities and to see that decisions were implemented. Shastri, in the absence of a portfolio, requires an autonomous secretariat to perform these functions. Viewed in these terms, then, the Prime Minister's Secretariat is merely the counterpart of the administrative arm of any other Ministry. In reality, however, it is much more, for the Prime Minister is Head of Government, not just one of sixteen Cabinet Ministers.

The main function of the Secretariat, in Jha's words, is ' to prepare drafts of important speeches, statements and letters '. But this seemingly innocuous role—which Nehru could dispense with because of an extraordinary capacity for work and superb drafting ability—carries with it the seed of influence, especially when the Prime Minister relies heavily on advice; the line between articulating someone else's ideas and intruding one's own is a very thin one. In the first three months alone, Jha drafted a major letter from Shastri to the Chief Ministers on the food crisis, his address to Parliament, in which he proclaimed his right to chart new paths if conditions so required, his statements on the need to re-orient Indian planning, with a greater emphasis on agriculture, and a host of others. Since Jha acknowledged that the Prime Minister consults him regularly on high policy matters, it is reasonable to conclude that he is not merely a Secretary of a Ministry.

It was natural, perhaps even inevitable, that the creation of an agency so close to the centre of decision would arouse concern in various branches of the bureaucracy, the Cabinet, and elsewhere in the Government of India. Jha acknowledged this; in fact, as noted above, he cited this as a reason for moving slowly. Yet he predicted compensations. Other Secretaries would welcome direct access to the Prime Minister via a fellow civil servant, for this would give them greater independence of their Minister; this was undoubtedly true, but as time passed some had qualms about substituting dependence on a super-Secretary. Ministers, too, he urged, would find merit in an efficient staff to expedite decisions, for Shastri's burden and disorderly work schedule were causing grave delay, especially in the early months; the Prime Minister's lack of punctuality and inability to terminate meetings, along with the newness of the office, were creating disruption in the Government machine. This was a plausible view, but Jha ignored the understandable ire of elected Ministers who were becoming dependent on the goodwill of a civil servant for access to the Prime Minister, especially Congressmen, with a deep-rooted distrust of those who had served the British *Raj*. As for his relationship to the Cabinet Secretary, traditionally regarded as the ranking member of the bureaucracy, he was reticent; but he revealed the shape of things to come when he remarked that, just as the Prime Minister co-ordinated the work of Cabinet, the Prime Minister's Secretary would become the co-ordinator of Secretarial activity.

It has happened thus. Within a few months Jha became a member of almost every committee at Secretary level in the Government of India. And the three relationships have evolved in the opposite direction to what he anticipated—jealousy among other Secretaries, chagrin among Ministers, and the decline of the Cabinet Secretary to the role of clearing house for Cabinet papers. Indeed, there is ample evidence to indicate that the Prime Minister's Secretariat, through the forceful personality of L. K. Jha, has become a major power centre in all-India politics, an interest group in its own right. It has exerted pressure on many issues, notably in the vital spheres of economic policy and foreign affairs. A few illustrations will suffice.

The first year of the Shastri transition witnessed a prolonged but inconclusive debate on the fourth Five-Year Plan, due to begin in the spring of 1966. The major points of controversy were: the size of the Plan; the division of resources between industry and agriculture; and the distribution of investment funds between the public and private sectors. On all these issues L. K. Jha stood squarely with the conservatives, as he made abundantly clear in the interview noted earlier. Thus he rejected the widely-espoused thesis that investment in heavy industry and agriculture are complementary, not competitive; at best, he declared, there is partial complementarity; hence, capital inputs into industry should be diverted into agriculture to stimulate that lagging sector of the economy. 'The Prime Minister feels', he remarked, 'that there must be something wrong with planning if it achieved so little for the common man'; he left no doubt that he concurred. Cautiously, but clearly, he favoured greater scope for the private sector. And on the size of the Plan he sided with those who stressed the shortage of resources—'realism'—rather than the imperative character of a larger total investment. He was (and is) not alone in these views. Nor is it suggested that his views were decisive—but he is, in fact if not in name, the chief economic adviser to the Prime Minister. Moreover, he drafted Shastri's key statements on economic policy. Thus, to the extent that Shastri moves Indian planning along a different path, Jha's influence is considerable. Powerful interest groups in the Indian polity also urge this shift—and the Prime Minister's Secretary is an effective advocate.

In this connection, Jha also expressed a bureaucrat's disdain for the 'non-professional' character of the Planning Commission. He acknowledged that planning performs an important function in a *federal* state, that of co-ordinating the planning mechanism in the Union and the sixteen States. On other grounds, however, he was bluntly critical, claiming that it tended to duplicate the work of the Ministries while examining their proposals and, most important, that it tended to make policy rather than tender advice. Hence its wings must be clipped—to allow it no more than a co-ordinating role. All this was reminiscent of Finance Minister John Matthai's objections to the creation of the Planning Commission in 1950, the basic cause of his resignation.[22] In a very real sense, then, the debate over the fourth Plan represents, among other things, a struggle between the professional Civil Service—which wants to restore the autonomy and power of the Ministry secretariats, especially Finance—and the economists who hold sway in a super economic policy secretariat, the Planning Commission. Nehru was the patron of the Commission; now that he is gone, the bureaucrats are likely to win. Here, too, the Prime Minister's Secretariat is altering the pyramid of decision and power.

In foreign policy, too, L. K. Jha has made his influence felt —despite his inexperience in this field, apart from attending

economic conferences and negotiating loans.[23]   The first notable
example concerns Shastri's maiden appearance before an international forum, at the Conference of Non-Aligned Nations in
Cairo in October 1964.   The Ministry of External Affairs prepared
a draft for his speech; unknown to them, the Prime Minister's
Secretary did the same; the latter was accepted.[24]   A more
conspicuous role was played by Jha during the lengthy negotiations over the Rann of Kutch dispute with Pakistan in the spring
and summer of 1965; C. S. Jha, the Foreign Secretary, was also
involved; but the more frequent, almost daily, press references
to discussions between the Prime Minister's Secretary and the
British High Commissioner in Delhi led many to wonder who
was the principal Indian official in foreign affairs.

This doubt became more pointed as a result of L. K. Jha's
successful penetration of the Foreign Office proper, in the
spring of 1965.   Largely at his urging, but with the backing of
other Secretaries, a high-powered Committee of Secretaries was
appointed ' to deal with foreign affairs '; the slight to the professionals of the Ministry of External Affairs was too obvious to
be ignored; nor was the Minister, Swaran Singh, spared.   And
this was accentuated by the composition of the Committee—two
of the six members came from economics Ministries; the other
four were the Cabinet and Defence Secretaries, L. K. Jha himself, and C. S. Jha, the Foreign Secretary.   The other two
Secretaries in the Foreign Office were conspicuously absent, as
was the Home Secretary, L. P. Singh, the most sophisticated and
urbane civil servant in Delhi.[25]   The result was deep resentment
among Jha's fellow bureaucrats, a predictable reaction to un-
abashed raiding of their domains.[26]   The taste of power appears
to have overcome his initial caution about offending colleagues.
Long before the end of Shastri's first year, then, the Prime
Minister's Secretariat had become not just an ' information pipe-
line ' to the Prime Minister or even merely a channel for the
reverse flow of decisions; [27] it was also a formidable influence in
the making of decisions.

At the level of high policy, the most significant development
of the Shastri transition is the emergence of an informal but

supreme decision-making organ for the Union as a whole. The
' Grand Council of the Republic ' [28] has no legal status or institutional form. It meets irregularly, at the discretion of the Prime
Minister. Its decisions can claim no sanction from the Constitution of India or the Constitution of the Congress. But it
exists; indeed, it occupies the summit of the all-India power
pyramid.

The membership of the Grand Council is nowhere clearly
defined; yet it is known, for this unique body has crystallized by
convention during the first year after the succession. In fact, it
emerged during that crisis and represents the continuing expression of the quest for consensus on issues of an all-India character.
What is more, it reflects the new balance of power between the
Union and the States and between the Government and the
Party. One may discern a structural antecedent in the National
Development Council, but the differences in composition, scope,
and power are much greater than the sole similarity—the
presence of Union and State Government leaders in both.

Ministers of Planning in the States and Members of the
Planning Commission sit on the Development Council but not
on the Grand Council. Similarly, members of the Working
Committee of the Congress are ex-officio members of the Grand
Council but do not, as such, attend meetings of the Development
Council. The Union Cabinet and the Chief Ministers participate
in both Councils, though some Cabinet Ministers ignore the
Development Council. As for scope, the Development Council
is confined to the Plan and general economic policy. The Grand
Council, by contrast, has no defined jurisdiction; but by convention it meets as and when any issue of all-India importance has
reached the stage of crisis or impasse; food and language are the
outstanding illustrations during the Shastri transition, as subsequent analysis will reveal. Neither Council is concerned with
foreign policy, though it is probable that the Grand Council
would be summoned if the Union Government were contem-
plating a major shift in India's orientation in world politics. The
effective power of the Development Council is limited, despite
its theoretical position at the apex of the planning pyramid; it
is, rather, more like a ' town hall ', with bargaining between

State and Union interests; real power, at least before the
succession, lay with Nehru, the Finance Minister, and the
Planning Commission. Again by contrast, Grand Council decisions have no formal sanction, but there is no effective appeal
from the consensus once reached. Members may nullify a
decision, however, by not carrying it out in good faith.

What makes the Grand Council powerful is its unique
membership—all the crucial wielders of influence in Party and
Government: the nineteen members of the Working Committee;
the thirteen Chief Ministers who are not on the highest executive
organ of the Congress; two representatives of the CPP; most of
the eight members of Cabinet who are not included in those three
groups, and a few special invitees, like Menon and Dhebar. The
Council's membership will vary, then, from 40 to 46, the combined Congress–Union Government–State Government élite. It
is small enough to permit effective deliberations yet sufficiently
representative to give its decisions the quality of finality. At the
end of the first year of Shastri's tenure (June 1965), its maximum
membership was as follows:

CONGRESS WORKING COMMITTEE

Fakhruddin AHMED (N)
Sadiq ALI (E)
Y. B. CHAVAN (E)
Morarji DESAI (N)
Mrs. Indira GANDHI (E)
Atulya GHOSH (N)—Treasurer
K. KAMARAJ (E)—President
T. MANAEN (N)
　　　　　—General Secretary
Gulzari Lal NANDA (N)
S. NIJALINGAPPA (N)
S. K. PATIL (N)
Biju PATNAIK (E)
Jagjivan RAM (N)
N. Sanjiva REDDY (N)
D. SANJIVAYYA (N)
Lal Bahadur SHASTRI (N)
Darbara SINGH (E)
Dr. Ram Subhag SINGH (E)
Mohan Lal SUKHADIA (E)

(N) nominated; (E) elected.

CHIEF MINISTERS

K. Brahmananda REDDY
　　　　　(Andhra Pradesh)
B. P. CHALIHA (Assam)
K. B. SAHAY (Bihar)
Balvantray G. MEHTA (Gujarat)
G. M. SADIQ
　　　　　(Jammu and Kashmir)
D. P. MISHRA (Madhya Pradesh)
M. BHAKTAVATSALAM
　　　　　(Madras)
V. P. NAIK (Maharashtra)
S. TRIPATHI (Orissa)
Ram KISHAN (Punjab)
Mrs. S. KRIPALANI
　　　　　(Uttar Pradesh)
P. C. SEN (West Bengal)
Governor of Kerala

(Nijalingappa of Mysore and Sukhadia of Rajasthan are on the
Working Committee.)

CONGRESS PARLIAMENTARY
PARTY
K. C. REDDY
Satya Narayan SINHA

SPECIAL INVITEES
U. N. DHEBAR
V. K. KRISHNA MENON

UNION CABINET (by rank)
T. T. KRISHNAMACHARI
Sardar SWARAN SINGH
A. K. SEN
C. SUBRAMANIAM
H. KABIR
M. C. CHAGLA
M. TYAGI

(Shastri, Nanda, Mrs. Gandhi, Patil, Chavan, Sanjiva Reddy, and Sanjivayya are on the Working Committee; Satya Narayan Sinha represents the CPP.)

A glance at this list reveals the enormous concentration of power represented on the Grand Council. Apart from the four key institutional interest groups—Working Committee, Chief Ministers, Cabinet, and CPP—there are spokesmen from every State; indeed, more than one from each State, except Jammu and Kashmir, Kerala, Mysore, and Rajasthan. The Caucus is there in full, as are all who contested the succession, and prominent individuals outside the institutional network. Thus, the Centre and the States, the Party and the Government, and diverse factions, groups, and ideological tendencies are all present, making the Grand Council a combined authority–power summit in the Indian polity.

It would be erroneous, however, to infer that this informal body has replaced the established institutions of India's democratic system, notably Parliament, Cabinet, and judiciary, or the Congress Working Committee itself. Rather, it must be viewed as a ' crisis committee ' to which is submitted any issue affecting the nation as a whole. It does not intrude into day-to-day decisions or into matters which are clearly within Union or State jurisdiction, or even all-India questions until all other forums of bargaining and decision have been used and an impasse has been reached. It is, therefore, a political ' court of last appeal ', where Union and State, Government and Party power constellations bargain at the highest level. There, much more than in Parliament or Cabinet, pressure groups meet on equal terms and resolve conflicts—by consensus. Seen in terms of the succession and its aftermath, the Grand Council of the Republic is the collective substitute for Nehru's charisma: what he could virtually decree by himself, for example on the language controversy, now requires their group consensus.

The passing of Nehru, the supreme arbitrator in Party, Government, and all-India affairs, has had another major consequence—the fragmentation of decision-making. This change emerges clearly from a comparison of the decision-making hierarchies before and after the succession—both in terms of the formal structures of power and different areas of policy.

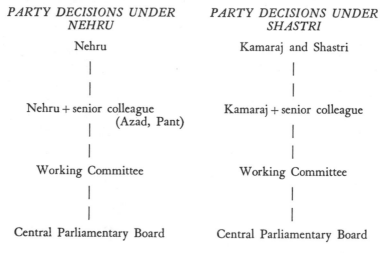

PARTY DECISIONS UNDER NEHRU	*PARTY DECISIONS UNDER SHASTRI*
Nehru	Kamaraj and Shastri
Nehru + senior colleague (Azad, Pant)	Kamaraj + senior colleague
Working Committee	Working Committee
Central Parliamentary Board	Central Parliamentary Board

The crucial distinctions here are: first, that Nehru's position at the summit of decision in *party* matters is now shared by Congress President and Prime Minister—in that order of importance; secondly, that the President, not the Prime Minister, takes the initiative on purely party affairs, usually in consultation with Caucus members, and that they have more influence than other members of the Working Committee; finally, though not apparent from this chart, the Working Committee, now free of the charismatic leader, has become a more genuine forum of discussion and decision.

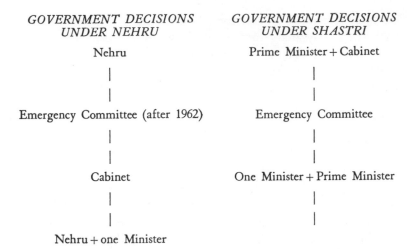

GOVERNMENT DECISIONS
UNDER NEHRU

GOVERNMENT DECISIONS
UNDER SHASTRI

Nehru

Prime Minister + Cabinet

Emergency Committee (after 1962)

Emergency Committee

Cabinet

One Minister + Prime Minister

Nehru + one Minister

Once more, the distinctions are evident: after the succession the Prime Minister is more 'first among equals' than 'first above equals'—decisions at the summit are shared between Prime Minister and Cabinet; secondly, Cabinet has restored its primacy over the Emergency Committee, except, as we shall see, in foreign affairs; and thirdly, while both Prime Ministers often made decisions on specific issues in collaboration with the Minister concerned, the role is now reversed, with much greater initiative and discretion in the hands of the Minister concerned.

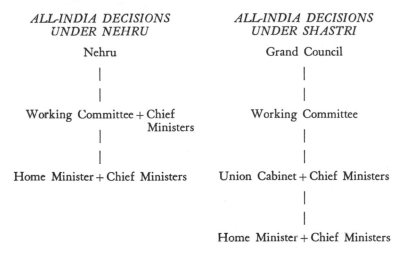

ALL-INDIA DECISIONS
UNDER NEHRU

ALL-INDIA DECISIONS
UNDER SHASTRI

Nehru

Grand Council

Working Committee + Chief
Ministers

Working Committee

Home Minister + Chief Ministers

Union Cabinet + Chief Ministers

Home Minister + Chief Ministers

The basic difference in this sphere, as noted, is the replacement of Nehru's charismatic power of decision by consensus in the composite oligarchy; a corollary is the elevation of the Chief Ministers to a position at the summit, as part of the Grand Council. The Council, however, is activated rarely. Thus, on many important all-India matters, the revived Working Committee is the inheritor of much of Nehru's power. Moreover, the Cabinet has become more important and has closer liaison with the State chiefs. With Nehru no longer there, and themselves as members of the Grand Council, the Chief Ministers bargain more frequently—and more successfully—with the Cabinet and the Union governmental establishment. What all this means is that, in the Shastri transition, the Chief Ministers have enhanced their influence *vis-à-vis* the Centre, a legacy of their role in the succession process itself. Decisions on lesser issues by conferences between the Home Minister and the State leaders continue as before, but again the balance of power has been altered.

The pyramids of decision in foreign and domestic policy have also changed as a result of the succession:

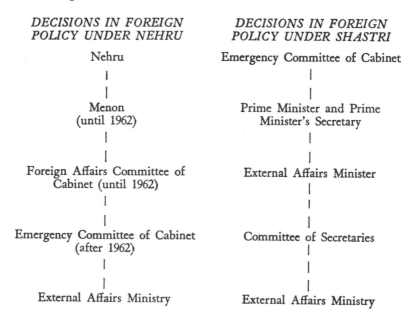

DECISIONS IN FOREIGN POLICY UNDER NEHRU	DECISIONS IN FOREIGN POLICY UNDER SHASTRI
Nehru	Emergency Committee of Cabinet
Menon (until 1962)	Prime Minister and Prime Minister's Secretary
Foreign Affairs Committee of Cabinet (until 1962)	External Affairs Minister
Emergency Committee of Cabinet (after 1962)	Committee of Secretaries
External Affairs Ministry	External Affairs Ministry

The contrast in the realm of foreign policy is the most striking of all. From 1947 until the Sino-Indian border war, Nehru had *carte blanche* and took full advantage of it, not only in shaping the broad guidelines of policy but also in making day-to-day decisions. Krishna Menon shared this power, by virtue of his unique relationship to Nehru, and translated many of these decisions into action, at the U.N. and elsewhere.[29] From about 1959 onwards the Foreign Affairs Committee acquired some importance, especially on China policy, though it had existed as early as 1950. In effect, however, foreign policy decisions until October 1962 were the monopoly of Nehru, assisted by Menon and the professionals of the Foreign Office. In the last eighteen months, the Emergency Committee became the principal forum for decisions though Nehru's primacy was never challenged.

This pyramid changed drastically after the succession. As before, Cabinet had no role, but its Emergency Committee became the supreme organ of decision, as revealed in the tense Rann of Kutch dispute in 1965.[30] Yet the Prime Minister himself has also taken the initiative in foreign policy, as with the decision not to produce the Bomb—which, by his own admission, was never brought to Cabinet. So too with his proposal for a nuclear shield in his discussions with Prime Minister Wilson in October 1964—which was unknown to his colleagues or staff.[31] A new variable, as noted earlier, is the Prime Minister's Secretary. Also new is a separation of function between Prime Minister and Foreign Minister, but the latter incumbent, Swaran Singh, has displayed neither forcefulness nor power during the first year. Apart from institutions and persons mentioned above, the Prime Minister's freedom of action is also limited by the new Committee of Secretaries. All this has tended to denigrate the influence of the External Affairs officials, for Nehru regarded himself, and was accepted, as a professional; civil servants outside the Ministry have acquired influence—at their expense. But the lines of decision authority had not fully crystallized in the first year after the succession.

The changes in domestic affairs are not readily apparent from a formal chart (see p. 128), for they are more in the nature of style and tone; but they are substantial nonetheless. Under both

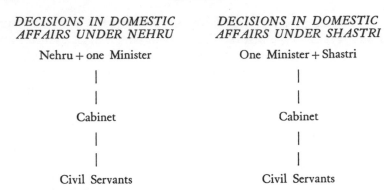

DECISIONS IN DOMESTIC AFFAIRS UNDER NEHRU	DECISIONS IN DOMESTIC AFFAIRS UNDER SHASTRI
Nehru + one Minister	One Minister + Shastri
Cabinet	Cabinet
Civil Servants	Civil Servants

Prime Ministers, decisions would often emanate from consultation with one of their colleagues but, as suggested earlier, the balance of initiative and influence has changed. Similarly, the Cabinet is now the key institution for domestic policy decisions. But most important is the enormous role now played by civil servants, who are far more influential in a wide range of middle-level decisions than in the past.

It will be noted that neither the Congress Parliamentary Party (CPP) nor the All-India Congress Committee (AICC) has been included in any of the pyramids of decision: the reason is that they are structures of authority but not of power; so too with their parent bodies, Parliament and the Annual Session of the Congress respectively. They are the institutions through which decisions are authorized, not formulated. And those pyramids of authority have not changed in the post-succession period. They remain as shown in the chart on p. 129.

The Legislature performs, as before, the authorization function and, formally, the formulation function in the Indian political system; the Executive formulates and implements policy. In both, the President stands at the apex of the authority pyramid. And the judiciary, in fact as in form, adjudicates the rules which are enacted. But this formalized structure conceals more than it reveals about the political process at the Union level. It is the decision pyramids which have changed, and these are the keys to an understanding of the impact of the succession on Centre and all-India politics.

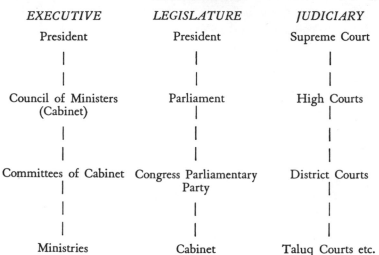

GOVERNMENT

EXECUTIVE	LEGISLATURE	JUDICIARY
President	President	Supreme Court
Council of Ministers (Cabinet)	Parliament	High Courts
Committees of Cabinet	Congress Parliamentary Party	District Courts
Ministries	Cabinet	Taluq Courts etc.

So too with the Congress Party structure of authority:

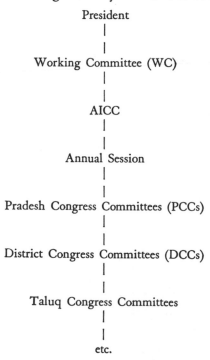

President
|
|
Working Committee (WC)
|
|
AICC
|
|
Annual Session
|
|
Pradesh Congress Committees (PCCs)
|
|
District Congress Committees (DCCs)
|
|
Taluq Congress Committees
|
|
etc.

This and the more elaborate Congress structural hierarchy have not changed. But the influence exerted by different organs has, notably the President and the Working Committee. The Annual Session and the AICC remain forums for the expression of opinion by rank-and-file delegates and middle-rank leaders respectively, as revealed at the various AICC Sessions and the 1965 Durgapur Session of the Congress. The domination of the High Command was no less in evidence, though articulate dissent was perhaps greater, in the absence of the charismatic leader.

The relations between Party and Government have long been a point of controversy in the Indian political system. Friction first arose during the experiment in constitutional government, from 1937 to 1939, when the Congress assumed responsibility in eight of the eleven Provinces of British India. Most of the national leaders, including Gandhi, Nehru, Patel, Azad, Prasad, and Bose, remained in the organizational wing and exercised broad supervision over the policies of the Congress Governments. Yet incidents arose, notably in the Central Provinces (Madhya Pradesh), and Nehru was led to define the proper relationship— the Party, through the PCCs, was to be consulted on policy issues but not to intrude into administration or day-to-day decisions.[32] Conflict erupted again on the morrow of independence, when Congress President Kripalani proclaimed the doctrine that ' it is the party from which the government of the day derives its power '. Prime Minister Nehru rejected this categorically, insisting that his Government was responsible to Parliament and not to the Congress or its President. This view prevailed and, as long as Patel was alive (until 1950), harmony between Party and Government at the Centre was maintained by the duumvirs. A year later, however, when Purshottamdas Tandon was elected Congress President—against Nehru's will—he attempted once more to assert the primacy of the Party. Nehru resolved the issue by resigning from the Working Committee and forcing Tandon's resignation.[33]

For the next thirteen years the autonomy of Government and its responsibility to Parliament remained unchallenged—whether

Nehru was Congress President (1951–4) or others held that office, Dhebar (1954–9), Mrs. Gandhi (1959–60), Sanjiva Reddy (1960–2), and Sanjivayya (1962–4): Nehru's special position as 'super-President' was acknowledged by all, as Gandhi's had been from 1920 to 1947. Reddy illustrated the position emphatically when he remarked, 'whatever Nehru wanted, we did; when Nehru wanted C. B. Gupta to be appointed Chief Minister of U.P., we simply had to work to do it'.[34] More bitterly, he told a friend that, as Congress President, he was treated as 'Mrs. Gandhi's chaprassi'! At the State level, however, friction between the Ministry and the PCC, i.e., the governmental and organizational wings, intensified over the years and became the dominant characteristic of State politics, a cover for the clash of interest groups, factions, castes, and individuals for power and patronage. So it continues in the post-succession period; but that aspect of the political system is beyond the scope of this study.[35]

The subordination of Party to Government—more accurately, of the High Command to Nehru—was so marked that Nehru himself attempted to enhance the prestige and importance of the Congress. Thus, early in 1959, he wrote to some of his colleagues:[36]

. . . Many people say that the Congress has become some kind of a camp follower of the Government. This is, I think, basically not true. It is inevitable that when leading personalities in the Congress and the Government are to a large extent the same, the direction of both should also be the same. But it has to be remembered that the push forward in regard to basic policies has come from the Congress organization, representing public urges, and the Government and the Planning Commission have followed these up and worked them out in detail.

This was true in one sense, for Nehru was not a dictator; nor was he impervious to pressure—from individuals, groups, or the public at large. But it is also true that the influence of Party *qua* Party declined steadily over the years of the Nehru era, certainly to 1963, and that the ultimate decision as to what policies to 'push forward' lay with the Leader, not with the Congress.

Nehru's position at the summit of power—in Party and Government—was ruffled, but not effectively challenged, by the dramatic failure of his China policy. Ironically, the fillip to change was his own doing—the purge initiated by the Kamaraj

Plan. When Kamaraj himself assumed the Congress Presidency, his leadership in the South, along with Nehru's declining vigour, invested that office with an importance unknown since independence. Further, it was that newly-acquired influence which enabled the President to play such a crucial role in the succession. And that, in turn, accentuated the influence of the organizational wing. Thus, in this respect, too, the succession was a great catalyst to political change—towards a new equilibrium between High Command and Cabinet.

When Shastri became Prime Minister, in June 1964, it was generally believed that a new duumvirate had come into being; many, in fact, predicted pre-eminence for the Congress President. Kamaraj had tried at the outset to put the stamp of Party and personal authority on the new relationship by his call for ' collective leadership '. But events dictated otherwise. For one thing, having made a king, the kingmaker lost half of his power. For another, Shastri knew that he was the genuine choice of the Congress and the country, regardless of the managerial skill of Kamaraj and the Caucus—and they knew it as well. Thirdly, the enormous power, prestige, and patronage inherent in the Prime Ministership in India's political system gave Shastri a marked advantage. And finally, Kamaraj had neither the pretension nor ambition to occupy the centre of the stage.[37]

Yet the ' duumvirate ' remains a valid concept for the Shastri transition, reminiscent of the Nehru–Patel relationship from 1947 to 1950—with three vital differences: the original duumvirs towered above their colleagues in Government and Party, occupying a unique place in the pyramid of power; Patel had substantial power as Deputy Prime Minister, as well as being Party boss; and, whereas Nehru and Patel differed sharply, Shastri and Kamaraj do not. For this reason, it is more accurate to view the post-succession relationship as an institutional duumvirate— the sharing of power by the two wings of the Congress or by Government and Party: the dispersion of power is real, but the recipients are not primarily individuals.

The restoration of the pre-1950 institutional equilibrium was inevitable—a natural assertion of autonomy by a party organization which had been long subordinate to a charismatic leader.

It was also healthy, for it induced frequent consultation and genuine harmony among equals which, in turn, strengthened the authority of a less secure and less gifted governmental leader.

It is difficult to assess precisely Kamaraj's role in decision-making. As he related in the spring of 1965, consultation with the Prime Minister ranges over a broad field—party organization, elections, economic policy, language, and Party–Government relations in the States; as to foreign policy, 'not much'. They have not always agreed, and Kamaraj acknowledged that his conception of 'collective leadership' had not fulfilled his expectations, i.e., co-operative discussion and decision between Cabinet and High Command on broad policy; he accepts fully Nehru's strictures about the Party's intrusion into day-to-day decisions. Nonetheless, there is ample evidence that the Prime Minister has not ignored the Congress President, if only because he knows that he needs the support of the organizational wing to implement his policies. Suffice it to note a few examples.

Press reports of their frequent meetings create the image of co-equals. Both were involved in the 'Punjab Crisis' following the resignation of Kairon in the summer of 1964; Shastri's candidate for the Chief Ministership, Ram Kishan, was chosen over Kamaraj's preference, Darbara Singh, but there was pro-longed deliberation. So too in the 'Kerala Crisis' at the turn of the year, with Kamaraj playing the leading role. Indeed, in purely party affairs, his primacy appears to be generally accepted by Shastri. The Congress President was intimately involved in the quest for a viable food-price policy during much of the year. His views on the fourth Plan, favouring a smaller total invest-ment, clearly expressed in his presidential address at the Durgapur Session, could not be, and were not, ignored; indeed, they strengthened the growing chorus of conservatism regarding economic policy. Kamaraj's role was no less prominent in the search for a consensus on language. Similarly, he was influential in the forced resignation of Biren Mitra as Chief Minister of Orissa, following the public revelation of corruption, and in the attempt to stem the tide of factional strife in various States.

Thus, his role is by no means inconsequential, though it may not measure up to the anticipated power of a duumvir. And it

is likely to grow, rather than diminish, in the light of his
re-election as Congress President for 1966 and 1967. As head of
the organization, he will supervise the allocation of election
tickets for Parliament and the State Assemblies, as well as direct
the Congress campaign throughout the country. The fact that
the Prime Minister strongly favoured a second term for Kamaraj
—which required an amendment to the Party's constitution—
suggests that harmony and co-operation will continue, perhaps
even increase, in the next phase.

There remains the question of Caucus power. Even more
than Kamaraj, its influence as a group declined once Shastri
assumed office. Members retain their influence as individuals
closely associated with the President, but no more.[38] Thus,
Atulya Ghosh was delegated to supervise the change-over in
Orissa, and Patil was delegated to try to prevent an open split in
the Kerala Congress. Yet these emissary roles do not flow from
the Caucus: Atulya has long had the position of party overlord
in eastern India, and Patil often served as a troubleshooter for
Nehru, notably during the crucial Andhra elections of 1955.
Should a new succession crisis arise and the Caucus be re-formed,
that special source of influence might be re-created. Until such
time, however, they remain Congress leaders in their own
right, with greater access to, and therefore influence over, both
President and Prime Minister. But it should be stressed that
Shastri himself is a leader of the Congress, as well as of the
Government.

The informality that obtains among Congress leaders is
illustrated by Caucus member Patil's ill-fated intervention in the
Kerala Party dispute. A group of Congress dissidents submitted
charges to Kamaraj about alleged corruption in the Shankar
ministry and sought interviews on various occasions; there was
no response, for he thought it would blow over. Finally, they
made the charges public and demanded a change in the State
Government; there was still no response. The dissidents then
announced that they would support a No-Confidence motion.
At that eleventh hour, Shastri telephoned Patil, who was in
Bombay, and asked him to proceed at once to Trivandrum. Patil
asked, ' do you want me to attend a political funeral? '; and

Shastri replied, 'after all, the Government of India should be represented'! Patil went and secured Shankar's offer to resign, but it was too late. Patil had also promised an inquiry into their charges, even if the ministry were brought down. Then came President's Rule. When, later, Kamaraj was told of Patil's pledge, he responded, 'did he promise? I must ask him'. No inquiry was ever held.[39]

Relations between Delhi and the States in the Nehru era were heavily weighted in favour of the Centre. There were many reasons for this. One was the unitary stress of the Constitution, which was evident in many sections: Article 3, giving Parliament almost unrestricted authority to alter the territory of the States— until 1956; Articles 352–360, detailing the formidable emergency powers of the President, extending to the legislative, executive, and economic spheres; Part XII, concerning the distribution of financial resources, revealing a marked dependence of the States on the Union for a steady flow of funds; Part XIV and the Seventh Schedule, setting out the distribution of legislative spheres of jurisdiction, again favouring the Centre; and Article 249, granting the vital residuary power to Delhi.[40] Another reason was the highly-centralized planning mechanism, with vast authority concentrated in the Delhi-based Planning Commission and the Union Cabinet; while the States bargained, often effectively, for larger allocations, they were ultimately dependent on the Centre. A third factor was the traditional role of the Congress Working Committee as the supreme decision-making organ for all-India policy, and the predominant presence of Union leaders on that body. And finally, perhaps most important, was Nehru's charismatic leadership and his undisputed position at the summit of power. The result was that all issues of a federal character were decided by recourse to the 'Great Source of Unity'; and Nehru, with his acute sense of history and, therefore, awareness of the powerful tradition of 'balkanization', used his multiple sources of power to foster the unity of India.

On the morrow of succession many predicted the resurgence
of 'fissiparous' tendencies, with ensuing danger to unity and
stability. Others, however, noted that Nehru had built wisely
and well, and that the foundations for unity were sufficiently
firm to withstand the challenge. After all, the basic pressures
for unity—constitutional, institutional, and economic—remained.
And the Working Committee, if anything, became more
powerful after Nehru's death. Indeed, the forces which were set
in motion, and later harnessed, during the first seventeen years,
could not be easily reversed: Nehruism in this sense perpetuated
itself.

This is not to suggest that Union–State relations were
unaffected by the succession. For one thing, the key role of the
Chief Ministers in the selection of Shastri gave them greater
leverage with the Centre. Closely related was the lesser stature
of the new Prime Minister and his penchant for consensus; in
all-India affairs, this meant the concurrence of the States. Moreover, the Chief Ministers as a group were elevated to the summit
of decision as members of the Grand Council of the Republic—
which partly reflected this trend to decentralization. The change,
then, was in both style and substance. Under Nehru, the Chief
Ministers would accept the Leader's advice and decision—and
would often delay or distort his intent in the process of implementation. Under Shastri, as Kamaraj, Sanjiva Reddy and others
testified, the relationship is more like that of co-equals: the
discussion is fuller and more genuine, with the result that the
decision process is slower but implementation is more effective.

This dispersion of power had already begun in the last years
of Nehru. And Nehru himself, despite his enormous power, did
not ride roughshod over the States. Thus, for example, the long-
standing border dispute between Mysore and Maharashtra, and
the river disputes in the South could have been solved by forceful
pressure from Delhi—but it was not exercised. What the
succession did, in essence, was to act as catalyst to the trend to
greater State influence and bring it to the surface. And yet there
are built-in limits to decentralization, for the Centre still controls
the purse strings and the States have a vested interest, financial
and other, in an efficient and strong Centre, from which they

can draw support. For the indefinite future, economic growth will remain the common core problem, and this is dependent on planning which, in turn, requires a stable and solid Union Government. There are healthy pulls in both directions.[41]

VI

IMPLEMENTATION

THE new equilibrium in Centre–State relations is a prominent feature of the Shastri transition; in fact, it crystallized during the prolonged debate on India's two major domestic crises of 1964–5 —food and language. An analysis of these issues has the added merit of uncovering the complex forces that enter into decisions on high policy at the all-India level—economic and ideological, institutional and regional, electoral and administrative, Party and Government. They provide exceptional data for a study of decision-making in the post-succession period.

While language dissension was the bane of India's polity, the food crisis dramatized the malaise of her economy. Neither was a product of the succession, but both served as crucibles for decision-making in the new era. Both have deep roots and have erupted periodically to challenge the ingenuity of men and the effectiveness of institutions, before as well as after independence. Indeed, they were part of the ' unfinished business ' of the ' Age of Nehru ', awesome legacies to the new régime.

The toll of India's famines in the nineteenth century was larger than the population of most sovereign states at the present time.[1] Even as late as 1943, the Bengal Famine took two to three million lives. And, while such disasters have not recurred, food shortage and malnutrition have been endemic features of Indian life. The competition between population growth and increase in food production has always been close, with the outcome uncertain from year to year. Thus, for example, when India was blessed with three favourable monsoons in succession, from 1952 to 1954, there was relative abundance. And when drought and flood were especially acute, as in 1957–8, scarcity reached a danger point. A massive import programme from 1960–4—16 million tons under the United States P.L. 480 Programme—created the illusion of adequacy. But the long-term problem remained, and an acute food-price crisis came to the surface on the eve of Nehru's death. It was to dominate the first year of the Shastri Government.

The facts are clear, the causes subject to varying interpretations. Thus, the index of wholesale prices for 'food articles' (base 1952–3 = 100) rose from 139 to 172 in one year. In many regions of the country retail food prices rose more than 50 per cent., causing acute distress, especially among the lower-income groups in urban areas. Long queues at 'fair price' shops and frequent attacks by hungry people on food 'godowns' in widely-scattered areas testified to the severity of the crisis.

The simplest explanation is a widening gap between demand for and supply of food since 1960. Effective demand has grown rapidly because of two factors: the growth of population at the rate of 2·2 per cent. per annum; and the income elasticity of demand for food, as a result of which about half the increase in income per person is spent on food. The Planning Commission estimated the effective demand for food at 72 million tons in 1960–1, with an annual rate of increase of 3·65 per cent. By contrast, the output of food was relatively static—81 million tons in 1960–1 and 1961–2, 79 million tons during the next two years; effective supply, including imports but excluding provision for wastage, seed, and feed, was stationary at about 75 million tons, and only 73 million in 1962–3. In short, there was a real scarcity in the last two years of the Nehru era, concealed largely by massive imports.[2] Other factors accentuated this shortage in the months after the succession.

A detailed analysis of the food-price crisis in 1964–5 is beyond the scope of this study. Suffice it to note some interpretations before turning to the decision process on food policy. At one extreme is the anti-statist school which asserts that there is no food shortage, acknowledges large-scale hoarding, and blames it on ill-conceived intervention against market forces. Its most articulate and influential advocate, S. K. Patil, noted that the peak of rice consumption was 32 million tons in 1962; production was 36 million tons in 1963, he said, with an expected output of 38 to 40 million tons in 1965. The surplus of 4 million tons was being hoarded by two million peasants, he claimed, because of lack of confidence: 'food is like stocks; confidence is the crucial factor '. The cause of the 1964 crisis, thus, is the Government's draconian policy towards the traders; measures like State trading frighten the trading community, and they hoard. Further, statutory rationing would be disastrous: 'in wartime, we suffered greatly from rationing '. The solution is complete free enterprise in food distribution along with higher prices to producers and massive imports to create a reserve stock.[3]

At the other extreme are those who attribute the crisis to massive hoarding by the middlemen. There is no *real* shortage, it is argued, rather, scarcity caused by a network of traders who withhold foodgrains from the market and thereby reap an enormous profit after prices have risen sharply. The solution, then, is as simple as the cause—stringent controls and State trading to ensure effective distribution of food to deficit areas and, especially, to the cities, which are being held to ransom by the evil men who control the wholesale trade. The Communist Party of India, leftist Congress M.P.s, and some intellectuals subscribe to this view.

Between these two emotionally satisfying explanations is a spectrum of more sophisticated analysis and prescription. Almost all acknowledge a real shortage of food and the prevalence of hoarding, but their policy proposals are more complex and diversified than either extreme. Among the political commentators, Inder Malhotra called for the maintenance of adequate buffer stocks through continued P.L. 480 imports; 'some measure of disciplined and controlled distribution and consumption '; Government responsibility to feed economically-vulnerable sections of the population in town and village; 'a dual policy of controlled distribution for the poor and a free market for the relatively affluent '; and the assigning of personal responsibility for agricultural production to the District Magistrate.[4]

One economic pundit stressed the need for stricter fiscal and monetary discipline and a greater sense of obligation by surplus States to deficit areas.[5] Another spelled out specific proposals:

Abolish [food] zones; enhance storage capacity to six million tons; build up foodgrain stocks through an aggressive purchase policy and even imports; fix floor prices above the post-harvest low in the recent past; respect the market mechanism and do not hesitate to buy above the floor level at the ruling market price in the off-season; do not ever force farmers to sell below the market price, for they will boycott the market and sell privately; since demand exceeds supply at the controlled price, ration major foodgrains in urban centres; operate the FTC [Food Trading Corporation] like an efficient, market-oriented business concern; take full advantage of large-scale economies in purchase, transport and storage, and finally, operate an integrated long-range agricultural policy, integrated at the village level, with strong emphasis on implementation.[6]

A third expert, the Vice-Chancellor of Punjab Agricultural University, saw the solution in less complicated terms: 'Full-scale procurement and rationing appears to be the obvious remedy, but it is neither practicable nor really necessary. Rationing in vulnerable urban areas and procurement in surplus areas is all that is really necessary. Legal and institutional remedies are practicable [but must be] set up on a long-term basis and recognized as an integral part of our food administration.'[7]

Among professional economists, Professor D. R. Gadgil called for the abolition of State food zones and a comprehensive policy of procurement of foodgrains and control of the prices and distribution of all essential supplies in an open manner.[8] Dr. Raj Krishna of the Institute of Economic Growth at Delhi University, whose thesis of real shortage was noted earlier, suggested four measures: 'a two-market system . . . consisting of the general retail market and the fair price market'; 'a reduction in the rate of growth of the supply of money'; continued imports—'an evil necessity'—to build up a buffer stock; and 'a genuine price support programme'.[9]

The most trenchant analysis was provided by Professor K. N. Raj of the Delhi School of Economics. The third Five-Year Plan had called for a rise in total investment outlay from Rs. 1,600 crores in 1960–1 to Rs. 2,600 crores in 1965–6, i.e., Rs. 1,000 crores; however, as this was scaled upwards in stages, the investment outlay in 1963–4 was about Rs. 450–500 crores above the 1960–1 level. To that had to be added an increase in defence expenditure of Rs. 525 crores above the 1960–1 level, as a result of the Emergency. Yet this additional investment in development and defence, in 1963–4 more than Rs. 1,000 crores, had to come from a much smaller increase in national output than planned for that year, only Rs. 1,400 crores. Thus, less than a third of the growth in total output was available for private consumption. As population had grown, this meant a reduction in per capita private consumption. And all this was accentuated by increased demand out of income generated by defence and development outlays. 'Some rise in prices was indeed inevitable in the circumstances.'

This is one reason for the rise in food prices. Another is the activities of trader-speculators. But a deeper cause, in Professor Raj's judgement, is the Government's import policy and its consequences. For one thing, of 12 million tons imported in 1960–3, only ¾ million was left as a buffer stock, hardly adequate to meet the additional demand. For another, the releases of imported food to the market kept agricultural prices low, a disincentive to production. Statistics reveal that, while the index number of wholesale prices for manufactured goods rose steadily, that of foodgrains fell sharply, especially for wheat, from 105 in 1958–9 to 96 in 1959–60 and 90 in 1960–1, remaining at that level during the next two years; the index number of the wholesale price for rice, by contrast, remained high. Significantly, this disparity in wholesale price trends for wheat and rice shows a marked correlation with disparities in retail price and in output. The price of wheat, whose production was supplemented most by P.L. 480 imports, rose 60 per cent. from 1962–3 to 1964–5, while that of rice, whose supply depended almost entirely on domestic production, rose only 15 per cent. in that period. In short, a policy of massive imports of wheat has had a disastrous effect on the price to the consumer. This is further evident in the disparity of domestic output. Rice production rose steadily, while wheat production fell steadily, from 12 million tons in 1961–2 to 9·7 million tons in 1963–4; the output of rice rose 5 per cent. in two years, while that of wheat declined 20 per cent. In Raj's view, this was the consequence of disincentive to wheat production, flowing from large-scale imports and the lower wholesale prices created by their entry into the market.

The sharp spurt in wheat prices is explained by other related factors. The decline in domestic output, he argues, had a more than proportionate effect on the amount of wheat marketed. As wheat prices rose, producers used their additional income to consume more of their own output. They may also have held back in anticipation of still higher prices. Thus, if 3 million tons, of a total output of 12 million tons, were marketed in 1961–2, only about 2 million of 9½ million tons of domestic output were marketed in 1963–4. And since, including imports, there were about 8½ million tons available in the market in 1961–2, it would have required 6½ million tons of imported food in 1963–4 to maintain the market supply; but such large buffer stocks were no longer available because of the indiscriminate releases of P.L. 480 wheat in the preceding three years. Hence the skyrocketing of wheat prices. The real culprits, then, were government policy in flooding the market with imported wheat and the dual consequences of lower domestic wheat production because of low wholesale prices and the destruction of an emergency buffer stock. Raj's prescription is threefold: ' a more far-sighted price policy ', i.e., higher prices for wheat producers to stimulate production; ' creation of an adequate machinery for market operations in foodgrains on a large scale '; and effective implementation of land-reform measures as an incentive to tenant-cultivators, specifically, ' compilation of a record of land holdings under close supervision, fixation of rent in absolute money terms, and introduction of arrangements by which rents are paid and received through some agency of the government '. These, and not a further extension of land legislation, are the remedies; if they are implemented, the outlook for agricultural output is optimistic.[10]

When Lal Bahadur Shastri assumed office, on 9 June 1964, the Indian economy was at its lowest ebb—stagnant agriculture, a major foreign exchange crisis, the slowing-down of industrial growth, and massive unemployment; worst of all, perhaps, was an enveloping crisis of confidence, as prices soared and food in the cities became scarce. Indeed, everything paled before the challenge of feeding India's hungry millions. It was an inauspicious setting for the new régime, despite the skilful and tranquil succession to Nehru.

It took four sessions of a modified Grand Council of the Republic, extending over a period of five months, to hammer out an all-India food policy: constitutionally, food is a State subject.

As with language, the process illuminated Shastri's style and the shifting pyramid of power in all-India politics. Within a fortnight of becoming Head of Government, Shastri summoned the Chief Ministers to Delhi. His address to the conference was in low key, revealing no fresh approach to the problem of run-away inflation in food prices; rather, it stressed making foodgrains available at fair prices, checking profiteering, larger internal procurement, and continued imports; there was a hint of the need for controls, but firmness was lacking.[11] The discussion that followed was in the nature of a skirmish and revealed conflicting interpretations. One specific proposal from the Centre was to take over existing rice mills; some viewed the consensus as favouring only the setting up of new mills in the public sector; others read it as sanctioning both measures; as subsequent events demonstrated, the minimalists were correct. There was also a clash on the proposed Food Trading Corporation, with anti-statists and most Chief Ministers succeeding in shelving the project. On the general question of controls, the State leaders served notice of their rightist orientation.[12] A month later, T.T.K. admitted the lack of clarity in Government policy; he also attacked the widespread hoarding—which could only be uncovered and disgorged if traders were forced to sell grains to the Government.[13]

Early in August the Prime Minister wrote a long and respectful letter to the Chief Ministers, pleading for co-operation and more forceful measures on the food front; the effect was nil, for the new men of power were in no mood to yield to Centre direction. Shastri then tried to head off the politicization of the food problem by holding a conference with Opposition leaders in Parliament; as in the first meeting with the Chief Ministers, he allowed Food Minister Subramaniam to present Government policy—and to bear the brunt of criticism. The gesture was unsuccessful for, from 24–28 August, the right-wing CPI (Communist Party of India) launched a nation-wide agitation against rising prices; on the first day, more than 1,300 were arrested. By that time, too, Shastri's period of two weeks' grace, to enable hoarders to bring their stocks into the market, had proved futile; the traders were not prepared to sacrifice their interests so lightly.

At the end of August, the AICC dutifully approved the Government's food policy. So did the Lok Sabha, on 10 September, by a vote of 201 to 34, but not before a stormy fifteen-hour debate, in which the fragmented Opposition parties delivered scathing attacks on the Government's inaction. Subramaniam outlined an integrated programme that was being evolved—establishment of a Food Trading Corporation, fixation of remunerative prices for producers, a large-scale soil survey programme, improvement of seed, the rapid completion of all minor irrigation projects, and an ambitious plan for domestic production of fertilizers. But few were impressed, for all this had been said before—many times—with little effect; moreover, these measures could not deal with the immediate crisis, and many knew that the Centre and the States had only agreed to disagree on specific remedies for the short-run.[14] The impression of bargaining and drift continued.

It was, in appearance, an exact replica of the uncertainty and indecisiveness on food policy under Nehru. Indeed, self-criticism abounds in Panditji's frequent admonitions to his colleagues on the food question. A few extracts reveal this strikingly:

. . . Nevertheless I feel that the fault is ours also. Perhaps we were too complacent, perhaps we did not look far enough ahead. Perhaps there was lack of co-ordination. . . .   (1957)[15]

. . . It is a painful thought that after ten years of independence, an agricultural country like India cannot feed itself. It would be wrong for us to blame the gods or the stars or floods and drought. We must recognize that there must be something lacking in our approach which has led to this relative lack of success.   (1957)[16]

Let us confess that in spite of our frequent talk on this subject, we have neither made the big effort, nor have we been very vigilant. What is particularly astonishing is our failure to utilize the actual resources available to us. . . . The fault, therefore, was in the failure of our administration, and it was a serious fault with grievous consequences. . . .   (1958)[17]

. . . We have not given him [the producer] the confidence, the faith and the self-reliance to change these practices, and to adopt new techniques and a more aggressive and forceful attitude to his work. All the fine decisions we make at the top and all the appeals that we issue achieve little success by the time they reach down to the cultivator.   (1958)[18]

. . . But we see hoarding again and an attempt to push up prices.
. . . A government that cannot deal with obvious anti-social elements
has surrendered to them and can have no credit or effectiveness.

(1959) [19]

. . . The fact remains that the whole future of our Plan, and
indeed even of industrial growth, depends on agricultural progress.
. . .   (1960) [20]

And so it continued in the early months under Shastri, though
with greater justification, for the new Prime Minister had
inherited the crisis—and lacked the asset of charisma.

Towards the end of September there was a novel gesture of
defiance by consumers in the capital: patrons of the India Coffee
House in Janpath revolted against high prices and set up a way-
side café near by! The spontaneous, non-political movement
spread to other parts of Delhi but petered out soon after.[21] At
the end of October a second conference of Chief Ministers was
held in Delhi. Shastri admitted failure in the Government's
efforts to stabilize the food situation without recourse to controls
and made two drastic proposals: statutory rationing in eight
cities with a population of over a million; and summary trial of
traders who sell foodgrains at prices higher than those fixed by
the Government. Subramaniam spelled out the ' harder line '
in a five-point programme: cordoning off Calcutta, Bombay, and
six other cities, as well as the State of Kerala, where the food
shortage was grave; informal rationing in cities with a population
over 100,000; statutory rationing in the larger cities and revision
of prices of imported rice and wheat in ' fair price ' shops; revision of rice zones; and the establishment of machinery for the
procurement of foodgrains in surplus States, until the Food
Trading Corporation came into being.[22]

The *Indian Express* reflected the mood of many when it hailed
the proposals as ' Drastic but Welcome ', noting that ' public
support . . . will be overwhelming '; further, ' for nearly four
months the Centre has tried to be accommodating to the State
Governments, with results that are visible. Any further wobbling
[might be disastrous].' [23] The Chief Ministers remained un-
moved, however; the only specific decision was to cordon off
Kerala and introduce statutory rationing there—a dire necessity.

As for the general proposal of rationing, they agreed only to discuss it again at the next AICC session early in November. All Chief Ministers of the States concerned were opposed. And the surplus States succeeded in pressing their view that there should be no free movement of rice to deficit States, a setback for the Centre's plan for equitable distribution—and a further illustration of where the power of decision lay in this crucial sphere.[24]

In the midst of the impasse with the State leaders, the Centre resorted to direct action. On 5 November it promulgated the Essential Commodities (Amendment) Ordinance to combat hoarding and profiteering. The basic provision was for summary trial of traders and officials, by magistrates and special judges respectively, for certain types of offences regarding the supply, distribution, and sale of foodstuffs. The maximum sentence was to be one year's imprisonment, but where the sentence did not exceed a month or a fine of Rs. 2,000, or both, the right of appeal was withdrawn. To many, it seemed long overdue; to others, draconian and dangerous.[25] The pressures that led to this hard line are not easy to identify, apart from the accumulated resentment of the public, both mass and attentive, the exploitation of the food issue by Opposition parties, and the increasing concern within Party and Government at their growing isolation from the electorate on a grave public problem. In any event, the Ordinance remained a dead letter, apart from the arrest and brief detention of some important middlemen in West Bengal—the traders were too strongly entrenched. The threat was not implemented, largely, perhaps, because of unwillingness to alienate that class which was the base of Congress power and finance. And by mid-January 1965 it was reported that the Union Government had concluded that drastic action would be ineffective in the state of food conditions then existing; as long as supplies were inadequate, market prices would have to obtain.[26]

The shift in policy was made possible, indeed necessary, by the nature of the consensus on food, which was finally reached in November. A third conference of Chief Ministers, held at the AICC session in Guntur on 7–8 November, failed to break the impasse; opinion remained divided, and mainly hostile, on the crucial issue of rationing. Thus the AICC resolution on food, in the words of its mover, Sanjiva Reddy, was 'not comprehensive and was couched in general terms'.[27] Reports of distress in Kerala, scene of a virtual rice famine, could no longer be ignored. The press, too, mounted further pressure. Even the conservative *Times of India* declared that 'the Union Government should have the good sense and the courage to use the emergency powers with which it armed itself almost two years ago'.[28] And Subramaniam reportedly expressed the opinion that food rationing would be necessary for five to seven years.[29] A decision could not be delayed much longer.

When it came, however, at the fourth Chief Ministers' Conference, on 17–18 November, the Centre's capitulation seemed complete. Whereas Shastri had proposed statutory rationing in eight major cities, it was agreed that this would be introduced in Calcutta only, and even that, reportedly, at the insistence of West Bengal's Chief Minister P. C. Sen; Bombay, Kanpur, and Ahmedabad would continue with the system of informal rationing, and Madras, Hyderabad, and Bangalore were to be permitted, if their State Governments so desired, a system of 'regulated distribution'; one newspaper aptly termed this, 'rationing as you like it'.[30] The States also scored a victory in the decision to make each State a closed rice zone, from which rice would move on a Government-to-Government basis, at the discretion of each; only the northern rice zone (Punjab, Delhi, and Himachal Pradesh), where little rice is grown, would remain intact! There were also to be continued zonal restrictions on the movement of wheat, at least until the following March. The only concession made by the surplus States was to contribute two million tons of rice to a Centre pool for distribution to the deficit States during the next year; Andhra, 800,000 tons, Madras, 200,000 tons, Madhya Pradesh, 400,000 tons, the Punjab, 250,000 tons, and Orissa, 300,000 tons, with a small contribution from the U.S.; restrictions on the movement of pulses and oilseeds were also to be withdrawn.[31] Some weeks later, Subramaniam candidly told Parliament that no proposal for statutory rationing was under consideration because of general opposition by the States.[32]

The Press, like many other observers, was dissatisfied with the consensus. The *Hindustan Times* took the Centre to task for yielding to the States: 'The time has come for the leadership at the Centre to assume the political responsibility for an all-India policy on food and divest the local leadership of both the initiative and the responsibility for it. The interminable parleys with the Chief Ministers are a pathetic exercise in evasion.'[33] The *Times of India* lashed out at both authorities: '. . . there is hardly a single State in the Union which is not guilty of subordinating the national interest to its own narrow, regional considerations. The conflict among the States is no longer a covert struggle. . . . What is alarming is that hardly anything is being done by those in authority to reverse the current dangerous trends.'[34] The occasion of this editorial was President Radhakrishnan's equally blunt remarks on the dismal state of the nation in a speech at Baroda, which was commended to politicians and public alike. And when Subramaniam told the Lok Sabha that statutory rationing was opposed by the Chief Ministers because it was not 'generally favoured' by the people, the *Statesman* chided him: 'Might one ask which people?' More bluntly, it added: 'There is no way out other than determined procurement at the village level and unyielding firmness towards the trade in the market towns and cities.'[35]

All these cries of despair, however well-intentioned, missed the real significance of the decisions on food. It was not as if the Centre wanted to yield or that the States were misbehaving: the Centre had no choice—because of the fundamental change in the equilibrium of power within the Union after the succession; and the States were protecting their basic interests, like all interest groups in a free polity; to expect them to do otherwise is to misunderstand the essence of the political process in a democracy. And in a vast federal state like India such bargaining, especially over something as basic as food, is natural—and healthy; it testifies to the reality of an open and competitive political system, as the language decision was to reveal later. In the short run it suggested weakness, but it also revealed sound underpinnings of democracy; and it is the price that must be paid if the system is to survive. Moreover, in the longer run, the Centre could arm itself for more effective future combat. The struggle over food was also a classic illustration of Shastri's style—decision by attrition and exhaustive—also exhausting—consultation. The outcome was a hotchpotch, representing a victory of the States over the Centre and of the surplus over the deficit States.

The November consensus on food policy was, at best, an interim agreement; at worst, an illusion. Certainly it did not end the crisis or the debate. A month later an eye-witness reported: ' The recent Chief Ministers' Conference was nothing more than an exercise in futility, if the lukewarm attitude of the authorities in Kerala towards the implementation of its decisions is any indication.' [36]   At the end of the year, the Executive Committee of the CPP decried the non-implementation of the consensus and the failure of the surplus States to fulfil their obligations. Even Subramaniam, who had privately termed it a ' gentleman's agreement ' which was likely to be implemented because it represented a genuine compromise of conflicting interests,[37] acknowledged that there were difficulties in getting full co-operation from the States.[38]   And in January 1965 the debate raged again in the CPP Executive Committee; more important, two senior members of Cabinet reportedly took opposing stands before the Committee— T.T.K. favoured control of the trade and Subramaniam argued that adequate enforcement machinery was not available.[39]

By the spring, the question of food receded into the background, because of prospects of a favourable crop. One commentator aptly remarked: ' Food Crisis Goes But Danger Remains.' [40] It returned in the summer of 1965. Chief Minister Naik of Maharashtra, supported by P. C. Sen of West Bengal, attacked the Centre's policy as ' either ignorant of basic matters with regard to food or . . . callous to the sufferings of the people '.[41] Further discussions by the Chief Ministers in July and August led to a ' firm decision ' to introduce statutory rationing in the eight Indian cities with a population exceeding one million.[42] Yet the crisis mounted, for the monsoon was late and inadequate. In 1964 there had been talk in Delhi of ' shortage '; towards the end of 1965 there was fear of ' famine ', and statutory rationing had not yet been implemented.[43]   Food remains the Achilles' Heel of India's economy.

The 'language question' has bedevilled Indian politics since independence, and even earlier: its roots are deep in India's culture, society, and history. Language was the most contentious issue during the drafting of the new Constitution. It was the motive force in the demand for States Reorganisation, which sapped the nation's energy from 1952 to 1960. It caused widespread fear in the South and a persistent clamour in the Hindi hinterland for a rapid change-over from English to Hindi as the Official Language. It has led to deep fissures in the Congress élite and in the Parliamentary Party. To many, it is a formidable threat to Indian unity.[44]

Our concern here is primarily with one facet of the problem —the Official Language—especially with the way in which an historic decision was reached at the close of Shastri's first year. Some background material is necessary, however. India is regarded by some as a Babel of languages, for no less than 1,652 'mother tongues' are mentioned in the *Linguistic Survey of India*; but of these, 87 per cent. are covered by the fourteen languages specified in the Eighth Schedule to the Constitution. In a broad delineation, the 'mother tongues' may be grouped into four linguistic families: Indo-Aryan (73·3 per cent. of the population); Dravidian (24·5 per cent.); Tibeto-Chinese (0·73 per cent.); and Austric (1·5 per cent.). Only the first two families are recognized in the Constitution, with ten Indo-Aryan languages and four Dravidian tongues. According to the 1961 Census, the distribution is as follows (in millions): [45]

INDO-ARYAN		*DRAVIDIAN*	
Assamese	6·8	Kannada	17·4
Bengali	33·9	Malayalam	17·0
Gujarati	23·0	Tamil	30·6
Hindi	133·4	Telugu	37·7
Kashmiri	1·9		
Marathi	33·5		
Oriya	15·7		
Punjabi	10·9		
Sanskrit	·002		
Urdu	23·3		

The nature of the language problem is evident in three facts: first, the Official Language as proclaimed in the Constitution—

Hindi—is claimed by 30 per cent. of the population as their mother tongue; if one adds Bihari (16·8 million) and Rajasthani (14·9 million), both variations of Hindi, the Official Language covers about 40 per cent. of the population; secondly, Hindi is concentrated in four States—Bihar, Madhya Pradesh, Uttar Pradesh, and Rajasthan; and thirdly, the four Dravidian languages, spoken in the four southern States of Mysore, Kerala, Madras, and Andhra respectively, differ in script, vocabulary, grammar, and syntax from the Sanskrit-derived Indo-Aryan languages of the North—though Sanskrit has penetrated deeply into Malayalam and, to a lesser extent, into Kannada and Telugu. Not without reason, the centre of language agitation in the South is Tamilnad, Madras. To this should be added the fact that English, while claimed by only 223,781 as their mother tongue, is known by about 11 million and has served as the working official language at the Centre and in most of the States since independence, as under the British *Raj*.

The major events leading to the crisis of 1965 may be noted briefly. First was the acid debate among the Congress members of the Constituent Assembly over the language provisions to be inserted into the Constitution. Many from the South opposed Hindi altogether, but even among the Hindi protagonists there was a fierce dispute over the script—Devanagri (Sanskrit) alone or both Devanagri and Persian; the latter would have implied an acceptance of Hindustani, a mixture of Hindi and Urdu, favoured by Gandhi and Nehru among others, but the purists triumphed. The price was a dual concession: a directive (of January 1950) that Hindi must be enriched by borrowing from India's other major languages so as to represent her composite culture; and, more important, the continued use of English as an Official Language for another fifteen years, i.e., until 26 January 1965. The Hindi enthusiasts wanted a five-year transitional period but finally yielded to pressure from the South. And yet, when the Official Language clause had been put to a vote on the floor of the Assembly, on 14 September 1949, it had reportedly been approved by one vote—78 to 77.[46]

The next stage came in 1957–8, following the publication of the Report of the Official Language Commission, after two years of inquiry.   The thrust of its majority recommendation (there was also a dissenting note by two members from the South) was that steps should be taken forthwith to ensure the effective change-over to Hindi on the appointed day.   Agitation erupted in Madras, a prelude to the outburst of 1965, and Congress M.P.s from the South pressed for the indefinite continuation of English. Nehru responded at the Gauhati Annual Session early in 1958 with the pledge that English would remain the ' associate official language ' for as long as the non-Hindi-speaking people wished—and the agitation subsided.

It is interesting to note Nehru's attitude to the language controversy at that time : [47]

During the last few weeks, the language controversy has become more acute, more especially in Madras.   I must say that this development has distressed me.   I quite understand the feeling of people in Madras or elsewhere in India against anything being done which puts them, from the linguistic point of view, at a disadvantage.   But what I have regretted is the aggressive manner in which views have been expressed.

How much more apt these words were for the explosion seven years later !

As for his governing principles on this problem :

. . .   These principles are (1) that decisions can only be largely by consent and cannot be imposed by a majority over a minority, (2) that every language should be given full scope and, in our Services, nothing should be done which puts a person from a non-Hindi area at a disadvantage.   So far as English is concerned, I am all in favour of the study of English being continued and even made more widespread. But I confess that I do not understand how we can lay down for the future that English should be our all-India language.   It may continue as such for some time, and even later it will no doubt play an important part.   But it seems to me rather humiliating for us to adopt a foreign language as the official all-India language.   I say so even though my training and predilection would be in favour of English. In any event, I see no reason why we should hustle any decision or fix strict time-limits in a matter of this kind.

There was a remarkable consistency in Nehru's attitude to the ' language question ', as evident in his speeches to the Constituent Assembly in September 1949 and to Parliament in April 1963. On the former occasion, he said : [48]

While English is a great language—and while English has done us a lot of good—nevertheless, no nation can become great on the basis of a foreign language. Why? Because no foreign language can become the language of the people.

He also administered a rebuke to the champions of Hindi.

Is your approach going to be democratic or authoritarian? . . . in some of the speeches I have listened to here and elsewhere, there is very much a tone of authoritarianism, very much a tone of the Hindi-speaking area being the centre of things in India . . . and the others being just the fringes of India.

In 1963, when the Official Languages Act was passed, he remarked:

I have been convinced for a long time, and am convinced today, that any real upsurge in India from the people, an awakening of the people cannot take place through the English language. . . . Then inevitably we have to deal with Hindi . . . for the simple reason that Hindi is the most feasible for this purpose. [And while encouraging Hindi] it becomes necessary and almost inevitable for English to continue to be a link language. The process is not a sudden thing that you fix a date for. . . .

Ever conscious of the danger of linguistic emotionalism, he wrote to some of his colleagues in 1963: ' . . . essentially the overriding reason for it [the retention of English] is the necessity of not encouraging any disruptive tendencies in India '.[49]

Despite his sense of satisfaction at the Gauhati Resolution in 1958—' I think we are entitled to congratulate ourselves and the nation for this broad vision ', he wrote at the time [50]—it took five years for his pledge to become law, because of the powerful pressure of Hindi fanatics. And even when this was achieved, it fell short of an iron-clad guarantee. Section 3 of the Official Languages Act, 1963, provided that English ' may ' continue to be used after 1965, in addition to Hindi, for all the official purposes of the Union and for the transaction of business in Parliament. Nehru added his own personal assurances on the floor of the House—and the South seemed satisfied. And so it remained until Nehru's death. When Prime Minister Shastri, who had carried the main responsibility for the Act as Home Minister, was asked after the 1965 upheaval why Nehru's assurance about the indefinite continuation of

English was not embodied in the Act, he replied that Nehru and he felt the phrasing of the Act was 'sufficient' to satisfy the non-Hindi-speaking people.[51]   The language crisis proved otherwise.

With Nehru gone and the change-over to Hindi rapidly approaching, the anxiety of the South came to the surface once more. The precipitating cause was a seemingly innocuous directive from the Home Ministry to all Union Ministries to report by 15 October 1964 on the steps taken so far to promote the use of Hindi for official purposes and to indicate what steps they proposed to take to use Hindi after the appointed day, 26 January 1965. The Delhi Secretariats were also instructed to issue some communications in Hindi to the Hindi-speaking States from that day; and all letterheads and printed forms were to contain headings in both Hindi and English from the day of the change-over, Hindi appearing first. To mark the change, it added, a few printed forms in Hindi should be introduced even before 26 January—in order to create the 'necessary psychological atmosphere'.[52]

The *Statesman* reflected the fears and annoyance of many with a broadside full of sarcasm—and prescience: [53]

. . . each Ministry in New Delhi will be engaged in an identical exercise on January 27, 1965—composing an epistle in Hindi. The preceding holiday, it is hoped, will enable senior officials to acquire strength and skill for this task . . . many of the employees may soon be making lists of notes they have written in Hindi and claiming an extra allowance for the performance. . . . [And if, as suggested] PIB Press releases for Indian language newspapers [are] in Hindi, it would be interesting to watch how they are received in Bengal and Tamilnad.

All this would be Gilbertian if it were not so regrettable. . . . If the pace of the changeover to Hindi is forced, the results can only be chaos.

At the other extreme was pundit Inder Malhotra, who misread the atmosphere totally—as did many in seats of power: 'On the eve of the change-over . . . strong emotion is conspicuous by its absence, which is a matter for congratulation.'[54] The Prime Minister had, on various occasions, cautioned the Hindi champions against any deeds or words which might cause concern or resentment among the non-Hindi-speaking people; [55] but, as the date approached, he echoed Nehru's oft-stated view—in less-charged contexts—by declaring that the retention of English as the Official Language for all time seemed to him 'a deeply humiliating position '.[56]

A month before the change-over, Home Minister Nanda tried to allay the fears of southern M.P.s by assuring the Lok Sabha that there was no question of any compulsion anywhere in regard to the adoption of Devanagri as a common script for India. And, at a meeting of the Grand Council of the Republic in December, the Chief Minister of Madras informed his colleagues that all was quiet in Tamilnad; no trouble was expected by the State Government.[57]

Beneath the surface, however, tension was building up: as so often, students were in the vanguard. The initial protest took a dramatic, wholly un-Indian form: two stalwarts of the Dravida Munnetra Kazhagam (DMK), the premier anti-Hindi organization in India, emulating the Buddhist monks of South Viet Nam, burned themselves to death in the streets of Madras City, on 25 and 26 January. By that time, too, a well-organized Students' Agitation Council had been formed, with branches all over the State. In Chidambaram, the home of Annamalai University, where Tamil nationalism flourishes, police firing dispersed a student crowd which had halted a train, killing one and seriously injuring another. Violence also erupted in Madurai, Tirunalveli, Coimbatore, and Vellore, with Congress volunteers assisting the police. At the very outset, on the night of 25 January, the police took into preventive custody some 500 active workers of the DMK, including its leader, C. N. Annadurai. Colleges were closed for a fortnight the same day, and many student leaders were arrested, but these, along with most DMK detainees, were released after the first wave of agitation subsided on the 27th. Delhi remained curiously silent, complacent, and seemingly oblivious to the widespread resentment.

It took a recrudescence of violence—on a much more massive scale—and the dramatic resignation of a member of Cabinet to move the stolid Shastri Government, and even then the response was halting and inadequate. The Students' Council had marshalled its forces during the two-week lull and, from 10 to 13 February, let loose a fury of agitation. All over the State students picketed post offices and held up trains in a symbolic protest against the change-over to Hindi. Violence begat violence, with responsibility shared yet obscure. It began in the town of Tirupur, in Coimbatore District, where police firing killed four, perhaps more. As elsewhere in anomic displays of pressure politics, the mob responded by burning any public property in their path. In the nearby town of Kumarapalayam ten were killed by police firing, and in Coimbatore City, another three; similar scenes were enacted in Tiruchi District. Sporadic violence occurred on the 11th. And then a day of *hartal* was proclaimed; intended to be peaceful, it witnessed battles between police and agitators in almost twenty towns, notably in Pollachi, the constituency of Food Minister Subramaniam, Chennimalai, and the former French Pondicherry. The total number killed in this explosion of passion and fear was variously estimated from 70 (official) to 500 (foreign observers). By the 13th calm was restored; the Students' Council suspended the agitation, having made their mark on New Delhi.[58]

The first step on the road to decision in the language crisis was taken by the Prime Minister in the face of massive pressure. On the evening of the 11th he set out a four-point policy, in a broadcast to the nation: first, every State would have complete freedom to continue to transact its own business in the language of its choice; secondly, inter-State communications would continue to be in English or would be accompanied by an authoritative English translation; thirdly, non-Hindi States would be free to correspond with the Centre in English, as in the past; and fourthly, English would continue to be used in the conduct of business at the Centre.[59] This was a welcome reiteration of past assurances, but these were no longer sufficient to satisfy the Tamils. Conspicuously absent was even the slightest hint that Nehru's assurances might be given a statutory form, a proposal pressed by Food Minister Subramaniam at a tense Cabinet meeting just before the broadcast. T. T. Krishnamachari had already left for Madras, at Shastri's request, but Subramaniam remained in Delhi, in the absence of any new concessions.

Indeed, that evening he submitted his resignation, along with Alagesan, a Madrassi Minister of State. The shock treatment had the desired effect. The next day Shastri accepted the idea of codification in principle, leaving a decision to a future meeting of the Grand Council; the Law Ministry was to provide guidance on procedure. The resignations were then withdrawn, as was the student-led agitation. Act I of the 1965 language crisis was over.

The Madras upheaval was caused by various pressures and fears, partly deriving from insensitivity and policy errors. The *Times of India* noted some acts of omission: first, 'a sad failure . . . to inform and educate public opinion about the language question'; secondly, the gap, since 1947, between intense advocacy of Hindi and the lack of its effective propagation in the non-Hindi States; and thirdly, the total failure of Government and Party, in Delhi and Madras, to appreciate 'the basic emotional resentment of the people towards what they believed to be the official policy', and, therefore, the inability to foresee the disturbances.[60] Kamaraj stressed the concern among Madrassis caused by various statements and circulars from the Centre which, he said, created the impression that Hindi was being effectively introduced on 26 January.[61] Sanjiva Reddy, by contrast, placed the blame on the Madras Government, which was 'complacently confident'.[62] Other Cabinet members concurred.

Two of the principal protagonists, Hindi enthusiasts and the DMK (the third was the English-educated middle-class student community of Madras), offered simple and self-satisfying explanations. Speaking for the former, Professor Bal Raj Madhok of the Jan Sangh stressed three factors: the failure of those in authority to prepare for the change-over since 1947; the nefarious activities of separatist forces; and the use of the language issue by politicians in Madras and Bengal. At the other extreme, a DMK M.P., Serian, attributed the crisis to the attempt to impose Hindi on a multilingual country; the reorganization of States in 1956, he remarked, had given dignity to the regional languages, and this was being undermined by the forced change to Hindi.[63] Neither view is convincing, for the roots lie deeper and the causes of the upheaval are more complex.

One dimension was political, for language in Madras was enmeshed with the struggle for power between Brahman and non-Brahman, dating at least from the 1920s: the latter identified Hindi and Sanskrit with North India, with Aryan, Brahman domination, and made the revival of a purified Tamil a sheet-anchor of their political strategy within Madras; in reality, this reflected a prolonged inter-caste battle for control of the State. A derivative in time was emotional antagonism to Hindi, based on the carefully-nurtured idea that Tamil was a vastly superior tongue, with an ancient and rich literary tradition. There was truth to this view; and while Sanskrit was recognized as an equal, Hindi seemed to many proud Madrassis an unworthy claimant to the linguistic throne of India; it was as if a venerable aunt was being asked to yield primacy of place to an unsophisticated niece!

No less important was the economic dimension: non-Hindi aspirants to the Services, always a major source of employment and status, would be at a distinct disadvantage in the examinations; this, in time, could lead to a redistribution of regional-linguistic representation in the Services, to the detriment of Madras and the South generally. Among students—who took the lead—this was the dominant consideration, and with good reason: in 1965, Madrassis occupied 18 per cent. of the posts in the all-India Services—an even higher proportion of senior positions—though they constituted only 8 per cent. of the total population, a disparity based on their superior knowledge of English.[64] The future of Tamilnad's educated class was at stake; to many, the larger issue of Tamil culture was also involved. And, through changes in the composition of the bureaucracy, the Hindi hinterland would enhance its political hegemony as well.

The precipitating cause of the 1965 explosion was the total lack of finesse in the Centre's campaign to create the proper 'psychological atmosphere' for the change-over, notably in a provocative circular of the Ministry of Information and Broadcasting. Within Madras, a disquieting role was played by some anti-Congress mill-owners: they financed the students' agitation and used the language unrest to vent their grievances against the State (Congress) Government's economic and tax policy. The ineptness of the Bhaktavatsalam Ministry assisted disorder. And police firing, in many instances, provoked violent reactions. The role of the DMK, the scapegoat of authority in Delhi and Madras, was marginal, though it had the most to gain from the agitation; its leader, Annadurai, showed restraint and moderation in the black flag protest of 25 January, though some of his followers pressed for a more militant line. In the background was the accumulated discontent with the rising cost of living and the serious food crisis of 1964, accentuated by the State Government's grave mismanagement. Another contributing factor was the strong feeling in the North, especially in U.P., that the time had come to secure a larger share of public posts. Like all political upheavals, then, it was a complex web with many strands.[65] Of its wider significance, Nehru's remark about the earlier language disturbances is not without relevance: '. . . that indicates how skin-deep our nationalism is and how we lose anchorage over relatively small matters. . . .'[66]

Act II of the decision process on language began soon after the Madras fury subsided. On 17 February the President's Address to the Budget Session of Parliament contained the following pledge: 'We wish to state categorically that the assurances given by the late Shri Jawaharlal Nehru and reaffirmed by our Prime Minister will be carried out without qualification and reservation. . . . While Hindi is the official language of the Union, English will continue as long as the non-Hindi-speaking people require [sic] it.' Parliament was to deal with the legal, administrative, and executive aspects, it added, and the Chief Ministers would consider the situation shortly.[67] The setting was thereby created for the stage of pressure politics.

Congress President Kamaraj, a Madrassi, took the lead by advocating an amendment to the Official Languages Act of 1963 to provide for the continued use of English as long as the non-Hindi-speaking people *wanted* it.[68] This proposal was discussed inconclusively in Cabinet on the 20th; and, a few days earlier, Shastri had assured the ever-watchful Congress Parliamentary Party that the final decision would be theirs—after the Chief Ministers made their recommendations the following week. He also pledged consultation with Opposition leaders, in an effort to reach a national consensus.   On the 20th, too, the Hindi extremists pressed their claim: the Delhi State Jan Sangh launched a movement against English by defacing hundreds of signboards in the capital with coal-tar and black paint; thirty-two persons were arrested.   Ironically, its official statement condemning the continued use of English was issued in English.   More revealing, speakers at the public meeting preceding the agitation did not know the Hindi equivalents of such words as ' symbolic ', ' compulsory ', ' survey ', ' signboard ', ' plank ', ' condemnation ', ' political interest ', ' emergency ', ' minority ', ' training colleges ', ' democracy ', ' Chief Minister ', ' violence ', ' conference ', ' party ', ' statesmanship ', ' peace ', and others.[69]   Spokesmen for the *Arya Samaj* and *Akali Dal* (a Sikh communal political party) backed the anti-English campaign.   In the Rajya Sabha, too, the deep fissures over language were evident, as spokesmen for the South and the Hindi States echoed the widely-held fears and aspirations.   Indeed, during the week of 17–24 February 1965, as one commentator observed, ' the language issue is now occupying national attention and energy almost exclusively, indeed obsessively.   From New Delhi, at any rate, it seems that the country has no time for anything else.' [70]

The pressure mounted by diverse interests was designed to influence the Grand Council, which held protracted discussions on 22, 23, and 24 February.   At the end of the second day the deadlock over statutory guarantees remained unbroken.   As so often in the past, the burden was shifted to a carefully-chosen sub-committee; in this instance, it comprised Morarji Desai and Chief Minister D. P. Mishra of Madhya Pradesh, representing the Hindi enthusiasts, Subramaniam and Chief Minister Nijalingappa of Mysore, representing the South, and former Congress President Dhebar as a neutral; noteworthy was the fact that all three major institutional interest groups in the Grand Council were represented—Working Committee, Union Cabinet, and Chief Ministers.

The upshot was an uneasy compromise, as evident in the key passage of their report, a four-point assurance:

. . . every State will have complete and unfettered freedom to continue to transact its own business in the language of its choice

which may be the regional language; communications from one State
to another will be either in Hindi accompanied by an authentic
English translation or in English. Thirdly, non-Hindi States will be
free to correspond with the Central Government in English. Fourthly,
in the transaction of business at the Central level, English will continue to be used as an associate official language in the intervening
period. No change will be made in these arrangements without the
consent of the States.

Yet this was merely a re-affirmation of the Nehru assurances, to
which the Working Committee once again declared ' the firm
resolve of the Congress to adhere '. And even then, vagueness
was conspicuous: there was no definition of ' the intervening
period ', nor was there any procedure indicated to ascertain ' the
consent of the States '. The only concession to the South, also
very vague, was the recommendation that the Union and State
Governments ' examine the steps that should be taken, including
amendments to the Official Languages Act of 1963, to give effect
to the assurances given by Mr. Jawaharlal Nehru . . .'. In
response to pressure from the States, the Committee also recommended that examinations for all-India Services should be held
in Hindi, English, and the regional languages ' as soon as
possible '. There was also a plea for effective implementation of
the three-language formula as accepted by the National Integration Conference of 1961, though here, too, the resolution glossed
over the basic difference between the two protagonists: the South
had accepted the idea of Hindi as the third language in their
States' educational system, the others being the regional language
and English, but Hindi States had interpreted ' another Indian
language ' as permitting Sanskrit, so that southern languages
were not being widely taught in their schools.[71]

Prime Minister Shastri's statement in the Lok Sabha on 25
February accentuated the impression that the decision process
was still in mid-stream—decisions were reached, but there were
still wide areas of disagreement—by pointed reference to further
' study ' and ' examination ' of the ' issues '.[72] Kamaraj and many
Chief Ministers expressed their ' satisfaction ' with the resolution,
but it was clear that agreement on the specific contentious issues
had not been reached. As the *Times of India* remarked: ' It
is true that the Working Committee's resolution has to all

appearances reduced the area of disagreement. . . . But this
reduction had in fact occurred some time before. . . .' [73]

Opposition party leaders were critical of the 'resolution:
comments ranged from 'disappointing' (Vajpayee of the Jan
Sangh) to the drastic suggestion by Madhu Limaye of the PSP
that Hindi-speaking States be allowed to abolish English at all
levels for Central purposes immediately.[74] Morarji Desai concurred, in a memorandum to the Education Commission made
public during the Grand Council's deliberations.[75] But most
disturbing was the Hindi 'backlash' within the CPP: the day
after Shastri's statement to Parliament, a delegation of Congress
M.P.s, headed by Bhagwat Jha Azad, K. D. Malaviya, and A. P.
Jain, all from U.P., submitted a letter signed by 106 M.P.s
demanding that no amendment to the Official Languages Act
be made.[76] As is his style, the Prime Minister listened politely,
without comment; the strategy was to allow all interested persons
and groups to air their views and let the issue simmer—decision
by attrition. This was apparent in his reply to the debate on the
President's Address: there was frequent reference to the need to
'fully and carefully examine' all aspects of the question; and
while he had 'clear and categorical views', he did not feel it
appropriate to express them yet.[77]

Act II of the decision process on language was slow to unfold.
In perspective, the Prime Minister appeared to be waiting for the
Hindi antagonism to statutory guarantees to talk itself out. There
was criticism of 'drift',[78] but he refused to be hurried. He conferred with Opposition leaders in Parliament at the end of March
and stressed the need for a national consensus.[79] The first serious
move came early in April, with the formation of a six-member
Cabinet sub-committee headed by Nanda to draft a proposed
amendment to the Official Languages Act; the other members
were Patil, Sen, Chagla, Sinha, and Tyagi, the last two representing Hindi enthusiasts; the others were prepared to go far in
the way of allaying southern fears, with Nanda himself openly
advocating 'prolonged bilingualism'.[80]

Two proposals dominated the sub-committee's deliberations
in April and May. The Sen formula, backed by the West Bengal
Government, provided that English would continue for all

official purposes of the Union, in addition to Hindi, until three-fourths of the States, through resolutions passed by their legislatures, endorsed the complete change-over to Hindi; this procedure is prescribed in the Constitution for certain types of constitutional amendment affecting the rights of the States. This would give the four southern States a veto, but if one was persuaded to yield, Hindi could be imposed on all of them; such was the fear expressed by Madras Congress leaders. S. K. Patil's formula went further: each State would be free to use English in communications with other States or the Centre indefinitely; it could retain English even after the rest of the country had adopted Hindi as the link language; moreover, English would continue to be used in Parliament until it decided by a two-thirds majority to conduct its proceedings in Hindi only; and even then, the President would have discretion to authorize the continued use of English in consultation with the non-Hindi States. Inevitably, this aroused the hostility of Hindi enthusiasts, who argued that Patil's proposals would perpetuate English. The problem, in essence, was to avoid the imposition of Hindi on the non-Hindi States and of English on the Hindi States. More important, the task was to secure a national consensus lest India's unity be seriously impaired.[81]

The Grand Council was summoned once more, on 1 and 2 June 1965. It was an historic session, for a consensus on language was finally reached, though not without intense bargaining and heated debate. Ironically, the hitherto core issue of the continued use of English aroused the least controversy: the Patil formula, recommended by the Cabinet sub-committee, was now accepted with little dissent. The only aspect that aroused distrust and concern was the provision in the official draft which gave the Union Government discretionary powers to specify the purposes for which English would be used in Union affairs in the future; both linguistic interest groups expressed apprehension that such rule-making powers might be used to their detriment; the compromise was that the specific items in which the use of English would be compulsory would form part of the Bill, with residuary items left to Union Government discretion.

The most contentious issue, with profound implications for the future of the Indian polity, related to the media of examination for all-India Services. Here, the Hindi enthusiasts exacted a heavy price for their concession, with the passive support of the non-Hindi States—i.e., examinations in all fourteen major languages. No less significant was the striking demonstration of a change in the balance of power in all-India affairs in favour of the States. The Cabinet sub-committee had opposed any change, and most Union Government spokesmen on the Grand Council stressed the great practical difficulties in the use of Hindi and the regional languages for examinations. But the advocates of multilingualism in recruitment to the Services pressed their case. Taking the lead were Morarji Desai and Ram Subhag Singh of the Working Committee, the Chief Ministers of the Hindi States, and Hindi spokesmen in the Cabinet, notably Tyagi; representatives of the non-Hindi States, who would thereby retain equal access to the Services, did not take issue with them. Only on the brink of linguistic chauvinism did the high ' national interest' assert itself; the proposal for State quotas in the all-India Services was rejected, its only advocate being the Andhra Chief Minister, Brahmananda Reddy, ' quotanand ' Reddy, as he was called.[82]

The upshot was a ' package deal': the South was given an iron-clad assurance on English, through the Patil formula; the Hindi enthusiasts enhanced the status of Hindi; and all linguistic interest groups scored a victory on the crucial point of the Services. The key points of agreement in the Working Committee resolution were:

1. ' It will be obligatory for all the States to introduce the three-language formula in their educational curriculum, extend it to the university stage and to apply it strictly.'

2. ' UPSC [Union Public Service Commission] examinations will be conducted in English, Hindi and other national languages mentioned in the Eighth Schedule ' of the Constitution, i.e., in all fourteen major languages.

3. To maintain parity in qualifications, there will be compulsory papers in Hindi and English, and for Hindi candidates a paper in ' any other language in the Schedule '.

4. 'A phased programme for the development of Hindi and . . . of other national languages'; and

5. the use of the regional language in each State as 'the medium of administration as well as instruction at the university stage as early as possible'.[83]

Reaction to the consensus was mixed. Chagla and Patil reportedly were concerned about the effect on national integration and the difficulty of implementation respectively. The Chief Minister of Madras saw 'nothing new' in the resolution. Naik of Maharashtra termed it the best solution 'under present circumstances'. The Chief Minister of Andhra said it was a 'good resolution'. Kamaraj concurred.[84] Press comment, too, was cautiously optimistic. As the *Times of India* observed, the resolution 'does not answer every doubt in every mind but it certainly represents a broad and wise decision'; it noted, with pleasure, that no time limit had been fixed for the complete change-over to Hindi and that this would be by consent, but added, 'the real danger lies in a political and emotional balkanisation of the country'.[85] Among the pundits, Inder Malhotra decried the 'overstatement . . . that the seemingly intractable and manifestly explosive language issue has been solved'; rather, he saw the resolution as paving the way 'for a sound and sensible solution . . . over a period of years'.[86]

Sharp criticism came from the Independent (Anglo-Indian) M.P., Frank Anthony: he termed the idea of multiple media of examination 'one of the last nails in the coffin of national integration', and the extension of the three-language formula to the universities 'educational nonsense', as well as a breach of Nehru's assurances.[87] More sober criticism was levelled by G. C. Chatterji, a former member of the UPSC: the use of regional languages for Service examinations, he said, will bring in the quota system by the back door.[88] On the whole, however, the Grand Council's consensus was welcomed as a respite from internal squabble; many recognized that it would take fifteen to twenty years to implement the complex settlement;[89] in the interim, the country could concentrate on more pressing problems.

Thus, Shastri's style—patient and broad consultation among all major interest groups—had succeeded in averting a language war, which could have destroyed the fabric of Indian unity. It had also given the protagonists a greater feeling of security and dignity, allaying fears and mistrust. Yet decision by compromise may have opened a Pandora's box, with linguistic chaos a distinct possibility, if the formula is implemented in full. Shastri's approach to decision-making and the new equilibrium of power in all-India affairs had led to short-run tranquillity at the probable cost of long-term disunity.

Fears were aroused at the outset of Shastri's second year in office. With customary zeal, the Home Ministry submitted a Note to Cabinet recommending that the UPSC be asked to hold examinations for all-India and Central Services in *all* regional languages from September 1966—at the same time acknowledging that the introduction of each new medium would add ' one more dimension to the complexity . . .'.[90] The *Statesman* reflected the concern of many by predicting a ' fresh demonstration of its potential for creating major confusion' and warned that it ' will only serve to accentuate inter-regional differences and conflicts '.[91] The Bill to amend the Official Languages Act was scheduled for the Monsoon Session of Parliament in August 1965, but dissension within Cabinet was not wholly absent on the precise phrasing of the draft.[92] Moreover, as the Indo-Pakistan war unfolded, the demand for immediate enactment became subdued. The historic decision on language, product of interest-group politics *par excellence*, was set aside, at least until the spring of 1966.

The changing pattern of political influence among India's interest groups has been discussed in various sections of this study. It remains to bring these strands together and to note the effect of the succession on others hitherto neglected. Among the institutional interest groups, the greatest beneficiary was the bureaucracy, especially its élite, the Secretaries. This was evident in many spheres: the creation of a powerful Prime Minister's Secretariat as the pervasive link between the Head of Government and the Ministries; the emergence of L. K. Jha as policy adviser to the Prime Minister; the formation of a Committee of Secretaries to oversee foreign policy; the conspicuous role of civil servants in vital negotiations, as with the two Jhas in the Kutch dispute—External Affairs Minister Swaran Singh was nowhere in evidence; the more pronounced influence of bureaucrats in the formulation of economic policy, exemplified in the debate on the Fourth Plan; the more frequent delegation of responsibility for drafting key decisions, as in the language question, and a host of lesser forms of influence. It would be an exaggeration to term this ' Civil Service Raj ', as some thoughtful observers did, but the spirit and substance of power, long associated with the bureaucracy in the British era, have been reasserted. Three factors are responsible for this change, as suggested earlier: Shastri's self-conscious reliance on his professional advisers, to an extent unknown in Nehru's day; the passing of a towering national leader, whose ambivalent attitude to civil servants included mistrust, especially of those who had long served an alien régime; and the partial vacuum in authority, incompletely filled by a lesser political leadership.

The impact of the succession on such institutional interests as the Cabinet, the Congress Working Committee, the Chief Ministers' club, and the CPP Executive has been dissected in depth. We have noted the changes in the spirit and process of Cabinet—the atmosphere of debate, decision-making, the relations between Prime Minister and his colleagues, and the restoration of the Cabinet's primacy over its Emergency Committee—as well as the continuities: procedure, the special position of the Finance Minister, functions, committee system, and structure, in four concentric circles of influence. Most significant has been the diffusion of influence within Cabinet and its ascent in the hierarchy of decision, at the Union and all-India levels. Similarly, the Party's autonomy and the vital role of the Congress President and Working Committee in the formulation of high policy have been striking developments of the Shastri transition; this was evident in the food and language controversies, among others; with the passing of charismatic leadership, an institutional duumvirate—Cabinet and Working Committee—has emerged.

The most notable accretion of influence, however, has been to the State bosses; through their collective presence in the Grand Council of the Republic, they have exerted massive power, as the ultimate consensus on food and language amply reveal. The Parliamentary Party, by contrast, has remained inconsequential, both in the succession struggle and in the developing pattern of decision on national policy.

The last of the major institutional interest groups, the Military, was not directly affected by the succession and its aftermath. The process of rebuilding, after the débâcle of 1962, had already begun and was neither hastened nor retarded by the coming of a new régime. The main criterion, budgetary allocations, revealed no change. Nor was there any change in India's China policy, where the Officer Corps might have been expected to make its influence felt. On the Rann of Kutch affair, the Army leadership exercised moderation, thereby strengthening Shastri's policy of peaceful settlement. And in the full-scale war over Kashmir, in August–September 1965, there is no evidence to indicate that the Military acted other than as the traditional instrument of civilian authority. It is true that the search for equipment went on, as evident in Defence Minister Chavan's journeys to Moscow and London, but these were planned before the succession; the pace did not quicken. In the short run, at any rate, there was no discernible change in the role or the influence of the Military in India's political system.

The future role of the Military in Indian politics is beyond the scope of this study. Suffice it to make certain observations. First, effective civil control over the armed forces in India has been unchallenged since independence. Secondly, until 1963, the Army was small and ill-equipped, as the border war with China revealed; to many, in fact, it seemed to be starved of funds and weapons. This has changed as a result of defeat in battle, but even the five-year Defence Plan for expansion and modernization sets the modest target of 825,000 men for the Army and 45 squadrons for India's Air Force.[93] Thirdly, the Military are preoccupied with two powerful and hostile neighbours, a formidable challenge at any time. Moreover, even if the Officer Corps were so inclined, the task of taking over India, let alone governing it, would seem awesome to an army of that size—and it would require perfect rapport and co-ordination among the four widely-scattered Commands and their GOC-in-Cs with Army Head-quarters in Delhi.

To hold together a country of 470 million people with fourteen major languages and cultures is difficult enough for a deeply-rooted Congress machine and Civil Service extending to the village; for the Army alone to do it is inconceivable, though it might succeed with the total co-operation of the Civil Service. There is no evidence of such an alignment at present; nor is it likely in the near future.   Much depends, of course, on the stability of the political system.   Stating it schematically, India's unity and stability rest on three institutional layers—the political establishment, including the parliamentary and party system, the administrative services, and the Military.   If the first should be shattered by corruption and/or external challenge, a civil dictatorship, backed by the Army, would not be unlikely; but even in this contingency the Army's role would be secondary. If the civil services, too, became ossified and utterly inefficient, the assumption of power by the Military would probably take place.   But even this, if senior Army personnel are to believed, would take the form of a constitutional dictatorship, i.e., at the behest of the President.   None of these contingencies appears to be on the horizon: the two other establishments are far from decay and collapse as India begins to think of her fourth general election in 1967.[94]

Associational interest groups in India are of two types: occu-pational and community.[95]   The trade unions remained relatively quiescent, except for agitation on the rising cost of living and food shortage, notably in the one-day general strike in Maharash-tra in August 1964; but such demonstrations were no different in size, frequency, and effect than in the past.   Indeed, the four organizations of urban labour—Indian National Trade Union Congress (INTUC), All-India Trade Union Congress (AITUC), Hind Mazdoor Sabha (HMS), and United Trade Union Congress (UTUC)—continued to act as arms of their parent political parties, Congress, Communist Party of India, Praja Socialist Party, and the Marxist Left respectively.   If the shift in economic policy is any test, the collective influence of the trade-union movement declined.

Peasant organizations, too, did not reveal any growth of influence or activity during the Shastri transition. There were occasional anomic forms of pressure among landless labour and share-cropping tenants, but these were typical of India's vast, subsistence agriculture. There was no organized effort to weaken the trader stranglehold over the marketing of food, with its inequitable distribution of returns to producer and middleman, now accentuated by the price spiral. The associations of peasants remained extensions of parties: Kisan Sabha (CPI); Farmers' Forum (Congress); Kisan Panchayat (PSP); and United Kisan Sabha (Marxist Left).

Among students, however, there was a dramatic display of effective pressure. The Students' Council of Agitation succeeded in merging its specialized interests with the larger cultural, linguistic, and political interests of Madras and, in a sense, of the South as a whole. By means of superb organization and sophisticated strategy, it virtually imposed its will on the Centre, to the extent of protecting its vested interest in English for access to the Services and as a working language of administration. This student association cut across the all-India organizations— Youth Congress (Congress), All-India Student Federation (CPI), Socialist Student Organization (PSP), and Progressive Student Union (Marxist Left)—and channelled the energies of ideo- logically diverse students into a united agitation on behalf of their occupational-linguistic interests; the student arm of the DMK took the lead. There were also organized strikes in the univer- sities over a variety of issues, but these were no different from the pre-succession pattern.

The most striking change in the influence-hierarchy among interest groups relates to the business community. We have seen how a strategically-placed interest group, the traders in food- grains, exerted a veto over a statist-oriented food policy. It rejected Shastri's plea to disgorge its hoarded stocks, in August 1964. It showed contempt for the anti-profiteering and anti- hoarding Ordinance of November, compelling the Centre to abandon a hard line. It successfully fought against monopoly

procurement and statutory rationing, supporting and strengthening the Chief Ministers' resolve on both these controversial issues.
And in the consensus on food, finally reached in November, it
scored a major victory—the Centre's concession on statutory
rationing, rice zones, and a diluted Food Trading Corporation.
On some of these points its interests merged with those of the
surplus States, and the ensuing alliance subdued the Centre; but
on others it fought alone, and triumphed.

The formal instrument of the trade was the wholesalers'
Grain Association, a network of rich and large distributors in
different parts of the country. It had other assets, however:
effective control over the marketing machinery for large supplies
of food; an inadequate administrative cadre to implement an
all-India control policy, along with Centre and State fear of the
unknown; the ideological aversion of the Congress élite to controls; and, most important, perhaps, the trade's influence in the
Congress Party, at all levels, by virtue of its financial contribu-
tions to the Party and its well-developed connections with officials
and politicians. The result was a classic illustration of interest
articulation in the political system and its dramatic effect on the
outcome of policy.

More generally, the business community emerged from its
subordinate *political* status under Nehru. This is not to suggest
that it lacked influence during the first seventeen years of
independence; but, for many reasons, its role in politics and
policy-making was indirect and, by and large, inferior to the
statist-oriented planners and political establishment—at least until
the last year or two of the Nehru régime. More than anything
else, Nehru had a deep-rooted emotional and ideological antipathy
to private enterprise; he acknowledged its importance but kept it
in a subordinate position as long as his power and vigour were
unimpaired, i.e., until 1962–3. But Nehru was gone now, as
were the two most vocal leftists in Cabinet, Menon and Malaviya.
Moreover, the new Prime Minister's Secretary championed the
business community's cause, as did others in the bureaucracy and
the Party, who had been careful not to offend Nehru.

The objective conditions of the Indian economy also
favoured businessmen and their ideas: stagnation in agriculture,

under-fulfilment of the Third Plan, a foreign exchange crisis—all this raised doubts about the efficacy of Indian planning and the stress on the public sector. Into this atmosphere of doubt and lack of self-confidence intruded an external pressure—the ' Aid to India ' club. Some of its members, led by the World Bank, began to intimate, gently and otherwise, that it was time for a change. A special Bank mission of a dozen experts, the largest ever dispatched to a client state, spent six months in the autumn and winter of 1964–5 surveying the Third Plan as a task force for Bank President Woods. The club renewed its allocation of slightly more than a billion dollars for the last year of the present Plan, 1965–6, but India's delegates were left with the unmistakable impression that the ' errors ' of the past would have to be rectified if large-scale aid was to continue during the Fourth Plan.

One expression of the change in business influence was the great debate on future economic policy, noted earlier. Another was the shift towards foreign private capital and the loosening of restrictions on collaboration ventures. The result was a stream of missions of Western industrialists and financiers, mainly American and German, seeking opportunities for joint enterprises. Some were consummated, others are in the process of maturing, and still others were abortive. The outstanding example of failure was the proposal of a U.S. firm, Bechtel, to build five huge fertilizer plants in the Fourth Plan period; this would have solved a major problem of Indian agriculture, but the Government of India, led by Finance Minister Krishnamachari, considered the price too high; [96] the swing to the Right had not yet reached the point of giving foreign capital a free hand. Nonetheless, the greater receptivity to foreign private investment inevitably spilled over to the benefit of the indigenous private sector. Its views became more vocal during the first post-succession year, and authority listened more attentively. And when the 20th Conference of the International Chamber of Commerce met in Delhi at the beginning of 1965, the road to a ' new economic policy ' was well marked. Thus, a complex of pressures, internal and external, enhanced the political influence of business interests in Shastri's first year. India will undoubtedly retain a mixed economy, but the share of the ingredients will undergo change in the coming years.   The business community has emerged as a powerful interest group—after Nehru.

A novel feature of India's political system is the array of community-interest groups, most of them highly articulate and some very effective. There are tribal parties such as the Jharkhand Party in Bihar, representing the Adivasis (recently merged with the Congress) and the Naga National Council. The remnant of the Indian Muslim League still flourishes in Kerala, and the *Akali Dal* remains a factor in Sikh politics in the Punjab. Almost every major language group has a specialized association, such as the Hindi *Prachar Samiti*; and caste associations abound. As in the Nehru era, some have been persistent participants in post-succession politics, others spasmodic actors.

The Naga insurrection began more than a decade ago and continued during the Shastri transition.   But the change of leadership at the Centre has altered its form—from a ' dirty war ' to conventional bargaining. Whether from weakness—pressure from China and Pakistan—or from conviction, the new Prime Minister broke fresh ground by agreeing to a cease-fire with the Naga underground, in September 1964; this has been extended periodically and continues in force. More significantly, and illustrative of Shastri's style, the Government of India has accepted the good offices of a three-man Peace Mission as mediator with a group of Indian citizens—and the Mission includes a non-national, the Reverend Michael Scott. The outcome is still uncertain, but the succession can be said to have enhanced the status and bargaining power of those who represent Naga claims to autonomy or independence.

Muslim interests were articulated at two controversial conventions, one in Lucknow in August 1964, the other in Delhi in February 1965. These were not innovations, though their tone suggested growing concern that, in the absence of Nehru, their trusted protector, Muslim interests—in education, the Services, and Urdu—might suffer. There is no concrete evidence of greater disability, but many Muslims—and others—detect a change in atmosphere in India's polity, which can be summed up as Hindu revivalism.   Subtle as it may be, Muslim interests are adversely affected.   And the partial victory of the Hindi enthusiasts indicates that this concern is not unfounded. As for the Sikhs, the pressure for ' Punjabi Subha '—a Punjabi-speaking State, masking the demand for a Sikh State—was quiescent during Shastri's first year, though it was revived soon after.

The most active—and successful—community-interest groups in 1964–5 were linguistic, as the debate and decision on language revealed. The Hindi group made the most striking advance in status and influence, the first real breakthrough in the virtual monopoly of English as the Official Language since the Constitution was adopted in 1950. Implementation may be delayed ten to twenty years, but the demand for Hindi as the all-India link language has been conceded afresh, despite renewed agitation in Madras. The vested interests in English have also been protected, at least in the short run; and the status of the regional languages has been enhanced, far beyond what their most fervent advocates thought possible. Indeed, all linguistic interests have gained—at the expense of India's unity; so much so that, if balkanization becomes a reality, its prime agent will be linguistic chauvinism. Yet, of all the beneficiaries, Hindi is the greatest, and with it the Hindi States. Their political influence in the Union will grow proportionately—some think, disproportionately—with the spread of Hindi as an effective all-India medium of administration and communication. As for caste associations, there is no evidence to indicate greater influence—or less; in any event, they flourish at State and sub-State levels much more than at the Union and all-India levels of politics, the objects of inquiry in this study.

Among the non-associational interests, Vinoba Bhave and his Bhoodan Movement have declined in influence, largely because of his illness and enforced isolation from the stream of politics. He spoke out on language, but few listened; his message has atrophied. More articulate has been Jaya Prakash Narayan, whom some consider the ' lost leader ', and others, the ' moral conscience of India '. In the early months Shastri was attentive to his views and consulted him frequently, especially on Kashmir. Narayan's plea for a fundamental re-thinking of India's policy on Kashmir gained ground in parts of the political establishment; his goodwill mission to Pakistan in early September 1964 seemed to have the Prime Minister's blessings; and the latter's pause in Karachi on the way home from the Cairo Conference in October was made after strong urging by Narayan. But internal Indian opposition to any change on Kashmir, combined with later developments— Sheikh Abdullah's behaviour abroad in the spring of 1965, the Rann of Kutch episode, and renewed hostilities in Kashmir—made Narayan's views unpalatable. So too with his suggestion, in the autumn of 1964, that India grant China a long-term concession to Aksai Chin as a way out of the impasse. Narayan was an articulate advocate of unpopular ideas throughout the Shastri transition but his influence diminished after a few months, except on the Naga question.

It is difficult to assess the influence of the fourth estate under Shastri. He is undoubtedly more sensitive to the views of press and pundits than Nehru ever was, perhaps because his position is less secure. He confers with leading editors more frequently and has created the impression that their views are weighed with care. This was reciprocated at the height of internal and external crises, food, language, and Kutch, though criticism was not wanting. Whether press influence has increased or not, leader writers and commentators are persuaded that it has. Among the major interest groups, then, the three principal beneficiaries of the succession have been the bureaucracy, business, and the language groups.

VII

LEGACY

MORE than a year has passed since the succession to Nehru. To actors and observers alike, it was a year of turmoil in the political system and of deep malaise in the economy. But most disquieting was widespread pessimism, verging on morbidity, about the future. The initial act—succession to a charismatic leader—was consummated with skill and tranquillity; a note of pride was thereby injected into the three major élite groups, political, bureaucratic, and communications, as well as into the small but vigorous attentive public. Almost at once, however, awesome problems confronted the new régime, with a persistent demand for decision, if not solution: in rapid succession, these comprised food, the Naga insurrection, Kerala, language, the Rann of Kutch, and Kashmir, along with a host of lesser issues.

The response varied. At times it was halting and fumbling, as the Shastri Government sought a viable compromise with the States on food and language; the price was high, for the Chief Ministers asserted their newly discovered influence, but a consensus was reached, at least until new coalitions of pressure groups demand revision. At other times there was a display of firmness, as on Nagaland and Kutch, and even forcefulness, as on Kashmir and Pakistan. There was also ample evidence of ineptness and vacillation, as with the Sheikh Abdullah passport fiasco and the dismissal of Orissa's Chief Minister on corruption charges.

The new phase of India's politics induced a stream of assessments, extending over a broad spectrum. The most powerful criticism came from an unexpected quarter—Nehru's sister. In the spring of 1965 she delivered a scathing indictment of the successor Government, terming them 'prisoners of indecision'. The country was ready to move ahead, but leadership was wanting. Shastri himself was taunted with a rhetorical plea: 'What is the Government afraid of? The whole country is behind it, wanting the Government and the Prime Minister to mould the destiny of the people.' And there was pointed reference to India's declining position in the world: 'We had a very fine position in the world yesterday. If we want it tomorrow, we had better look to it today.' [1]

There was nothing new in this criticism, except the source: Opposition M.P.s had used even harsher language in the food and no-confidence debates in the autumn and again during the budget session. To some, it was the stilled voice of Panditji, proclaiming, 'J'accuse'; to others, it was simply the expression of accumulated resentment at India's plight; and still others detected a challenge for leadership. Many, indeed, considered the attack in bad taste and unfair. They recalled that India's 'fine position in the world' had been shattered by the China débâcle and that Shastri had inherited a tarnished image of India. They also recalled Mrs. Pandit's bitter reflections on the abysmal state of the nation at the close of the Nehru era—'I am oppressed with a feeling of shame—shame that after seventeen years of independence the strong united nation we dreamed about is a chequerboard of disintegrating States hostile to one another. . . . How long will the hungry and disappointed men and women listen to the reasons that are offered for the failures?' [2]—and asked: 'If these were the conditions under India's charismatic leader for almost two decades, how could one expect drastic change under a new Prime Minister in eight months?'

Shastri was visibly moved by this assault. To the Congress Parliamentary Party he reportedly said: 'What is happening these days is very painful to me. . . . In Parliament, in future, we should be more cautious.' More pointedly, he added: 'What is this propaganda about indecision? It hurts me. We should not harm the Party. The Party has been consulted often and we meet usually once a week.' Mrs. Pandit apologized, 'if my speech hurt anybody. But I do not take back a single word.' And to Shastri she said: 'I have affection for you as though you were my brother'; but 'you are too busy. Occasionally, you should share your views with other people. . . . I renew my loyalty to you.' [3]

Others shared Mrs. Pandit's disenchantment, among them Jaya Prakash Narayan. The new Government had started well,

said the Sarvodaya leader, but after a few months it declined
steadily into ineptitude, indecision, and uncertainty. He decried
Congress factionalism, the lack of a sense of purpose, and the
absence of thinking about India's future.[4] Among the pundits,
Nandan Kagal was the most outspoken. 'The Shastri Government is barely ten months old', he wrote, 'but it already has a
tired and dispirited look.' As for the mood in Delhi, 'despair
is perhaps the wrong word. . . . [It] is rather one of urbane
frustration concealed by cynical boredom.'[5]

Defenders of Shastri were no less emphatic. Caucus member
Sanjiva Reddy declared, soon after Mrs. Pandit's onslaught, that
he was certain of the wisdom of the choice of Shastri as Prime
Minister, confident that the nation was in good hands, and convinced that all the problems besetting India were legacies of
Nehru: 'They were dormant during the last five years, so that
it would be unfair to blame Shastri.'[6] Atulya Ghosh concurred:
'All the current problems—food, language, Kashmir, etc.—were
inherited by Shastri. During the last six or seven years, the
country was allowed to drift. How can Shastri be expected to
solve them so quickly?''[7]

This theme was echoed by many Congress politicians. Most
commentators, too, were sympathetic but perceived a mixed
record. Frank Moraes acknowledged 'some notable and con-
structive achievements', such as the Indo-Ceylon Agreement of
October 1964 and the Nagaland negotiations. However, there
was discordance in statements by Ministers; and 'it is necessary
to bring the Chief Ministers . . . to order'. Most important,
'the Prime Minister must show that he can be tough. His
policies should develop teeth.'[8] Mulgaokar commended Shastri's
new direction in planning, the Naga problem, and relations with
Pakistan; but 'striking failures' were more conspicuous—the
Centre's concessions to the States, continued factional strife in
the Congress in the Prime Minister's home State, corruption, the
food crisis, and lack of co-ordination in Government. 'Mr.
Shastri's six months have been too much of a mixed bag. . . .
The period of alibis is over.'[9]

The most sophisticated appraisal came from Pran Chopra.
At the outset, he discerned 'two valuable assets from the Nehru

era: a reasonably complete and distinctive framework of policy
. . . and a climate of moderation . . .'. Set against these, however, were formidable problems: creating a harmonious team
within Cabinet; forging a new relationship with State leaders;
rooting out corruption and misrule; and surmounting a grave
economic crisis. The greatest liability was the lack of charisma:
' At Mr. Nehru's bidding people were more willing to wait; they
might be less willing at Mr. Shastri's.' On the prospects, he was
cautiously optimistic.[10]

At mid-stream, Chopra wrote a persuasive indictment of the
cynics and the critics. Many alleged weaknesses of Shastri were
termed legacies of Nehru: stagnation in agriculture; corruption
in politics; the dwarfing by China; the state of the Congress; and
disharmony between Delhi and the States. Further, there had
been no failure in foresight as costly as Nehru's China policy; no
rupture in Government as dramatic as the resignations of Deshmukh in 1956 and T.T.K. in 1958; no Ministry as feebly directed
as some in the past; no greater division in the Congress than in
1950–1; and no greater inter-State antagonism than between
Bengal and Assam in the early sixties. In more positive terms,
there were new initiatives on Nagaland, Ceylon, Nepal, and
Kashmir, and an attack on corruption. To the dispirited he
remarked, acidly: ' The process of normal growth continues—
only the pains are not eased away now by a charisma and there
is no remedy for the fear of growing up.' Democracy was bound
to flourish now because Nehru's ' large presence was comforting,
but it was also debilitating'. On balance, then, ' Mr. Shastri's
record has not been bad '. The real danger is the prevailing
gloom within the body-politic.[11]

At the end of the year of transition, press evaluation was even
more favourable. The *Times of India* observed: ' The very fact
that Mr. Shastri has come through this testing time without too
many bruises is in itself a significant commentary ', though it
called for more forceful leadership.[12] The *Statesman* was more
fulsome in tribute: ' Much sooner than Mr. Nehru and more
often within a year, Mr. Shastri has had to face the hard choice
between what is sensible and what is popular. His preference
has always been for the sensible course. . . . Despite the

compromises, delays and hesitations . . . in the end he has nearly always taken the best decision consistent with circumstances.' The consensus on language and moderation on the Rann of Kutch dispute were cited in this connection. As so many others, however, it warned of the need for a more popular image: ' The exhilaration of decisive action is also needed.' [13] All agreed that, by the beginning of his second year in office, Shastri's position was even stronger than on the morrow of succession.[14] Indeed, barring some national upheaval, such as military defeat at the hands of Pakistan, his tenure in office is assured at least until the 1967 elections, probably beyond.

The succession was universally hailed as a major achievement, and correctly so. But tranquillity is not an unmixed blessing in a society torn between the pulls of tradition and modernity. This is especially true of an innately non-revolutionary society like India, bound down by an age-old way of life, encrusted with passivity, caste, and archaic barriers to change. As with the first transfer of power, in 1947, continuity made for political stability, but at an enormous price. The administrative system, devised in another age, for other purposes, was retained, even strengthened. Inertia remained, and the sheer weight of paper in an inefficient and outworn bureaucracy continued as a massive barrier to progress. The political *mores* were given a new lease of life, and they too obstruct more rapid and purposeful action. The *status quo* acquired a new sanction, when dynamism was the first requisite.

The politics of democracy, with its attendant techniques of bargaining, persuasion, and compromise, is a major value *per se*; and the vast majority of India's élites so regard it, a legacy of the British *Raj*. With Nehru, its supreme advocate in the nationalist movement, they placed it at the summit of their value pyramid. During the Nehru era, its underpinnings were carefully built and nurtured, through three general elections: the rules of the parliamentary game, adherence to the Constitution, responsibility to the elected representatives of the people, etc. The contribution of the succession was to strengthen the system's viability and the élites' commitment to its processes. Yet this also entailed a disincentive to change in the attack on the paramount problem of economic growth.

If progress in that sphere was inadequate under a charismatic leader committed to modernization and economic planning, and possessed of vast personal power, what are the prospects for more rapid growth under Shastri, operating within the same political framework? It may well be that the unity of India can be maintained only by the politics of compromise, given its vast size and multiplicity of competing interest groups—though some would question this thesis. And it is true that political stability is a condition of economic progress. But stability is not coterminous with democracy. The dilemma of two competing values in a new and developing society—the ordering of civic behaviour by consent and economic improvement—remains in post-succession India. The outcome will emerge in the next ten to twenty years, with many unknown variables, internal and external, still to assert themselves.

There are also imponderables in the narrower realm of the political system proper. A concomitant of tranquillity is complacency. Pride in the Shastri succession is legitimate; self-satisfaction is not. There is ample evidence that more established democratic systems, with deeper roots in their societies, succumb to pressures from within and without, and give way to some form of authoritarian government. Few countries in the world can compare with India in terms of the variety and gravity of such threats to democracy. Thus, the succession to Nehru cannot be regarded as a definitive assurance of the system's survival.

There is a related question—whether the succession can be regarded as a precedent for a pattern of political change at the summit of Indian government or merely as a political freak? It may be argued that skilful management of the 1964 succession will make it relatively easy for a non-ideological Congress élite to repeat the performance. That assumes, however, that the distinctive variables of that transfer will remain unchanged or will reproduce themselves: fear of chaos; a superb manager; a caucus of able, determined politicians backing one person; a docile Congress Parliamentary Party; a President committed to the 'dignified' rather than the 'political' view of his office; the perpetuation of a one-plus or two-party system; and a candidate ideally suited to unlock the door. These might persist if a new succession were to occur within a year or two, but even that is uncertain, for such a complex constellation is the product of a specific set of circumstances, and these do not readily recur.

Hence the equally, perhaps more, plausible view that the dangers inherent in a post-Shastri succession would be greater, especially because Kamaraj and the Caucus had ample time to arrange an orderly succession. As one member of the Caucus remarked candidly: 'We were lucky last time, but who knows if we can pull it off again. The audience will know that it is a trick next time.' The issue remains in doubt, but two things seem clear: it would be an illusion to assume the existence of an established pattern, on the basis of the 1964 experience; and, secondly, complacency will only heighten the probability of the 'freak' interpretation being verified.

A distinctive feature of India's democracy is its party system: it conforms neither to the classic two-party pattern of the United Kingdom and the United States nor to the multi-party type of the French Fourth Republic; rather, it is a one-plus party system, comprising a governing party with a massive parliamentary majority and a scattering of opposition groups which, even in co-operation, cannot wrest power from the Congress. The system functioned because of two special factors: one was Nehru's commitment to the democratic process and his tolerance of criticism within Parliament and elsewhere; the other was the heterogeneous character of the Congress, a movement rather than a party, which embraced powerful pressure groups and thereby acted as a quasi-legislature with built-in brakes on the power and initiative of Cabinet. As long as these factors obtain, the inherent danger of a formalized one-party system is remote—but the temptation is ever-present. The growth of an effective opposition party is, therefore, a *desideratum*, if not an essential safeguard for the perpetuation of democracy.

The year of transition did not alter the dual role of the Congress—as Government and Opposition—or the tradition of tolerance. It did witness, however, the declining strength of opposition parties. No period since independence was more conducive to the growth of the lesser parties. For one thing, Nehru's death removed a cushion against popular discontent with the party in office. For another, the widespread shortage of food and the price spiral provided an ideal issue for anti-Congress propaganda. And thirdly, a series of by-elections during the year of turmoil provided a legitimate forum for the expression of dissent. Yet the evidence points to a reverse trend.

The Communist Party split in the autumn of 1964—over the China issue; and, despite the impressive performance of the Left CPI in the Kerala election in March 1965—it received the largest number of votes—the far Left opposition is weaker than ever before. The democratic Socialists are in even greater disarray: a projected union between the Praja Socialist Party and the Socialist Party, under the designation Samyukta (United) Socialist Party (SSP), disintegrated in the spring of 1965, at the point of consummation. Nor has the right-wing Swatantra Party displayed any vitality; indeed, its Bihar branch under the Raja of Ramgarh, with fifty-six seats in the State Assembly and eight in the Lok Sabha, attempted to move *en masse* into the omnibus Congress. Only the communalist Jan Sangh held its own. This trend is evident in by-election results. In seven parliamentary contests during 1964, the Congress made a net gain of two seats. And, in ninety-five State Assembly by-elections since the 1962 general election, it gained seven seats, most of them towards the end of 1964.

The gap between the Congress and all other parties appears to be growing. What is more, the internal squabbles among Congress factions and leaders is deflecting attention from the real challenge to India's political system. All this led to an acid commentary by one of India's most perceptive analysts: [15]

The real politics of India is the politics of poverty and development. All else is dross. The tensions of linguism, casteism, communalism, regionalism and economic discontent are essentially by-products of poverty. . . . The tragedy of the Indian situation today is that just when an economic breakthrough is within sight, the poverty of Indian politics threatens to brake development by fastening attention on secondary distractions, by promoting a sense of defeatism and failure, and by its growing irresponsibility and triviality. . . . And in this sorry situation, the Congress is able to give full rein to all its petty intrigues, factional quarrels and manœuvring for personal position in a manner reminiscent of the KMT [Kuomintang] and the Wafd.

This view may be too optimistic about India's immediate prospects for economic development and somewhat exaggerated in its assessment of the Congress; but it brings into sharp focus the dilemma of growth and stability noted earlier and the question of the survival capacity of India's one-plus party system.

Another disquieting development of the first post-succession year was the tarnished image of Parliament. A rash of incidents in the legislatures of West Bengal, Rajasthan, Maharashtra, and U.P. occurred in August 1964. Two examples will suffice. In Bengal, the Speaker was compelled to adjourn the Assembly after several days of disorderly behaviour by both Opposition and Congress members. And in U.P. the Speaker suspended twenty-eight Opposition members on one occasion and ordered seventy Opposition members to leave the House on another, both for defying the Chair.[16] More ominous was the spate of unruly scenes in the Lok Sabha during the spring of 1965. Within two months, erring members were suspended on nine occasions, and others were asked to withdraw from the House on seventeen occasions. The frequent absence of Prime Minister Shastri, in marked contrast to Nehru's daily presence during parliamentary proceedings, did not enhance the prestige and status of Parliament. As one commentator remarked: 'Parliament today is faced with the crucial problem of survival as the focal point of democracy. It can be saved only by itself and not by an external authority. . . . A great deal is on trial in India at the moment, and the future of parliamentary democracy is one such test.' [17] The working of Parliament during the post-succession year did not augur well for the future.

The most striking innovation in India's political system was the Grand Council of the Republic: during a year of permanent crisis it performed well, notably on the issues of food and language. Yet the institution and its rationale—consensus among the oligarchs—are fraught with imponderables. To what extent can a system based on consensus solve the fundamental economic and social problems gnawing at India's polity? Is the price of formal consensus so high as to induce stagnation in spheres demanding dynamic initiative? Has the Centre, through the Grand Council, conceded so much power to the States as to undermine effective all-India Government? If, as seems likely, the Grand Council becomes the permanent organ of decision on *any* controversial issue of national importance, will it not render Cabinet, Parliament, and the Congress Parliamentary Party super-fluous or, at best, lesser components of the system? Does not the strengthening of the Grand Council and the broadening of its jurisdiction presage an undermining of India's precarious unity, reversing the unitary trend sanctioned by the Constitution of 1950 and sought relentlessly by Nehru? And, finally, is there not a danger that the States, now homogeneous linguistic-cultural units, will press their new position of influence to the point of demanding revision of the distribution of legislative and financial powers, with dire consequences for the Union?

Indeed, this points up one aspect of India's democracy which has not been tested—the effect of a probable future dispersion of power in the States among various parties while Congress remains in control at the Centre. Given India's federal system, what kind of language policy could be evolved, for example, if the DMK captured Madras and/or the Jan Sangh secured power in one or more Hindi States? Could the Grand Council function in these circumstances? All these are possible consequences of the Shastri innovation; none is certain.

The experience of the first year suggests that consensus tends to mask basic disagreement and to delay the inevitable clash, with the Centre in an increasingly weak position. The problem lies deeper, namely, in the absence of clear directions of policy, whether because of the *mélange* character of the Congress—in its class, regional, factional, and ideological composition—or because of the sterility of thought. To complicate matters, Shastri seeks a near-total consensus when, in fact, a 65 per cent. to 70 per cent. consensus is sufficient to develop and carry out a policy; the result is, not infrequently, the abdication of decision and drift. But, as one writer observed, ' consensus cannot bridge unbridge-able gulfs; whatever appears to do so from time to time is not

consensus but confusion. . . .   Consensus can take care of the
legitimate divergence on specific issues . . . not so to diffuse the
meaning of policy that it should mean all things to all men.' [18]

The succession of 1964 answered the question, ' after Nehru,
who? ', at least in the short run.   But how much of the Nehru
legacy remains after the year of transition—and what is likely to
continue in the decade to come?   The four pillars of ' Nehruism '
were Democracy, Planning—with a moderate socialist orientation, Non-Alignment, and Secularism.   There have been many
changes in the political system, as noted earlier—a new duumvirate between Cabinet and Working Committee, a new equilibrium between the Centre and the States, a new relationship
between the Prime Minister and his colleagues, a new decision
body at the summit, and the undermining of Parliament; but
Democracy as such remains rooted in the consciousness of India's
élites, its attentive public and, no less than before, in the mass
public as well.   Yet its survival is far from certain.   Either of
two contingencies could terminate—or suspend—the experiment:
a massive external threat, which the civil government is incapable
of meeting; and prolonged economic stagnation.   The first is
more likely and more dangerous, as the Sino-Indian border war
and the Indo-Pakistan war of 1965 reveal; the second is possible,
but its effect on the political system is slow to mature.
     Planning as a method of achieving sustained economic growth
is implanted in the Indian polity.   Some aspects were challenged
in 1964–5—the role of the Planning Commission, the relative
emphasis on industry and agriculture, and the distribution of
investment funds to the public and private sectors.   In that sense,
a subtle process of ' de-Nehruization ' has begun, as will be
evident in the fourth Five-Year Plan.   And, indeed, the trend
towards capitalism in the Indian economy, with greater influence
exerted by the business community, will almost certainly continue
in the years to come; with Nehru's passing, the greatest barrier
to private enterprise has vanished.   But national planning is
accepted by almost all sections of the nation; even the Swatantra

Party, were it to achieve power, could not dismantle or discard the system as a whole.

De-Nehruization is most evident in the sphere of foreign policy, notably in the withdrawal of India from intense involvement in the outer perimeter—the global system—to the inner perimeter—India's neighbours. As one commentator remarked: ' More attention has been devoted to our relations with our neighbours during the past 17 weeks than during the preceding 17 years.' [19]   It is true that Shastri attended the Non-Aligned Conference in October 1964, visited the Soviet Union, Canada, and Yugoslavia in the spring and summer of 1965, participated in the Commonwealth Prime Ministers' Conference, and made periodic pronouncements on Viet Nam. But the thrust of India's foreign policy changed drastically—to a preoccupation with its neighbours. This had already begun in the last year of Nehru's life; now it assumed new dimensions. It will become more marked in the future. Non-alignment remains the formal basis of India's policy, but this has been transformed, in practice, into bi-alignment with the super-powers; equidistance from the United States and the Soviet Union has been replaced by equal proximity; such was the impact of the China débâcle and India's lesser prestige in the world. Thus, the Nehru era in foreign policy has become an historical relic.

The last of the Nehru pillars, Secularism, was the least firmly established during his tenure of office as Prime Minister: the barriers of society, history, and psychology were too great to be overcome in seventeen years. Shastri seemed no less committed to the principle and to the protection of minorities. But powerful forces, partially repressed by Nehru's active stress on secularism, came to the surface after the succession; a subtle Hindu revival was in the making. This, too, seems likely to continue and to gather momentum, for traditional Hindu tolerance is not synonymous with the secular ideal, and Nehru's commitment was respected, but not shared, by the majority of the Congress élite. This does not necessarily suggest a formal change in the Constitution, nor is this necessary; but pressures from below will increasingly manifest themselves. And as Shastri, a weaker leader, more in tune with popular, traditional feelings, seeks to reflect, and yields to, those feelings, the secular ideal will probably wither.

Nehru will join the pantheon of Indian Gods, as Gandhi has already done. Some of his ideals will atrophy, others will be modified, and the core—Democracy and Planning—will probably remain the lasting legacy. The succession marked the end of an era but not a rejection of its charismatic leader's goals for India.

VIII

THE SECOND SUCCESSION [1]

LAL BAHADUR SHASTRI died at the height of his power and prestige on 11 January 1966; it was a mere nineteen months and two days after he had succeeded Jawaharlal Nehru. Thus was India faced once more with the task of selecting a new Head of Government in a period of travail. As in 1964, the process of decision was mature and tranquil, though not without friction in the governing party, which on this occasion was overt and sustained. A multitude of pressures clashed and coalesced in the public view, culminating in the election of Mrs. Indira Gandhi, Panditji's daughter, as Leader of the Congress Parliamentary Party and, therefore, Prime Minister-designate, on the 19th of January.

The setting for India's second succession was pre-eminently one of drama, poignant and historic—an Indo-Pakistani summit conference in the fabled city of Tashkent, with Soviet Premier Kosygin playing the novel role of mediator between two non-Communist states. A week of tense and implacable negotiations had suddenly, it appeared, been rescued from impasse.[2] The fundamental sources of conflict between India and Pakistan were not removed by the 'Tashkent Declaration'; and Kashmir was not even discussed in a spirit of accommodation. Nor is it known whether Shastri and Ayub reached agreement through persuasion or whether they yielded to cajolery and coercion, real or implied; probably all three ingredients were involved. But all this was obscured by the tragedy soon to follow, and the 'spirit of Tashkent' was hailed by an anxious world as a new beginning in the long, bitter, and costly conflict.

News of the Tashkent communiqué reached Delhi around 5 p.m. on Monday, 10 January. The initial reaction was relief and approval, but before the day was out a tone of anger became evident in scattered discussions among the political élite. Archnationalists in the Congress and the bureaucracy bitterly opposed the withdrawal of troops to the 5 August line without Pakistani acceptance of a 'no-war pact', and the Indian abandonment of the strategic Haji Pir Pass, gateway to the Vale of Kashmir and symbol of the triumph of Indian arms, without formal Pakistani renunciation of future guerrilla warfare in the struggle for Kashmir. Some Indians called it an act of treachery and declared that, if Shastri had returned alive, there would have been a torrent of abusive criticism; in the words of one member of the Grand Council of the Republic, 'the Working Committee session on Tashkent would have been one of the stormiest on record '.[3]

Shastri himself was not unaware of this possibility, as evidenced by his remarks to a group of Indian journalists in Tashkent late on Monday afternoon. To the question, 'Are you sure that Pakistan will implement the Agreement? ', he replied simply, 'I hope so '; and further, 'some Pakistanis have their doubts that *we* will implement it '. And, when someone asked, 'Do you expect trouble back home of the kind that happened over the [Rann of] Kutch Agreement? ', he expressed his concern with a gentle plea: 'It is for you gentlemen to set the tone of the comment.'[4] The confrontation with his critics never took place; eight hours later Shastri was dead. He died of a heart attack at 1.32 a.m. Tashkent time (2.02 a.m. Delhi time), just seven minutes after he woke with a coughing spasm and staggered out of his bedroom in search of help.

The grave news reached Delhi within fifteen minutes. Home Minister Nanda was the first to be informed because there was no immediate response at Rashtrapati Bhavan (President's Home). Within hours, Congress leaders all over India had begun the trek to the capital. Shock was the pervasive mood at the sudden passing of a man who had begun to display the qualities of leadership, if not of greatness.

As in 1964, the constitutional vacuum was filled swiftly and smoothly. Nanda was summoned to Rashtrapati Bhavan, and the President re-enacted the scene that had immediately followed Nehru's death—in accordance with his view that the office of Prime Minister must not remain vacant. As the senior Minister in the Union Government on both occasions, it was Nanda who assumed the post; this time, however, the Emergency Committee of the Cabinet played no role, for its members were scattered in India and abroad; nor was it constitutionally necessary. The initial swearing-in ceremony took place at 3.15 a.m., but only three Ministers were present—Nanda, Mrs. Gandhi, and Sachindra Chaudhuri, the recently-appointed Finance Minister. Five other members of the Cabinet, along with thirteen Ministers of State and fourteen Deputy Ministers, were sworn in at 10 o'clock in the morning; all others were absent and were inducted when they returned to Delhi. In the interval, Dr. Radhakrishnan delivered a eulogy to the fallen hero in a broadcast to the nation (at 7.40 a.m.). Nanda added his tribute an hour later. There was a casual reference to constitutional precedent in the President's speech—' the Congress Parliamentary Party elected Lal Bahadur as its leader . . .'—but no one doubted, then or later, that this procedure would be followed.

The plane carrying Shastri on his final journey home touched down at Palam airport at 2.31 p.m. By that time many of the principal actors in the succession drama of 1966 had already reached Delhi: Congress President Kamaraj, by special plane from Madras; Atulya Ghosh, from Calcutta; S. K. Patil, from Bombay; and the Chief Ministers of Madhya Pradesh (Mishra) and of Rajasthan (Sukhadia). Mrs. Gandhi, Nanda, Jagjivan Ram, and the Chief Minister of Mysore, Nijalingappa, were already there; so, too, were lesser actors, like Patnaik of Orissa, Subramaniam and Krishna Menon. The only important figures who were absent at this time were Morarji Desai, who heard the news in the town of Koraput, Orissa, and returned by special plane; Sanjiva Reddy, also on tour in the south; and Chavan, who had been with Shastri in Tashkent. All were present in Delhi before the day was out.

The mood of the crowd at the airport was sombre but without visible expression of grief, which may reflect the Hindu attitude to death and the fact that people rarely display grief over the passing of public figures, except for members of the immediate family and close friends. After a brief scene of prayer and chanting, the body was placed on a caisson and moved slowly to the Prime Minister's residence at 10 Janpath. Then began the long file-past, as a million persons paid their last respects to 'the man of the people'.

Outwardly politics were suspended the day Shastri died. Behind the scenes, however, certain moves were set afoot, thoughts were spoken, and events occurred, which all indicated that self-restraint was incomplete in the pursuit of power. Cynics observed that the struggle for the succession began as early as 6 a.m. on that day, Tuesday the 11th, and there is evidence to support this view. Nanda took the lead. He telephoned D. P. Mishra, the Chief Minister of Madhya Pradesh, at that hour and asked when he was coming to Delhi. More important, he sought Mrs. Gandhi's support in an early morning conversation: he asked whether she wished to be Prime Minister and was told that she would not be a candidate; further, that 'you have just been sworn in, you must carry on'; and she added that she would support him, provided he had support from other leaders and groups in the Party. That evening, Mrs. Gandhi went to Kamaraj and told him of her conversation with Nanda, including her conditional support for his continuation in office. The Congress President replied, 'just leave things as they are; I will consult with many people'.[5] Nanda interpreted her remarks to mean unqualified support and was dismayed to learn, two days later, that her position had changed. Kamaraj himself had already decided, *from the very outset*, that Mrs. Gandhi was the most suitable candidate, though he *never* said so publicly and did not even let it be known indirectly for two days or more.[6]

Just before 9 a.m. on Tuesday, S. K. Patil arrived from Bombay and drove straight to Nanda's home, setting in motion a rumour, later confirmed by Patil himself, that he favoured Nanda's continuation in office, at least until the 1967 general election.[7] Later that morning, Nijalingappa of Mysore telephoned Patil and Atulya Ghosh and sought their views; all agreed that the matter should not be discussed seriously yet, for Shastri's body had not even returned. Yet Atulya recalled that, during his flight from Calcutta that morning, in the company of Bengal Chief Minister P. C. Sen, the idea was broached that Kamaraj should be asked to become Head of Government, a proposal that was publicly aired only two days later.[8] And around 3.30 in the afternoon, just after the airport reception of the dead leader, Nanda drove off with Mishra and told him that he would like to stay on as Prime Minister for one year; he added, significantly, that if he accepted second place in any Cabinet, it would be one headed by Mrs. Gandhi.[9]

The first of many condolence meetings was held in the Central Hall of Parliament at 5.30 p.m., with a small number of M.P.s in attendance (Parliament was then in recess). There was one noteworthy—and noticed—aspect to the proceedings, as Kamaraj remarked jocularly to some correspondents soon after: ' What's this I hear, Nanda spoke in English and Chavan in Hindi! '

In the evening the ubiquitous round of consultations began, with activity concentrated on the homes of Nanda and Kamaraj. To the latter came the following, between 4.30 and 8.45 p.m.: the Chief Ministers of Madhya Pradesh, Maharashtra, Madras, and Punjab; Patnaik, Sanjiva Reddy, Patil, and Atulya—together, and Mrs. Gandhi; (the Congress President also received Soviet Premier Kosygin and called on Dr. Radhakrishnan).[10] Many termed these ' courtesy calls ', but it is reasonable to assume, in the light of the evidence cited above, that the succession issue was not totally ignored by India's leaders. Discussions were not systematic; they were more in the nature of preliminary probes and soundings of attitudes to the task ahead. By Tuesday evening four names were already in the air—Nanda, Morarji, Mrs. Gandhi, and Defence Minister Chavan; the first two were self-conscious candidates—' it was obvious that I would be a candidate ', said Morarji, and his mind was made up when he heard the news,[11] though he did not declare his availability at that stage, to avoid the costly blunder of 1964; and Nanda entered the ring at once, with the feeling, ' I can't be a stepney * Prime Minister for ever '—as Head of Government he did not have to proclaim his candidature.

At the end of the first day, then, the struggle was in confused motion, its contours blurred by the shock of Shastri's death. Some of the candidates were known, as were the rumblings of dissent from ' consensus '; nor was there a need to summon the oligarchs, for a meeting of the Working Committee had been fixed for

* Spare wheel in a car.

Friday 14 January—to hear Shastri's report on Tashkent. Now it would be transformed into the Grand Council and set the rules for the choice of his successor.

To those who were conscious of the 1964 precedent there were, at this early stage, at least three observable differences: a pronounced feeling of self-confidence, expressed most candidly by one close associate of Nehru and Shastri—'there is the feeling that if Shastri could govern India these past nineteen months, any one of us can '—a dangerous self-delusion; secondly, there was no compelling sense of urgency for, unlike 1964, ' the eyes of the world were not upon India '; and thirdly, the struggle was bound to be more complex because the Caucus did not have an agreed candidate; indeed, they had not given thought to ' after Shastri, who? '

The public posture of restraint until after the funeral was respected by the Congress élite in both successions. Yet there were two episodes of note on Wednesday morning, 12 January. Nanda called on Kamaraj at 8 o'clock and made a bid for interim continuity—until the 1967 elections; in tone and spirit, if not in these exact words, the Acting Prime Minister reportedly said to the Congress President, ' why not try me out for a year, you can always chuck me out then '. Later in the day, too, Nanda pressed his claim with Kamaraj by saying that he saw no reason why he should step down this time.[12] The taciturn but brilliant master of political change at the summit of India's Government in 1964 and 1966 said nothing, and Nanda, erroneously, took this to mean acquiescence, just as he misinterpreted Mrs. Gandhi's initial support as permanent and unconditional. These two miscalculations, along with excessive and premature zeal, weakened his claim among his colleagues. That morning, too, a consensus was reached among members of the Syndicate and others that Morarji must be excluded; in fact, from that point onwards the struggle for the succession assumed the character of ' Morarji versus the Pack '.[13]

There was also a brief condolence meeting of the Congress Parliamentary Party (CPP) Executive in the morning. The general sense was that, unless it heard otherwise from the Working Committee—which it recognized as a superior body— the Executive should summon the Parliamentary Party into session, as in 1964, an implicit indication of concern and expectation about the role of the parliamentary wing in the choice of its leader. Sensing the probability of a contest, some members suggested an informal secret ballot followed by unanimous, formal election by the CPP; but, as in 1964, the initiative lay with Kamaraj and the organization. That evening he indicated that the Working Committee would summon the CPP after *it* had decided on the procedure to be followed.

The funeral, too, followed the pattern of 1964. The cortège left 10 Janpath at 9.30 a.m. on the 12th and made its way to the banks of the Jamuna, just 150 yards from Nehru's cremation site. The crowd was very thin in many places and not nearly as large as the Press or All-India Radio suggested. Grief was almost nowhere to be seen, not even in the VIP enclosure next to the *Samadhi*, a reflection of the fact that Nehru was the last of the giants of the nationalist movement and that, unlike Shastri's, his passing marked the end of an epoch; Shastri was denied the time to create that profound impact. The final ceremony was longer and more ritualistic. And then, at 12.32 p.m., the pyre was lit by Shastri's eldest son, Hari Kishen; the crowds began to disperse almost at once.

The faint and muffled probes of the first twenty-four hours now became open skirmishes and manoeuvres. When Chief Minister Sukhadia of Rajasthan visited him soon after the funeral, Atulya suggested Kamaraj as the ideal Prime Minister—in an election year. Sukhadia concurred but asked whether Mrs. Gandhi might be a second choice if Kamaraj declined; it was the first occasion in the nine-day drama that she was 'sponsored'. The Bengali leader suggested that she be approached, and Sukhadia reported to him that 'her mind was in a fluid condition', that she 'left it in the hands of the Congress leaders'.[14] This incident, confirmed by Mrs. Gandhi, destroys the myth, circulated then and later, that she was a reluctant candidate; as early as Wednesday the 12th she was not averse to the idea of becoming Prime Minister.

Another visitor to Atulya on the afternoon of the 12th was D. P. Mishra. All names were rejected—except Kamaraj; Mrs. Gandhi was not yet on the list. And, at 9.30 p.m., Atulya went to the Congress President to say, ' you have to accept '. ' He did not reject the idea ', added Atulya; he merely said, as was his way, ' let us consider '. They then decided to meet with their colleagues in the Syndicate—Patil, Reddy, and Nijalingappa—at Reddy's home later in the night.

Before that important conclave, however, at least two other episodes had taken place. Nijalingappa went to Morarji after the funeral to explain why he was unacceptable to the Caucus —his aloofness, rigidity, authoritarian bent, his extreme Hindu orientation, and the like. That afternoon, too, Nijalingappa received a visit from Chief Minister Naik of Maharashtra, who made a bid in favour of Chavan, the outstanding Congress leader of that State. There was much friction between Mysore and Maharashtra, especially over Goa, Marathi-speaking border areas, and river waters. The Mysore Chief Minister did not conceal his annoyance with the parochial attitudes of Chavan but he assured Naik that ' if Chavan is the choice of the other leaders, I will not stand in his way '.[15]

Before the Caucus met, Kamaraj had a steady stream of visitors at his home—some twenty consultations between 4.30 p.m. and 9.30 p.m. All sections were represented: Chief Ministers (of Andhra, Orissa, Jammu and Kashmir, and Madras); Union Cabinet (Chavan, Ram Subhag Singh, and Sanjivayya, the Untouchable spokesman); the Syndicate (Sanjiva Reddy and Atulya); the Left (Menon and Malaviya); and State leaders (Darbara Singh of the Punjab and Kamalapathi Tripathi of U.P.). On the basis of these discussions he let it be known to the press that the Chief Ministers and other leaders whom he had met on Tuesday and Wednesday ' generally ' favoured a ' unanimous election '; he acknowledged some dissent but added, ' I hope there will be unanimity '. It was the first public statement by the Congress President on the succession issue—inoffensive but pointed: Kamaraj's way of saying that it should be an organization decision rather than by a free vote. It was also a rejoinder to Morarji whose declared motto, then and later, was ' no

unanimity at the expense of democracy '. ' Let us take the contest to an open vote, for this is true democracy ', he told newsmen
on Wednesday evening; with the Congress High Command
opposed, he knew that the only possible forum for victory was a
secret ballot in the CPP. Kamaraj was quick to counter, and his
views were conveyed to all the actors by All-India Radio in its
10.30 p.m. news bulletin: the conflict between the two men and
the forces they represented, an enduring feature of the 1966
decision process, had now entered the public arena.

The Syndicate's first ' formal ' session, late on Wednesday
night, was inconclusive: there was no pre-eminent candidate, as
in 1964, except perhaps Kamaraj who was resisting the ' call '.
Neither Mrs. Gandhi nor Chavan had declared their intentions
and, in any event, there was strong opposition to both from
different members of the Caucus; Morarji was unacceptable, and
that left Nanda—for whom there was no enthusiasm. Patil
recommended his continuation in office, on the grounds of
administrative experience and minimal disruption to Government
and Party. Reddy was not opposed. Nijalingappa had reservations. Atulya urged Kamaraj to stand and, as noted, had rejected
all other names. And Kamaraj, as usual, was silent. The names
of Patil and Reddy were floated, in what seemed like an act of
desperation, but no one took these ' red herrings ' seriously. Thus
it was that, by a process of elimination, the mood of negative
consensus at the end of the second day favoured the interim
Prime Minister. The fact that he was supported by Rajagopalachari, leader of the conservative Swatantra Party, openly, and by
the Left privately, may have made him more acceptable—but also
more suspect.[16] Caucus backing for Nanda, then, was fitful and
uncertain. More important, disunity and indecisiveness were to
weaken the role of the group that had managed the 1964
succession with skill and finesse.

Thursday, 13 January, began on a note of confusion and
fluidity. No less than eight names were now in the air, with
varying degrees of commitment and support: Morarji, Nanda,
Mrs. Gandhi, Chavan, Patil, Reddy, Kamaraj, and Jagjivan Ram

—who had cautiously entered the contest the previous night.[17] The blur was evident in the first round of press comments that morning. No names were mentioned, though the *Statesman* ('The Succession') delivered an unmistakable rebuke to Morarji: 'Resilience, poise, finesse, a known freedom from self-righteous attitudes . . . are also qualities statesmanship needs.' Kamaraj, it added, 'faces an even more intricate task in finding a consensus'. The *Times of India* ('The Challenge') urged that 'unprofitable controversy over the procedure' be avoided, for both the consensus technique and a secret ballot were acceptable. The *Tribune* ('After Shastri, What?') declared that 'the task of choosing his successor . . . is a national concern'. And the *Patriot* ('Choice Problem') concurred, with a crude insult to India's parliamentarians: the selection—no preference was indicated—should not be left to 'a brute majority in the Congress Parliamentary Party . . .'. The *Hindustan Times* ('Picking Up The Threads') was non-committal on procedure but stressed that 'no time should be lost'. Among the political analysts, only two offered their views at this early stage. Malhotra advocated the appointment of a strong Deputy Leader,[18] and Krishan Bhatia bluntly opposed an open contest, as well as a stop-gap arrangement.[19]

The tempo of political activity increased sharply that day, for the crucial meeting of the Working Committee was drawing near. There was a myriad of consultations and conferences at various levels—almost all dominated by the compulsion to find a candidate who could defeat Morarji: despite the pressure for unanimity, he held his ground and made it clear to all who would listen that he would insist on a trial of strength in the CPP. Thus, as on the third day of the first succession, Thursday was a day of bargaining, courting, and lobbying.

The nerve centre was Kamaraj's home at 4 Jantar Mantar Road: no fewer than five Chief Ministers (of Rajasthan, U.P., Madras, Jammu and Kashmir, and Orissa) called on the Congress President in the morning. Another focus of activity was the home of Atulya Ghosh at 19 Canning Lane: there the Chief Ministers of eastern India gathered between 6.30 and noon to debate the widely-shared predicament—how to stop Morarji; the only way out, they agreed, was to draft Kamaraj. Throughout the day a powerful campaign was mounted to this end. First, the idea was leaked to the press. Then Orissa's Biju Patnaik was informed of the growing consensus at a luncheon in the garden of his sumptuous house at 3 Aurangzeb Road, attended by Reddy, Bengal's P. C. Sen, and others. Patnaik had been Morarji's staunchest supporter in the first succession; now, he hedged astutely. As he remarked that day, he favoured Morarji, except in two contingencies: if Mrs. Gandhi became a candidate, he would support her wholeheartedly; and, if Kamaraj entered the contest, he would reconsider his position. On Thursday the 13th, then, Patnaik was amenable to persuasion. Yet the previous day he raised no objection to Nanda continuing in office: 'After all, he has been in the Cabinet for a long time and knows the intricacies of administration; he could carry on just as well as anybody else.' More revealing about the state of mind on Thursday morning, before the 'draft Kamaraj' proposal took shape, was his remark that 'we are all amused by the thought that, by a process of elimination, we end up with Nanda staying on'.[20]

A concerted move to persuade Kamaraj came in the evening. Once more, Atulya was the spearhead. Just after the Working Committee condolence meeting, from 6–6.30 p.m., a small group was gathered about the Bengali lynchpin of the Syndicate—Sen of Bengal, Chaliha (Chief Minister), and Fakhruddin Ahmed (Working Committee representative) of Assam, Darbara Singh of the Punjab, and Naik, Chavan's right hand in Maharashtra. 'We must decide', said Atulya, conscious of the Working Committee meeting just seventeen hours away; 'you go to Kamaraj'; and he added, in his account, 'my stand throughout was that it should be Kamaraj or his nominee; this is an election year'. At 7.30 in the evening the first three, accompanied by Nijalingappa of Mysore, carried Atulya Babu's suggestion to Kamaraj. 'It is not possible', he replied simply; on the previous day he was less restrained: 'for Heaven's sake, don't drag my name into this'. Atulya persisted at the second 'formal' Syndicate session that night—Kamaraj was not present because 'we asked him not to be', but the Congress President would not be moved.[21]

To many who know the ways of Indian politics at the summit, this seemed like an Atulya ploy to move into the Congress presidency, the key to vast patronage and influence in an election year—perhaps even to undermine Kamaraj's authority. Kamaraj apparently sensed the trap and shrewdly understood the perils of yielding to pressure: his authority and prestige among Congressmen could—and would—be impugned by the charge of using his office as a lever to the Prime Ministership; moreover, even if he were chosen, he would be immensely handicapped in Parliament, Cabinet, and the world by the language problem; as one of his closest colleagues remarked, with a straight face, ' he knows no known language—and therefore he cannot read! '; thirdly, such a move would deprive the Hindi heartland of all three senior posts in the country—President of India, Prime Minister, and Congress President—and the Congress cannot afford any further weakness in that area; and finally, as he remarked, ' I am not interested in the Prime Ministership; in an election year the Congress Presidency is the most important office.' [22]

Morarji was haughtily inactive during the first three days of the succession battle. Having been badly burned in 1964, he skirted the issue of availability; recalling the incident on Wednesday evening, he declared that he would not allow himself to be misquoted again—by saying nothing about his candidacy. More important, he spurned the entreaties of his followers to canvass for support and seek allies—in short, to engage in political action. As late as Thursday he showed utter contempt for coalitions with other persons and interests, calling them ' undignified, contrary to my principles; they involve dirty bargaining and conditions which tie one's hands; I will not do it '.[23] He changed his mind on canvassing for support, from Friday onwards, but he did not display resilience or finesse on the vital issue of forging alliances for the election and beyond; he did not, in short, understand or resort to one of the core features of democratic politics—the bargaining process—and for this he paid dearly. Until that day only one Chief Minister, Nijalingappa, had visited him, and only to tell him why he was being denied the prize. Patnaik, C. B. Gupta, a long-time ally who controlled half the U.P. votes, Patil and others came too; but it was a trickle, compared to the flow elsewhere; Morarji was waiting—in vain—for the ' call '.

It was on Thursday, too, that Mrs. Gandhi and Chavan, the ' quiet ones ' among the major actors, made their move. They met at 3.15 p.m. and, in effect, formed a pact: ' if you wish to be Prime Minister and you have the backing of other leaders, I will withdraw and my votes will go to you ', was the essence of Chavan's pledge; Mrs. Gandhi reciprocated. Nor was this unexpected, though it was not reported, for, among all Congress leaders, there is a known affinity between these two in policy outlook; indeed, along with Subramaniam and Asoka Mehta, they have been meeting informally together since early 1965 (the language riots in Madras) and may be regarded as a ' New Force ' in all-India politics, a counterweight to the Caucus. Now all four are in the Union Cabinet, and one of their number is Prime Minister; it will be a force to reckon with.

The same afternoon Mrs. Gandhi told D. P. Mishra that ' if there is near-unanimity and Kamaraj asks me, I would stand '; by near-unanimity she apparently meant all except Morarji. Mishra also spoke with Patil, who indicated his continuing support for Nanda; the Chief Minister of Madhya Pradesh reiterated his backing for Mrs. Gandhi. He also met Jagjivan Ram, who said he intended to play the role of peace-maker, though he still favoured Morarji; he was to try later—and fail, and then shift allegiance, as in 1964.

A new centre of activity from Thursday onwards was the Central Hall of Parliament. Normally deserted during the recess, it became at once a focal point for M.P.s of all camps, as well as those who wished to assert the primacy of the Parliamentary Party in the decision. As time went on, and an open contest seemed certain, Central Hall became the forum of intense canvassing. On the 13th, however, it was merely a convenient meeting place for random discussion.

Kamaraj continued his relentless round of consultations. Apart from the Chief Ministers' deputation sent by Atulya, he received visits from Cabinet Ministers Sanjivayya and Sachindra Chaudhuri, as well as Nanda, a number of M.P.s, CPP officials Gopala Reddy and Satya Narayan Sinha, dissident State leaders like Kamalapathi Tripathi of U.P., and a few Pradesh Congress Committee representatives. Once more, that evening, he indicated his hope for unanimity—as he was to do consistently until Monday the 17th—and rejected a draft: 'please don't drag me into this controversy', he told the press.

When the Caucus met at Sanjiva Reddy's home on Thursday night there were three constants in the developing decision process: Morarji's determination to contest to the bitter end; the resolve of Kamaraj and the Syndicate to keep Morarji out; and Kamaraj's firm resolve not to stand—despite Atulya's lingering hopes and continued pressure. Of the remaining candidates, Patil, Reddy, and Jagjivan Ram were either not serious or marginal. This left Nanda, Chavan, and Mrs. Gandhi. Once more the Caucus was split and failed to reach agreement.

Nanda was the most palatable of the three alternatives to Morarji, in terms of Syndicate interests. His strength, ironically, was his weakness—the lack of an independent base of political power, which made him more amenable to influence. Indeed, the willingness to entertain the idea of his continuing in office appeared to be based on a realistic power calculus: through key positions in the Cabinet (Patil in External Affairs, Reddy as Home Minister, and Chaudhuri, Atulya's nominee, in Finance) the Syndicate would acquire massive control in the Union Government. Thus, while all disparaged him, they recognized his value. Offsetting this 'asset', however, were two glaring liabilities—it was doubtful that he could defeat Morarji in a straight contest within the CPP and, even if he did, his would not be the most potent Congress image in the general elections of 1967.

Chavan's weakness was his strength—his power base in Maharashtra, making him less reliable as Prime Minister, i.e., more independent. Moreover, he had offended Mysore by what it regarded as a parochial attitude to Goa—his intervention from the Centre in favour of his own State's claim—and the South more generally by his attitude to the Krishna-Godavari rivers dispute. There was, too, a long-standing animosity with Patil in Bombay politics. Nor did he have the compensation of a link

with the Hindi heartland—though he had sought to establish
this by his speech in Hindi at the parliamentary condolence
meeting.

Mrs. Gandhi's shortcomings, in Syndicate eyes, were formidable: administrative inexperience—some felt, incompetence;
indecisiveness and access to the Left; haughtiness—which some
Caucus members had felt in the past and deeply resented; youth;
frailty; and independence. But her assets were even more impressive: certainty that she could defeat Morarji in the pending
contest; wide popular appeal, enhanced by the Nehru name and
mantle; the best possible public image of the Congress in the
general election, heightened by her association with U.P., the
largest State in the Union.

This assessment was not shared by all members of the Syndicate; indeed, different persons had different preferences which,
stripped of the nuances, may be portrayed as follows:

	Mrs. Gandhi	Chavan	Nanda
Atulya	Critical but not unalterably opposed	Open to persuasion	Opposed
Nijalingappa	In favour	Opposed	Reservations
Patil	Opposed	Opposed	In favour
Reddy	Opposed	Favourable but not enthusiastic	Favourable

The only firm decision that appears to have been taken on
Thursday night was the elimination of Chavan, largely because
of his alienation of the South and personal animosity. As for the
other two, Kamaraj's gentle prodding and the knowledge that
most Chief Ministers favoured Mrs. Gandhi began to have their
effect—a shift in the mood of negative consensus away from
Nanda to the ultimate victor.[24] Kamaraj's patience and the tactic
of 'allowing them to talk things out' had begun to turn the
tide. But the issue was still open when the Caucus adjourned: if
Morarji yielded to the pressure for unanimity the political impera-
tives would change and Nanda's hopes, strongly supported by
Patil and others, including a section of big business, might yet be

realized. The Working Committee on the morrow would force the Syndicate's hand.

Friday 14 January was a day of extraordinary complexity and significance in the struggle for the second succession. The major event was a meeting of the Working Committee, really the Grand Council of the Republic, at 11 a.m. But, unlike the parallel meeting of 31 May 1964, which adopted the consensus principle and thereby assured Shastri's triumph, the 1966 session merely laid down the rules for an open test of strength, growing more bitter by the hour. From that point onwards the pattern of decision diverged sharply—from the politics of unanimity to the politics of overt conflict; the climax of 1964 had become the watershed of 1966. With the gates now open, the battle assumed a new dimension of intensity. And before the day was out the contending forces had crystallized; confusion had given way to clarity.

The Grand Council meeting was brief, a mere forty-five minutes, compared with the three-hour discussion leading to the consensus formula in 1964. According to Patnaik, ' the whole thing (the substantive part) lasted five minutes; then we joked about '. Present were the eighteen members of the Working Committee, the thirteen Chief Ministers not on that body, four special invitees—Dhebar, Krishna Menon, Subramaniam, and T.T.K.—and six representatives of the CPP—the Chief Whip, the two Deputy Leaders, and the three General Secretaries—a total of 41 persons.

Accounts of the discussion are fragmentary—it was all over so quickly. Kamaraj opened the proceedings by referring to the consensus formula of 1964 and wondered aloud whether it might be adopted again. At that point Morarji reacted ' violently ' and insisted on a vote in the Parliamentary Party; he was supported by two or three Chief Ministers. In the desultory exchange of views that followed only three themes were recalled: Patil, followed by Jagjivan Ram, suggested an informal sounding of CPP members—each M.P. to write the name of his choice on a ballot paper, a process of elimination, and the unanimous 'election' of the majority candidate by the Parliamentary Party; the idea remained still-born. Dhebar pleaded for an early election; then Sanjiva Reddy suggested that the leaders try to reach a consensus in private consultations. Various names were tossed out, and within seconds an informal 'committee of four' came into being—Kamaraj, Morarji, Nanda, and Jagjivan Ram; it had no formal status, it was obviously a face-saving device, and it never met. Thereafter, the mechanics were thrashed out.

The only firm decision of the oligarchs was that the successor to Shastri would be elected by the CPP on Wednesday, 19 January, with Kamaraj presiding. Kamaraj was *instructed* to *seek* a consensus but he was not *authorized* to *ascertain* it, as in 1964—a momentary blow to his prestige. If these efforts were unsuccessful there would be a secret ballot—based on the French Fifth Republic Presidential election: the winning candidate would require 51 per cent. of the votes, though it was not made clear whether this meant total possible votes or votes cast, whether it included invalid votes, etc.; if there were more than two names there would be as many ballots as necessary to produce a majority candidate, the person with the least votes in each ballot being dropped; the balloting would be concluded in one sitting, presumably to avoid inter-ballot lobbying. No names were mentioned at the meeting; formal nominations were to be made on the 19th.

There were only three reported comments on the meeting. Kamaraj and Jagjivan Ram were cautiously optimistic about the prospects for unanimity. Morarji termed it 'a good decision' and, while acknowledging that genuine unanimity was desirable, 'a contest seems to be inevitable'. He had reason to feel pleased with the outcome, for the High Command had been successfully challenged, and the battle over procedure won; Morarji knew full well that a secret ballot was the *sine qua non* of victory. After the meeting he and Kamaraj drove together to the latter's house and spent twenty minutes together; in the light of subsequent events it is doubtful that any substantive discussion took place.

Morarji's veto of consensus unleashed new forces in the decision process and imposed compelling pressure to find a coalition candidate to defeat him. The rest of Friday and most of Saturday were dominated by this need. Quickly—and by subtle design, it would appear—the field was narrowed to the Congress President's consistent choice, Mrs. Gandhi. It was first necessary to establish beyond doubt Kamaraj's refusal to contest—in the Syndicate, the Chief Ministers' club, and the Parliamentary Party. This was accomplished by mid-afternoon on Friday. He told Atulya and the Chief Minister of Madras at or just before the Grand Council meeting that he definitely would not stand. He repeated this to a group of four Chief Ministers—Mishra of Madhya Pradesh, Sahay of Bihar, Sukhadia of Rajasthan, and Naik of Maharashtra —when they called on him at 1 p.m.

Mishra had taken the initiative that morning and had called his colleagues together at Madhya Pradesh Bhavan to consider the situation. All agreed that, if Kamaraj was prepared to stand, he must be supported. Whether Mishra, the spearhead of the Mrs. Gandhi campaign among the State leaders, proposed her as an agreed alternative at this gathering is not certain,[25] but it was certainly in his mind, as later events showed. In any case the psychological necessity of clearing the air was accomplished at the meeting of the four with Kamaraj. It was on that occasion that he said he considered the Presidency of the Congress that year more important than any other office in the country. When he was asked, ' is this final, may we give it to the press? ', he said, simply, ' yes '. He then spoke to each of the four separately and, to Mishra and Sukhadia, at least, he said, ' Nandaji has no chance '; he did not indicate a preference—but did he have to?

While Kamaraj and Mishra were preparing the ground for Mrs. Gandhi, Patil was making a keen effort to maintain the *status quo* and, incidentally, to avoid a contest. To a small group of Caucus members and others gathered at his home he submitted a proposal, in writing, for a ' Cabinet of Composite Talents '. Ten names were listed in the core group: Nanda, Mrs. Gandhi, Morarji, Patil, Chavan, Jagjivan Ram, Sanjiva Reddy, C. B. Gupta, Swaran Singh, and Sinha; five other places were left vacant, with the suggestion that these might be filled by Subramaniam, Chaudhuri, Chagla, Kabir, and Sen; no name was specified for the Prime Minister, but Patil later clarified his intent by saying, 'look at the first name on the list '—it was Nanda. No decision was taken at this stage, but when Kamaraj was told, he rejected the idea out of hand. Patil persisted at the Syndicate meeting on Friday night but to no avail. He had also told Mishra of his ' brain wave ' and the two discussed it with Mrs. Gandhi; she listened and merely said that she would consult Kamaraj, adding that Patil should do the same. According to Kamaraj, by the time the proposal came to him, Patil mentioned either Nanda *or* Mrs. Gandhi as Prime Minister; events probably required an adjustment to save the scheme in any form; Kamaraj was not convinced.

The net was virtually closed in the evening. Mishra sounded the Chief Ministers of South India and gathered that Chavan was not acceptable. Patil, apparently disquieted by these consultations, telephoned him and reportedly said, 'if Chavan is a candidate, I am a candidate', perhaps to caution against any Chief Ministers' move in Chavan's favour. This was really unnecessary, for Mishra favoured Mrs. Gandhi, as did Kamaraj; the Syndicate had rejected Chavan the previous night; and the Defence Minister had neither declared himself a candidate nor campaigned actively. It was left to Naik, the Maharashtra Chief Minister, to explore the terrain; and when it was found uninviting, Chavan let it be known that he was in the hands of the Congress President, which meant that, as he had pledged, he would throw his weight behind Mrs. Gandhi. Kamaraj himself maintained a public posture above the inter-personal rivalries. 'I have no particular preference for one candidate ', he told the press in the evening; 'all my efforts are to bring about unanimity.' Whether he thought this still possible on the evening of Friday the 14th, is unclear. It seems more plausible to interpret his remarks as pressure on the diverse anti-Morarji interests to settle upon a coalition candidate who could contest with optimum effectiveness against him for the CPP vote; in short, Kamaraj was anxious to avoid splitting the vote.

When the Caucus met at Kamaraj's house, between 9.30 and 10.30 in the evening, the stage was set for its acquiescence in the Congress President's choice. Any doubt that Mrs. Gandhi was prepared to compete for the prize, a factor assiduously cultivated by her detractors, was dispelled that evening. When a journalist provoked her, implying fear of a test of strength in the CPP, she reacted instantly that there was no harm whatever in a contest and, ' I am not afraid of a contest '. She would have preferred Nanda or Chavan to carry on, she added, but between Wednesday afternoon and Friday afternoon she had been approached by a large number of persons and asked to stand; she would abide by the Congress President's decision.

When the Syndicate foregathered, then, the air had cleared, with four known constants in the equation: Morarji's determination to force the issue to a vote; Mrs. Gandhi's unqualified availability; Kamaraj's preference, indirectly conveyed through the Chief Ministers; and the probability that Nanda would be defeated in a secret ballot. The Syndicate had no real choice, for the decision had been made elsewhere, induced by Kamaraj's brilliant strategy of building up massive pressure, through endless consultations with Chief Ministers and others—an unwritten, unstated, perhaps not even fully grasped alliance with the State leaders. But even then the Caucus was not fully prepared to yield to what amounted to an imposed decision. Patil still pressed Nanda's case, and Atulya maintained the fiction or illusion of a wide-open race for the coalition's blessing. He went to Nanda that night and told him what had happened, saying, ' We are in the hands of the Congress President; he will choose from a panel of five names [Nanda, Mrs. Gandhi, Chavan, Patil, and Reddy] —or someone else.' This may have been a sop to a crestfallen Nanda or wishful thinking; Kamaraj and others knew better. Another day was required to bring the Syndicate around. It had been outmanœuvred; what remained was to compel its adjustment to the situation, however reluctantly, by a *fait accompli*.

Saturday, the 15th, witnessed a dramatic breakthrough in the struggle for the succession to Shastri: eight Chief Ministers issued a Statement calling for the election of Mrs. Gandhi as Leader of the CPP. To onlookers at the time everything else paled into insignificance, and with some reason, for this act assured Nehru's daughter of the Prime Ministership. Yet there were many other events that day, before and after, which illuminated the dynamics of decision at the summit of Indian politics. Some, indeed, provided clues to the most perplexing question of the nine-day drama, with far-reaching implications for the balance of influence in all-India politics during the post-Shastri phase. Was this a revolt from below, a genuine initiative by the State leaders to impose their will and their candidate by a public display of collective strength, or was there collusion with the Congress President? Or, in fact, was it inspired, induced, even arranged, by Kamaraj to obliterate all remaining opposition to his choice? Stated in more impersonal terms, does this act mark a qualitative change in the distribution of power between the Centre and the units of the Indian federation or does it represent the reassertion, after nineteen months of the dispersion of power, of the primacy of the all-India organizational wing of the Party? The answers must, of necessity, be more tentative and qualified than the questions, for it is too early to pass final judgement on events so complex and so recent. But it is well to capture the flow of deeds and words for calmer reflection at a later date.

Atulya Ghosh, a major actor in both successions and a key member of the Syndicate, with vast influence in the Congress machine in the eastern States, dismissed the Statement as ' un-necessary ', ' impolitic ', and ' unwise ', adding that it ' created difficulties '. In his account, the issue had already been decided on Saturday morning—by the Caucus. Yet his disclosure of events that morning suggests doubt as to where the decision was made. No fewer than seven Chief Ministers (of Andhra, Assam, Bengal, Bihar, Mysore, Orissa, and Rajasthan) and the Punjab's Darbara Singh came to see him, one by one, and all *said* that they would support Mrs. Gandhi; nor can it be deduced that this was at his behest for, thus far, he had opposed her or, at least, had taken no steps to support her. Then Bengal's P. C. Sen, just before leaving for Calcutta, paused at Kamaraj's home. The Congress President said that ' so far, from the consultations I have had [mostly with the Chief Ministers], the majority is for Mrs. Gandhi '. Sen reported this to Atulya, who then telephoned

Sanjiva Reddy.   Reddy, on his own, said Atulya, went to Kamaraj and conveyed his support for Mrs. Gandhi.

According to Nijalingappa of Mysore, an ' associate ' member of the Syndicate and a member of the Chief Ministers' club, he and Reddy called on Kamaraj at 10.30 in the morning and indicated their acceptance of Mrs. Gandhi.   He then telephoned Atulya, who agreed, but was unable to reach Patil.   Kamaraj, too, specified 10.30 as the time of Syndicate acquiescence.   There can be no doubt, therefore, that the Caucus ' came around ' to the idea of Mrs. Gandhi as Prime Minister only *after* it was crystal clear that the overwhelming majority of Chief Ministers, Kamaraj, and others were supporting her.   The Caucus did not *make* the decision, as it did in 1964; it merely *adjusted* to compelling circumstances.

It is also evident that the Chief Ministers knew Kamaraj's mind when they gathered at Madhya Pradesh Bhavan in New Delhi's diplomatic enclave between 1 and 2 p.m.; the Congress President confirmed that he had conveyed his preference in the course of consultations with the State leaders.   Did Kamaraj instigate this ' show of force '?   He denied any knowledge of the meeting, and most persons interviewed concurred, including Mishra, who had taken the initiative.   As the Madhya Pradesh Chief Minister recalled the episode a few days later, he felt that the time had come to crystallize the developing situation and so he telephoned all Chief Ministers to come together for a ' free discussion '.   (Although a long-time supporter of Morarji, he had parted company during the first succession struggle when he was accused of disloyalty for attempted mediation [26] and he felt a debt to Mrs. Gandhi for rescuing him from the political wilderness in 1963.)

Of the nine Chief Ministers present (those from Andhra, Bihar, Jammu and Kashmir, Madhya Pradesh, Madras, Maharashtra, Mysore, Orissa, and Rajasthan), all but Sahay from Bihar agreed that they should go to Kamaraj and convey their support for Mrs. Gandhi.   Sahay asked for time to consult his faction-ridden colleagues.   Mishra's theme was, ' why leave the responsibility entirely to Kamaraj, we must share the burden '.   Tripathi of Orissa concurred but wanted to consult Patnaik, still the dominant figure in the State Congress; he did so and was told to join the deputation. Nijalingappa telephoned Patil from the meeting, and he came around. He also called Reddy who said, 'that's what we agreed to this morning'. The inter-personal élite network had now been integrated. One curious feature was the presence of Food Minister Subramaniam at a gathering of Chief Ministers; apparently he had come to discuss the food situation with Mishra and was still there when the Chief Ministers began to arrive; he was asked to stay on!

By the time the meeting adjourned journalists had gathered in strength. As the Chief Ministers set out for Kamaraj's home, Naik leaked the 'decision'—'we are for Mrs. Gandhi'—and the word spread rapidly throughout the city. When the deputation arrived, the Congress President seemed—or feigned—surprise: 'What's the matter?' he asked; they presented their Statement, and Kamaraj nodded. Mishra, spokesman for the group, said, 'We have tried not to give publicity to this; do what you will with it.' Kamaraj said he would tell the press in the afternoon, and did so: 'Almost all the Chief Ministers are in favour of Mrs. Gandhi', he announced—but he still refused to indicate his own choice (it was tactically wise not to do so) and reiterated his hope for unanimity, bearing the Chief Ministers' view in mind. Before the day was over the Chief Ministers of Bengal, Punjab, and Himachal Pradesh had added their support, and Bihar's Sahay added his approval—twelve of the fourteen Chief Ministers were now openly identified; only Gujarat, Morarji's home State, and U.P., whose Chief Minister, Mrs. Kripalani, owed her position to Morarji's ally, C. B. Gupta, remained aloof.

The impact of numbers, political strength, and psychological surprise was enormous, but Morarji refused to yield. The eight Chief Ministers went from Kamaraj's house to Atulya—'because he is a prominent man', said Orissa's Tripathi—and asked him to attempt to persuade Morarji to withdraw, in the light of over-whelming support for Mrs. Gandhi, and thereby to maintain party unity. The two leaders met at Morarji's home at 5 p.m., the first effort of the coalition to persuade him to concede, in the face of overwhelming odds.

What transpired was later communicated to the press by Morarji himself: 'Mr. Ghosh only conveyed to me the factual statement of the Chief Ministers'; to the writer he added, the following morning, that Atulya, like his colleagues in the Caucus, was unhappy—'go and see them and they will tell you'—and did not press him to yield. In fact, Morarji gave the impression of optimism that Atulya and others would release the 'whip' on their votes, to the extent of permissive voting on the 19th. He criticized the Chief Ministers' action as 'interference' with the rights and privileges of M.P.s and claimed that this would redound to his benefit because of widespread resentment in the CPP. He also derived comfort from the inclusion of only eight Chief Ministers in the Statement. And, as for his own intentions, 'I am firm. I will stand to the last. My stand has not changed.'

By Saturday evening the 'bandwagon effect' was in full swing. In fact, it had begun even earlier, around 4 p.m., when Patnaik went to Morarji and advised him to concede—he was playing the same role as on Friday afternoon, 29 May 1964! At 5 o'clock the first meeting of a State parliamentary group took place: Sukhadia met his Rajasthan M.P.s—only nine out of twenty-two were present—and tried to ensure their vote for Mrs. Gandhi by stressing Party unity, the coming general election, etc.; some resentment was felt for, as one of the participants noted, 'last time, at least, they consulted us, now they are not even doing that'.

This was accentuated by a noticeable feeling of elation within the CPP during the preceding twenty-four hours; with an impasse in the Grand Council on consensus, many thought their role in the selection process would be important, perhaps paramount; some even felt that the time had beckoned for initiative in establishing a meaningful precedent that the Parliamentary Party should function as an autonomous body; now the State leaders were throwing their weight about—and this in the year election tickets would be allocated by the leaders of the organization. Morarji had correctly sensed this mood and counted on it developing into a major 'revolt from below'; he was to be disappointed, for crass self-interest among the M.P.s was not likely to give way to a vague and only partly-shared principle of CPP autonomy—and the coalition leaders knew this.

The two other aspirants for support by the anti-Morarji forces joined the bandwagon, Chavan gracefully, Nanda less so. At 6 p.m. the Defence Minister telephoned Orissa's former Chief Minister, Dr. Mahtab, and said, in effect, ' Indira is their choice; I have given her my support, and Patil has come around.' Mrs. Gandhi confirmed Chavan's support in the evening and added to the press, significantly, that she and Chavan had been consulting all along; to the writer, the next day, she replied in the affirmative when asked whether it would be correct to say that they had been allies from the outset. Nanda announced his withdrawal ' in view of the wide measure of agreement over Mrs. Gandhi's candidature '. But his natural disappointment could not be easily contained. In the evening he telephoned Mishra and asked, ' what is all this happening? '; he was reminded of his remark four days earlier that the only other person under whom he would serve would be Mrs. Gandhi. Nanda acknowledged this but was troubled by a strain in his relations with Nehru's daughter caused, he said, by emissaries assuring him that she would not stand.

Mrs. Gandhi, too, confirmed this momentary friction, which came to the surface in a conversation with Nanda on Friday afternoon: Nanda claimed that he was certain of the support of a majority of the Chief Ministers; Mrs. Gandhi quietly dissented, on the basis of information available to her—and the events of Saturday proved her correct; there the matter ended. By Saturday evening Nanda adjusted to reality, as did his supporters on the Left, who had quietly canvassed on his behalf.

Mrs. Gandhi was not unaware of the Syndicate's reluctant acquiescence in her candidacy. She reportedly told one M.P. on Friday morning that she knew of Atulya's reservations and sought advice as to how to overcome them. The next morning she did something about it: Deputy Minister of Steel Sethi went to the Bengali leader and conveyed her concern; Atulya replied that he was in the hands of the Congress President—' any candidate of the Congress President is my candidate '. It is reasonable to surmise that by then, if not before, Atulya knew that Mrs. Gandhi was Kamaraj's candidate, and his knowledge of that fact must have been known to her. Efforts were also made to heal the breach with Patil—the Deputy Minister of External Affairs, Dinesh Singh, was the emissary. As for her relations with Kamaraj, who had steadfastly supported her behind the scenes, she publicly acknowledged his pre-eminent role to the press at the moment of her *de facto* triumph: ' He has asked me to stay at home until he calls me.' It was just as well, for on Saturday evening friends, admirers, and supplicants descended upon her home at 1 Safdarjang Road to celebrate her victory. She was quietly confident but she knew that the contest was not over.

By the night of the 15th the political fog had cleared: the intra-coalition struggle was over and the path set for a straight contest between Morarji and Mrs. Gandhi. There were some in the anti-Morarji camp who had hopes that unanimity could still be imposed. And that, indeed, was the only issue at the close of the day of breakthrough—consensus or contest; but even if it went to a secret ballot in the CPP, no one, except perhaps Morarji, had any doubt about the outcome.

The press set the tone. ' Indira Gandhi Likely to be Next Prime Minister' was the lead in the *Times of India* account of Saturday's events: ' The succession issue was practically settled today', it began. And the *Hindustan Times* wrote: ' . . . Mrs. Gandhi's election . . . should be considered assured.' The *Indian Express* pundit, Argus (Frank Moraes), concurred: ' Bar the tumult and the shouting, it looks as if Indira is in ' and Morarji ' will be badly beaten '. On the issue of consensus versus contest, the press, like the Party, was divided. The *Hindustan Times* favoured the latter in its Saturday editorial, ' Looking For A Leader': ' A straight contest . . . will be preferable . . . to a formal unanimity which only papers the cracks in the party. . . .' The *Statesman* (' Consensus or Contest ') demurred: a free vote is ' unexceptionable in principle ' but the ' search for consensus may have greater relevance '—because the Prime Minister represents the whole country and must have broad-based support. The *Patriot*, organ of the Left, virtually called for an imposed decision (' Objectives '): ' the Working Committee should assert its right to lead the party . . .'. On this point Morarji was to have the last word.

In terms of significance within the decision process as a whole, Saturday, 15 January 1966 was comparable to Sunday, 31 May 1964. The analogy is imperfect, however, because of the breakdown of consensus in the Grand Council during the second succession. One was a day of breakthrough, the other a day of decision, though, in perspective, their function was the same. Other themes bear attention at this point.

Patnaik's role, as noted, was identical; when he realized that the coalition had broken through the morass of disunity, he urged Morarji to withdraw. Morarji's role-change was the most striking: in 1964 he had yielded, now he was determined to fight. Thirdly, the Syndicate's pre-eminent role in the first succession was not repeated; at most, it delayed the formation of an effective anti-Morarji coalition and ultimately had to yield to pressures created by other power centres in the Party. One result was declining influence, still to be manifested. Another is that the coalition candidate, Mrs. Gandhi, owes nothing to the Caucus, unlike Shastri at first; her debt is to the Congress President and the Chief Ministers.

Kamaraj's role was undoubtedly important in the first succession—it was he who ascertained the consensus single-handed—but his influence derived, in part, from the solid and united backing of the Caucus. In the second succession, despite the apparent setback on the consensus issue in the Grand Council, he emerged as the towering figure by the close of the day of breakthrough : he forged a united anti-Morarji coalition, not only without the backing of the Caucus but in the teeth of sustained opposition. That he was able to do so was due partly to his extraordinary skill in the art of political management and partly to the co-operation of the Chief Ministers' club.

In objective terms, the second succession witnessed the emergence of an alliance between the head of the Congress organizational wing at the Centre and the State Government leaders; the organizational chiefs in the States played a marginal role. Few perceived it at the time, and some, including Kamaraj, denied it. But there can be no doubt of its reality—one of the most significant phenomena at the outset of the post-Shastri phase of Indian politics. How it will shape internal Congress politics and relations between the Union Government and the federating units will only gradually become apparent. Yet it should not occasion surprise for, as the decision process on food and language in 1964–5 amply revealed, there has been a marked accretion of influence by the States since Nehru's day; that trend was strengthened by the events from Tuesday, 11 January to Saturday, 15 January.

One cannot be certain of the precise distribution of influence *in this particular decision*. One might argue that Kamaraj was merely manipulating the Chief Ministers, as he had induced Syndicate acquiescence. One might also contend that the Chief Ministers' *démarche* was decisive in breaking Syndicate resistance and setting the bandwagon in motion. Almost certainly, each was 'using' the other, though not necessarily with conscious design. More relevant is the fact that there was a community of interests, mutually recognized, and it was that which served as the basis of the alliance. Both had two basic objectives—to beat Morarji and to create the best possible image for the general elections of 1967.

At one extreme were those who saw the Chief Ministers' meeting on Saturday as a mere instrument of Kamaraj's will and strategy. The *Hindustan Times* wrote: ' All this was obviously a matter of form. Long before the Chief Ministers' informal meeting was convened, it was known this morning that the Congress President considered Mrs. Gandhi the most suitable choice.' The *Economic Times* (16 January) echoed this view: Kamaraj's quiet diplomacy had led to several meetings between Chief Ministers and leaders of the High Command 'and eventually to this morning's meeting of Chief Ministers '.

This would suggest a superb illustration of ' controlled feedback ', with Kamaraj initiating and controlling the entire process. But this seems too rigid an interpretation of a complex inter-relationship of men and forces. One Chief Minister, obviously proud of the *démarche*, explained the discontent of the Caucus by saying that he and his colleagues ' had stolen their thunder '. But this, too, exaggerates the role of a specific component in the process. Closest to the mark, it would appear, is Nijalingappa's simply stated view: ' Kamaraj helped us to make up our minds ', referring to both the Syndicate and the Chief Ministers, and Kamaraj's remark, ' I allowed them to talk things out; I knew they would come around to the view that Mrs. Gandhi was the best choice.' It was through this continuous process of consultation, or ' talking it out ', in which Kamaraj was the pivot and the key listener, that the power centres in the Party arrived at an internal consensus. Kamaraj knew his mind, a distinct advantage. The Chief Ministers were concerned about the 1967 election and drew encouragement from the Congress President's views, gently conveyed. And the massive pressure built up by both induced acceptance by the Syndicate. The first two emerged stronger in the process—at the expense of the third.

Sunday, Monday, and Tuesday may be taken together as the post-climax phase of uneven contest: the Congress High Command and the Chief Ministers were ranged against the solitary Morarji, with a few allies scattered throughout the Party. Nonetheless, his attitude remained firm and consistent. To the remark by this writer on Sunday morning that ' the pressure on you is beginning to mount and will increase in intensity in the next few days ', he reacted casually: ' What does it matter, this pressure; I shall stand and I will win.' The rationale for his decision was that he would be doing a disservice to the country if he withdrew. ' And when I win, the democratic principle will become firmly established in the Congress.' As for his sources of strength, they were ' the rank-and-file M.P. in every State '. ' But will they vote freely or as directed ', he was asked. ' If they don't vote as they see fit, there is little hope for the Congress and the country.' The vivid impression he created on the morning of the 16th was a mixture of self-righteous principle—certainty that this was the right course of action—and stoic resignation—' whatever the outcome I shall persevere '. His communication network, as revealed by aides, was threefold: a stream of visitors to his home; [27] telephone conversations with numerous M.P.s; and an unidentified staff in the city campaigning on his behalf.

The bandwagon for Mrs. Gandhi gathered momentum on

Sunday, as a contest appeared more and more certain. Yet there was a comparative lull in political activity after the breakthrough of the previous day. Mrs. Gandhi was the first to visit Kamaraj on the 16th, followed by Subramaniam, Atulya and Reddy together, the Chief Ministers of Madras, Maharashtra, and Mysore individually, Krishna Menon, and CPP officials, Satya Narayan Sinha and K. C. Pant. But the most important caller at 4 Jantar Mantar Road, in terms of the succession struggle, was Jagjivan Ram, at 8.30 in the evening. His candidacy was obscure, his attitude to the two contestants even more so. When he emerged he promised to work for unanimity and remarked, ' I am sure that the Congress President will succeed '—a pointer to his action two days later, when he deserted Morarji and threw his support —estimates ranged from twenty to eighty votes—behind the coalition nominee. Nanda, too, reassured Mrs. Gandhi of his support, but he had not really given up hope: he telephoned Atulya in the evening and asked, ' what happened to the panel ' from which Kamaraj was to make a choice? The Congress President had selected one, was the reply, and he was advised to work for her; he agreed to do so. Atulya himself went to Mrs. Gandhi and conveyed his support.

The Morarji camp fought back by trying to exploit the under-current of resentment in the CPP and, perhaps, to set in motion a counter ' revolt from below '. Dr. Mahtab issued a Statement, the thrust of which was clear: ' . . . the responsibility of choosing the Prime Minister is that of the Members of Parliament. . . . While unanimous election of the leader is most desirable . . . election by vote is inherent in democracy. . . . To adopt all kinds of means in order to achieve apparent unanimity is the very negation of democracy. . . . [So too with] any kind of pressure or . . . any extraneous considerations to influence the opinion of members. . . .' Two Congress M.P.s from Assam, Chetia and Kakoty, echoed this view publicly, while others pressed the claim privately—in Central Hall and in private houses.

They were aided, ironically, by a group of seven prominent Opposition M.P.s who declared: ' It is strange that the voting rights of Members of Parliament are being virtually exercised by the Chief Ministers of States who are not even voters themselves.

This is a negation of democracy.' They also assailed All-India Radio 'for creating an atmosphere in favour of a particular candidate in the forthcoming contest', referring, apparently, to the 'Topic for Today' programme of Saturday evening which explained the Chief Ministers' role and the need to obtain their consent.[28] A former minister and publicist, K. Santhanam, also questioned the propriety of the Chief Ministers' role. But all efforts to mount a counter-offensive failed. Kamaraj merely expressed 'surprise' at the Opposition M.P.s' Statement and defended both the State leaders and All-India Radio; it was sufficient. Yet there was a conspicuous and important change in his attitude on Sunday evening: he told journalists he was not afraid of a contest nor even anxious to avoid it; his only desire was to avoid bitterness; by then he sensed that Morarji would not yield.

The controversy over the Chief Ministers' role dominated current comment during the last days of the drama. Argus (Moraes) observed on the 16th: 'It must be conceded that they [Morarjiites] have a point there.' Two days later there were three leaders on this topic. The *Hindu* ('Chief Ministers' Choice') termed their action legitimate because the Prime Minister 'represents the entire country' and the Union Government needs the co-operation of the States. The *Hindustan Times* ('In the Wings') concurred, in more expressive language: their role 'does not imply any attempt to usurp the rights of those entitled to appear on the stage. At best it only amounts to a claim to be in the wings instead of having to watch the scene from the gallery.' Nandan Kagal took the same view ('Choosing the Successor', in the *Times of India*): to call the Chief Ministers' act 'improper betrays a strange notion of the democratic process'. And the *Statesman* ('The Seat of Power') took a middle-of-the-road position: the CPP should be neither the sole elector nor 'relegated to the position of a mere ratifying body of a choice made elsewhere . . .'.

Monday was a day of hectic lobbying and canvassing for votes, as the coalition and Morarji mobilized their resources for the contest. Kamaraj appeared to be masterminding Mrs. Gandhi's campaign by getting State groups of M.P.s to meet and adopt resolutions favouring her for the Prime Ministership. This tactic of psycho-political warfare had already begun on Sunday: fourteen Punjab M.P.s met under the aegis of Swaran Singh and pledged their support; and Deputy Minister of External Affairs Dinesh Singh called a private meeting of some thirty younger M.P.s to enlist their support for Mrs. Gandhi. This technique gathered momentum on Monday. The parliamentarians from six States (Andhra, Bengal, Bihar, Delhi, Maharashtra, and Mysore) met separately with their Chief Minister or their State boss and, apart from Bihar, rallied to the coalition; Sahay of Bihar asked for unanimous support from his delegation; one man dissented, and the group dispersed without a vote. A corollary of this tactic was the exaggerated public claim by Chief Ministers that their M.P.s were solidly behind Mrs. Gandhi: Ram Kishan of the Punjab spoke of eighteen to twenty out of twenty-two votes; so, too, Sukhadia of Rajasthan; and P. C. Sen said only three or four of Bengal's M.P.s would stray from the path.

All through the day the pressure mounted, especially in the Central Hall of Parliament, where M.P.s whiled away the hours until most of the 551 eligible CPP voters had arrived, in response to a circular dispatched by the General Secretaries at the close of the Grand Council meeting on Friday. Another theme that day was the rebuttal of Morarji's allegation of interference by the Chief Ministers. Atulya took the lead. Democracy, he said, was not the mere counting of heads; it required consultation among all interested parties; he was 'vitally interested' in the outcome and had every right to advise his M.P.s. The Chief Ministers of Madras, Bihar, and Punjab echoed this view in separate statements—the Central Government, they argued, was not the sole concern of M.P.s. Morarji remained firm, describing himself as 'the M.P. candidate' and Mrs. Gandhi as 'the Congress President's candidate'. He was very active, telephoning a large number of M.P.s and holding a press conference in the evening, while his supporters in the CPP kept up an incessant campaign of canvassing among their colleagues. Mrs. Gandhi, by contrast, left the canvassing to her followers; one or two M.P.s from each State were given responsibility for getting out the vote.

Kamaraj's home remained the centre of coalition activity. No less than eight Chief Ministers called on him individually on Monday, as did Atulya and Reddy together. There were two other group consultations with the Congress President—Fakhruddin Ahmed of Assam, Darbara Singh, P. C. Sen, and Naik at 7 p.m., and the Chief Ministers of Bihar, Madhya Pradesh, Maharashtra, and Rajasthan at 8.30, all presumably to co-ordinate tactics.

There was an interesting rumour afloat on Monday afternoon —that Nanda would be an acceptable compromise if the two leading contestants withdrew. Morarji denied this publicly. And, when a Chief Minister relayed it to Kamaraj, with the added speculation that Patil was responsible, the Congress President brushed it aside as untrue: it was widely believed that Nanda himself had circulated the idea in a desperate bid to stay on as Prime Minister. In any event, Atulya buried it when he announced that, even if Morarji and Mrs. Gandhi and the whole Congress agreed to elect Nanda unanimously, he, personally, would contest the decision. Atulya was vocal on another rumour —that a Cabinet list had already been drawn up. 'Do you think', he replied, 'we are lacking in ordinary decency [and would] bargain about seats in the Cabinet [before electing a person]?' Opposition M.P.s also entered the fringes of the struggle that day. Bagri of the Samyukta (United) Socialist Party (SSP) declared that democracy required the Prime Minister to be a member of the Lok Sabha—which Bhupesh Gupta of the Right CPI denied—and termed Mrs. Gandhi's candidacy a 'conspiracy to install a weak person at the helm of affairs'.

Tuesday was much the same, with hectic canvassing by both sides. Almost all other State parliamentary groups met and proclaimed their support for Mrs. Gandhi. Morarji's technique was individual canvassing by telephone—around the clock. A tone of anger and sharpness, however, crept into his pronouncements that day, both at a press conference and in a three-page 'open letter' to Congress M.P.s: '. . . those who, by virtue of their positions had a special responsibility to be above personal prejudices and animus, seem to have decided that the search for unanimity should mean the elimination of all those whom they

do not like '. There was also reference to ' unhealthy precedents
. . . in the effort to claim unanimous support for the choice of a
few people who are in positions of authority ' and to pressure
' to foil the secrecy of the ballot . . .'; it was very close to the
bone.

Atulya took up the challenge and issued an equally pungent
rejoinder: it was ' an insult to every single Congress M.P. and
to the Congress organization as a whole ', for it was ' ridiculous
in this year of grace 1966 ' to suggest that anybody could get a
single vote through threats or pressure. He also propounded the
novel view that Morarji's act in becoming a candidate without
consulting his colleagues in the High Command was ' highly
undemocratic ', a symptom of the ' mother Congress ' syndrome
in Indian politics.

Jagjivan Ram made a brief entry on to the stage in the early
afternoon, when he called on Morarji in an effort to mediate.
Rebuffed, the Untouchable leader then announced his support for
Mrs. Gandhi. With the defections of Patnaik and Jagjivan Ram,
as in 1964, Morarji's prospects fell even further; but he held fast.

The climax to this phase in the struggle was a brief meeting
between the two real protagonists—Morarji and Kamaraj—at the
former's home shortly after 6 p.m. According to Morarji, the
Congress President did not make a specific request to him to
withdraw. He asked Kamaraj, ' Does unity mean that I should
withdraw? '—and got no reply. He then asked, ' What crime
have I committed? '—and again there was no reply. Kamaraj
merely expressed the opinion that ' the other candidate would get
a majority ', and Morarji countered, ' tomorrow the ballot box
will show '. Kamaraj's account, to his own press conference on
Tuesday evening, was essentially the same, though he indicated
that he had formally asked Morarji to withdraw; he also brushed
aside the question whether there were only two candidates.

It remained only to confirm the decision: this was done by
the CPP on Wednesday 19 January. By 11 a.m., when the session
was due to begin, 526 Congress M.P.s were present in the domed
Central Hall for the first contested election to the leadership;

twenty-six had come from hospital beds for the occasion. Kamaraj presided, with Nanda to his right and CPP officials all around him. He displayed the large, elevated—empty—ballot box and placed it in front of the presiding table.

The procedure was orderly—after Tyagi, who had just resigned from the Cabinet over the Tashkent Declaration, had walked over to the microphone and objected to the meeting being photographed and filmed, adding his own displeasure about an intra-party ballot. Mrs. Gandhi was nominated by Nanda and seconded by Sanjiva Reddy. Morarji was nominated by Hanumanthaiya of Mysore and seconded by Tika Ram Paliwal of Rajasthan; no speeches were made. The balloting then began: each eligible voter walked to the presiding table, received his ballot paper, walked to a concealed closed booth, cast his vote and then returned to drop it in the box. It was a slow process, including a rather long count—1½ hours to count 524 ballots twice. Eventually, just after 3 p.m., the Returning Officer, G. S. Pathak, fought his way to the microphone and said, 'I declare Mrs. Indira Gandhi elected . . .'; the rest of his words were drowned in the applause. The vote was 355 to 169; neither of the contestants exercised the privilege of casting their ballots. Then came the speeches: first, Kamaraj, who stressed the formidable problems facing India today—food, economic crisis, and tension on the borders; then Nanda, who invoked the memory of Nehru and Shastri, and called for complete support for the newly-chosen Leader; then Morarji, invited at the suggestion of Kamaraj. He offered 'full co-operation and good wishes and goodwill', repeated at the end of his remarks; but the main thrust of his speech was a thinly-disguised attack on the coalition, as he referred half a dozen times to the need 'to create an atmosphere of fearlessness' in the Congress. Finally, Mrs. Gandhi spoke, at first in Hindi, leading some to wonder whether the general election campaign had begun; she also spoke in English, more briefly and less well. There were appropriate references to the occasion and a declaration of faith in the capacity of India's people to meet the crises that now faced them, as so often in the past. Profusely garlanded, the victor made her way through the excited crowds massed near Parliament. The second succession was over.

After a ceaseless round of consultations, the Prime Minister-designate presented the list of her Council of Ministers to President Radhakrishnan at 2.45 a.m. on Monday 24 January. That afternoon they were sworn in. There were some changes: the addition of Asoka Mehta, former Congress Socialist and PSP leader, in the new post of Minister of Planning; G. S. Pathak, a U.P. barrister, to the Law portfolio; and Fakhruddin Ahmed, the Congress organization leader in Assam, to Irrigation and Power. The energetic Manubhai Shah was promoted to Cabinet rank, in the same portfolio, Commerce, and Jagjivan Ram returned, this time to Labour, Employment and Rehabilitation; there were also some changes at the Minister of State and Deputy Minister level, and some reorganization of ministerial responsibilities. Some expressed displeasure that more drastic changes had not taken place—they would have done if the effort to move Nanda from the Home Ministry to the post of Leader of the House and Minister without Portfolio had succeeded; he balked, even though he was assured of the No. 2 rank. Compared with Shastri's retention of the Nehru Cabinet virtually unchanged in 1964, Mrs. Gandhi's action seemed drastic, though to some not drastic enough. Yet a 'new look' had come to the summit of India's Government.

IX

COMPARISON

VIEWED in terms of political dynamics, the succession may be likened to a game. Both in 1964 and 1966 there appeared to be a multiple choice but in reality there were only two players—Morarji and the coalition; the role of all other individual actors must be seen as impinging upon, deflecting, blurring, and crystallizing the two real constants in the game. Yet the decision process differed markedly in India's experience of political change at the summit.

The proper designation of the 1964 game is 'Morarji *v.* a United Front'; in 1966 it was 'Morarji *v.* the Pack'. This contrast derives from the different setting in which the games were played and highlights revealing differences in decision-making. It was the psychological atmosphere and the manner in which the object of play—the Prime Ministership—became accessible that explains the change in environment and actions of the players.

Long before Nehru died the Congress élite had pondered the issue of succession with concern and disquiet: the towering position of Nehru for seventeen years, the entire period of independence, and the relentless uncertainty of a watchful world had created doubt, even fear, whether a smooth succession could be achieved. The gradual decline in vigour and health of India's charismatic leader had the political compensation, however, that steps could be taken to fill the vacuum—if not directly by him, then by careful planning among the Party leaders. And those preparations were made, with skill and finesse, as the analysis of the first succession laid bare. From Tirupathi (October 1963) onwards, certainly after Nehru's grave illness at Bhubaneswar (January 1964), a powerful coalition had come into being, the Syndicate, headed by Kamaraj, and with it an agreed choice, Shastri. Nehru's role in the game, objectively perceived and possibly consciously performed as well, was to ease the transition and tranquillize the play by casting symbolic approval on the choice—by bringing Shastri back into the Cabinet soon after he became incapacitated: it was not enough to foreclose the game but sufficient to shape its character. In perspective, Shastri was the partial recipient of Nehru's mantle. Thus, a combination of fear of the collapse of the political system, widely-shared and genuinely felt, time to prepare the ground, a coalition to direct the play, a pre-eminent player, and the charismatic leader's approval determined the flow of events, the character and the outcome of the game.

How different was the setting of the second succession, only nineteen months later. Fear had given way to self-confidence because India's political system had demonstrated ability of a high order in filling the void caused by Nehru's passing. Nor were the 'eyes of the world' upon the players, partly because of preoccupations elsewhere—notably the *coup* in Nigeria—partly because the death of Nehru was viewed as the end of an era and that of Shastri was not, and partly because of the precedent of stability in 1964. There was, then, no sense of urgency to fill the vacuum—'if Shastri could rise to the occasion, any one of us can'. Thus unity in the face of the unknown was no longer a compelling restraint on the actors. The suddenness of Shastri's death was a further variable, for little if any thought had been given to 'after Shastri, who?' and no preparations had been made for this contingency. Apart from the lack of time, the coalition of 1964 had eroded—Kamaraj had moved away from, and above, his Syndicate colleagues. Further, there was no pre-eminent candidate for the second succession, and the Caucus was unenthusiastic about any of the alternatives—except for united opposition to Morarji. Finally, the leader had not lived long enough to transmit, by word or deed, his mantle to any other player, for he was too busy establishing his own claim to primacy.

The result was a change in the set of rules and in the decision process, though the players were identical, except for Shastri. In the first game there was one smooth and relatively frictionless phase of decision-making between Wednesday afternoon, 27 May 1964, when Nehru died, and Sunday morning, the 31st, when the Grand Council accepted the consensus principle, leaving the decision, in effect, to Kamaraj and the Caucus. Morarji challenged the united front briefly but he displayed self-imposed restraint, both on Sunday morning and again the following evening when he yielded to the Congress President's judgement of the consensus. In the second game two phases were evident. The first was a struggle of wills among the anti-Morarji forces, with Kamaraj, Mishra, Nijalingappa and others favouring Mrs. Gandhi, the ' Big Three ' of the Syndicate opposing her, and the majority of players awaiting a lead; it lasted from Tuesday morning, 11 January, until Saturday night, the 15th. The second phase took the form of an open contest between Morarji and the coalition, pragmatically united behind Mrs. Gandhi, from 16 to 19 January. It is this which explains the difference in the duration of the games, three and a half days in the first, almost nine days in the second succession.

Decision-making in the two games may also be compared in terms of the power centres through whom the decision had to pass before it was consummated. In 1964 there were only two ' circles of decision '. The core group was the Syndicate, including Kamaraj, which had made its choice before the game began. Its task was relatively simple—to persuade the Grand Council of the Republic, in which it was the dominant pressure group, and this was accomplished swiftly and without much conflict on Sunday 31 May. In 1966, however, the process was much more complex and difficult. Four ' circles of decision ' can be discerned: the core was Kamaraj himself, with a clear and firm choice, though he may have wavered in the direction of Chavan when unanimity still seemed possible; the second circle was the disunited Syndicate which could not agree on any candidate and only did so when faced with a *fait accompli*; the third power group was the Chief Ministers' club which, partly on its own and partly under Kamaraj's gentle prodding, played an autonomous role in the process; and, finally, the Congress Parliamentary Party had to be convinced in a secret ballot. In numbers these four circles followed an ascending order, 1, 4, 12, and 526. In time-sequence the process was somewhat blurred, apart from Kamaraj at the outset and the CPP at the end of the game. The relationship of the Caucus and the Chief Ministers in both a time-sequence and the cause-effect flow is less orderly. Both accepted Mrs. Gandhi the same day, Saturday the 15th, but the first was passive and the second active in its approval. Indeed, as suggested earlier, the Syndicate acquiesced under joint pressure mounted by the first and third ' circles ', Congress President and the Chief Ministers' club. It is in this sense that the term ' alliance ' to describe the objective play of Kamaraj and the State leaders seems valid. There is no evidence to suggest that it was forged before the second game, as the Syndicate was before the first. Nor was there a pre-arranged candidate between these allies. Kamaraj took the lead, and the Chief Ministers, in their own interests, saw the wisdom of the choice. They then combined forces, with an indeterminate degree of collusion, to overcome the opposition, doubts, and reservations of the Caucus; this took five days, from Tuesday to Saturday. When the second ' circle ' was attached to the decision, it was a foregone conclusion that the fourth, the CPP, would approve as well. This occupied almost four days because of the insistence by one player, Morarji, that the game be played to the bitter end.

A comparison of the two successions in terms of ' phases ' and ' circles of decision ' leads one to some reflections on the forces at play in the two games. As noted earlier, some of the enduring forces in Indian politics were manifested in 1964: regionalism, State parochialism, caste identity, and factionalism. To what extent were these evident in 1966? Regionalism was certainly displayed in the attitudes to a number of players. Chavan was rejected largely because of his alienation of the South—in the interests of his own State, Maharashtra. Indeed, to say that he lost Delhi over Goa is not without an element of truth. Morarji, too, had deeply offended the South—in fact, the entire non-Hindi ' rimland ' of India—by this rigid espousal of Hindi as the national language. One of Nanda's liabilities was that he did not represent a definable region. And Mrs. Gandhi had the great asset that, of all the candidates, she alone came from the Hindi ' heartland '; even more, from its core, Uttar Pradesh.

State attachments were no less apparent in the calculations of the four power centres of decision. Chavan's main corporate strength came from Maharashtra. The one State whose bloc of votes Morarji could count upon, with few defections, was Gujarat. Nanda's weakness was evident here too, for he lacked an independent base of power in any State. And Mrs. Gandhi, though she eschews identity with her home State, could expect to draw a substantial number of votes from U.P.—and Kamaraj, the Syndicate, the Chief Ministers, and the CPP knew this. Nanda or even Chavan could not make the same dent in this bloc of 84 votes if pitted against Morarji, who championed the cause of Hindi and was supported by former Chief Minister C. B. Gupta; Mrs. Gandhi, as the ' favourite daughter ', could. And Nijalingappa's Mysore would probably have voted *en masse* against Chavan, with a possible multiplier effect in other States.

Caste plays a major role in State and local politics but is marginal at the all-India level; there is no evidence that it operated in either succession—except in so far as it was intertwined with factionalism, which was present in both. The Gupta group in U.P. supported Morarji in 1964 and 1966, though defections to the ' favourite son ' were expressed in advance of the Shastri consensus and, almost certainly, were reflected in the secret ballot of the second game. Chief Minister Sahay of Bihar was unable to join his colleagues in the ' draft Mrs. Gandhi ' Statement because of a strong anti-Indira faction in his State. And such dissident leaders as Mahtab of Orissa, Hanumanthaiya of Mysore, and Paliwal of Rajasthan backed Morarji.

The phenomenon of dissidence, widespread and widely known, came to the surface of all-India Congress politics on Wednesday 19 January—though there were precedents for such an eruption. No other explanation is possible for the surprising number of votes received by Morarji. The only bloc of votes assured to him was Gujarat, with 26, and even some of those went to the coalition candidate; but Morarji polled 169. The difference can only be explained in part by U.P. and Bihar factional support. What appears to have taken place was widespread individual dissidence reflecting resentment against direction from above, and the *secret* ballot made it possible to express this. Many who had a grievance—against Kamaraj or any member of the Syndicate or his Chief Minister—voted against their nominee. It was the first time that the dimensions of faction and dissent in the CPP could be gauged precisely.

For Morarji, perhaps, these factors provided the consolation of preventing rout and humiliation. The opposition vote, almost one-third, was not large enough to undermine the coalition or the victor but sufficient not to obliterate the vanquished. As Argus (Moraes) remarked aptly (*Indian Express*, 20 January), Morarji ' has lost the battle [but] has salvaged his political soul '. It would not be easy to ignore him or the dissidents in the future. For Kamaraj and others the degree of dissent must have come as a shock: a dozen estimates given to the writer in the two days before the poll ranged from 100 to 130; some coalition leaders had hopes that Morarji would secure even less than 100. Whether the ' upset ' will be reflected in an effort at reconciliation cannot yet be determined—but neither Morarji nor any of his followers was invited to join the Cabinet, as they were by Shastri. The distribution of Congress tickets for the 1966 Rajya Sabha election and the 1967 general elections will illuminate this point.

The forces that shaped the outcome of the second succession were not identical to those responsible for the Shastri consensus, though they were strikingly similar in terms of institutional interests. To use the lock metaphor once again, the succession to Shastri may be likened to a safe with a complex combination: the head of the Congress organization at the Centre plus twelve of the fourteen Chief Ministers plus (reluctant) support of the Syndicate plus an overwhelming majority in the Parliamentary Party plus a compulsion to keep Morarji out plus concern about the 1967 general elections. Only Mrs. Gandhi fitted that combination in 1966, and Kamaraj knew its composition. Stated in different terms, Mrs. Gandhi was the key to the second succession, and Kamaraj deftly unlocked the door. It was a brilliant feat of political management.

As in the first game, there was a sophisticated interplay of institutional interest groups, notably the Working Committee, the Chief Ministers' club, and the CPP Executive. But associational interests were marginal, apart from the factional type; organized caste and communal groups played no role. Nor did trade unions or business organizations influence the decision. And the Syndicate was a disturbing element in the smooth flow of the game.　Also, unlike 1964, the press did not back any of the players.

Analysis is always rendered easier by hindsight.　Yet the political assets of Mrs. Gandhi seem so formidable that the outcome of the game should have been apparent at the start of play. One member of the Grand Council put it succinctly: 'The Congress needs a winner in 1967—and she is it.　She is well-liked in the South [partly because of her dramatic Nehru-like gesture of flying to Madras during the language riots in January 1965], she has a following in U.P., Bihar, etc. [the Hindi ' heartland ']. She has a national appeal, the Nehru name in the countryside.　She is a natural leader for the Congress.　These qualifications also ensured a victory over Morarji—and were possessed by neither Chavan nor Nanda.

One of the Chief Ministers cited additional reasons: she has the widest international contacts of any of the candidates, an invaluable asset in the current state of food and foreign exchange crises; the minorities would feel more secure with a Nehru as Prime Minister than with any other Congress leader; and her link with Kashmir would strengthen India's claim and possibly create popular support in the disputed State.　A member of the Syndicate added a novel reason for the choice, namely, that the South and the non-Hindi area in general should not alienate the Hindi ' heartland ' further by depriving it of representation in the three highest offices in the country.　More to the point, he observed that the Congress is relatively weaker and more faction-ridden in the Hindi area and that it faces a serious challenge from the Jan Sangh; a Prime Minister ' who can speak to these people [voters] in their own language ' is essential.　Another person noted that the Nehru mantle would help to carry Mrs. Gandhi's words (and with it the Congress election platform) to large masses in the countryside, as well as to special communities like the Muslims and the Untouchables.

The case for Mrs. Gandhi as coalition candidate and Congress Prime Minister was overwhelming.　Morarji's appraisal—' as long as two men [Kamaraj and Mishra of Madhya Pradesh] know their minds and the others are uncertain, the two will triumph '—misses the crucial point.　The second succession was managed by a few people, but they represented powerful forces in the Indian polity. Like all players in a political game, their authority and roles derived from their constituency—region, State, and party organization.

The behaviour of the principal actors in the second succession has been dissected in detail. But the strategy and tactics employed require further elucidation. The principal player was Kamaraj, whose dexterity and skill in manipulating others in the game command respect. Yet his strategy remained obscure during the first five days. Reticent about his choice in public and within the Caucus, he strove to build a massive coalition which would compel surrender by the other principal player or, if necessary, defeat him in open battle. To accomplish this it was necessary to persuade or cajole other power centres in the Party.

First and foremost was the Syndicate, whose influence flowed from control over a substantial bloc of votes and the prestige acquired in the management of the first succession. Kamaraj knew of its disunity on all possible candidates of the coalition. Instead of applying the tactic of direct assault, he resorted to encirclement, using the Chief Ministers' club as his instrument. He avoided alienation of the Caucus by allowing them ' to talk things out' while building up relentless pressure in favour of Mrs. Gandhi which would feed back to ' the four' through the State leaders. At the same time, he used his prestige to persuade the Chief Ministers, not only that his choice was wise and in the best interests of the Party and the nation, but also that they should take the initiative in extending the network of support. By Saturday the 15th the strategic goal was attained—a viable and effective coalition had been created. It remained only to canvass in the CPP to achieve as dramatic a victory as possible. Whether he intended to eliminate the opposing player, Morarji, from all future games or merely to teach him a lesson is open to judgement. But the overall strategy was eminently successful.

Morarji's behaviour in the early days was a mixture of caution and disdain for the political game. Indeed, he revealed a desire for the crown but no strategy to achieve it. His only object until Friday was to veto a consensus, for this would have foreclosed further play. Thereafter, as the Kamaraj-led coalition took definite shape, he yielded to the urging of his followers and began to campaign actively. Having scored a tactical victory—an open contest—he tried to capitalize on resentment in the CPP and propel a 'revolt from below'. It was the only sensible strategy, for there had been a conspicuous erosion of his strength during the nineteen months of Shastri's tenure. The other three 'circles of decision' were beyond his reach, though he did try to mobilize dissident groups in the States to his side. His tactic was individual canvassing, bringing to bear his seniority in the Congress élite and his reputation for integrity, administrative experience, and decisiveness. The odds were heavily against him and he was defeated but by no means eliminated from the political arena.

Mrs. Gandhi's strategy, too, can be deduced from deeds and words. This time, she was keen from the beginning of the game and saw no reason why she should not be Prime Minister. One cynic in the Grand Council expressed the opinion that, in her view, only the Nehrus are fit to govern India. In any event, a shrewd political instinct led to caution; she did not push herself forward and never *formally* declared her candidacy. From the three stages of her gradual entry into the game—conditional support for Nanda, availability, and willingness to contest—it appeared that she was determined not to make a hasty commitment. She waited for the 'call' from Kamaraj and the Chief Ministers, for she knew that nobody could win without their support. Like Shastri in 1964, she did not canvass for votes or even for support in the power centres of decision—except for the understanding reached with Chavan the afternoon before the Grand Council met; nor did she have to, for there were many no less interested than she in her victory. At what point in the game she knew that the 'call to office' would be sounded remains unclear; but she felt sufficiently confident by Friday evening, the 14th, to enter the contest. Yet she never became an active player. The 'call' came the following day and, quietly, she set about to offset resentment in the Syndicate and thereby to make the coalition more secure—by sending emissaries to Atulya and Patil on Saturday, the day of breakthrough.

Chavan's behaviour was similar to that of Mrs. Gandhi: he was keen but cautious—and was never an active player in the game. He allowed his Maharashtrian supporters to make known his availability and to probe the reaction; Naik played the key role in this strategy. When it became apparent that a consensus among the anti-Morarji forces was crystallizing in favour of Mrs. Gandhi—but not before then—he offered her his support; but even then, on Thursday afternoon, the 13th, he left the door open for a shift in his favour by securing a reciprocal gesture. After the Chief Ministers' *démarche* on Saturday he withdrew gracefully, for he regarded Mrs. Gandhi as the most preferable alternative to himself. Of all the candidates, real and potential, apart from the victor, he emerged with his image and position intact—in fact, enhanced; and time is on his side: he is only fifty-three.

Nanda's strategy was simple—to maintain the *status quo*. And he could press his claim with greater plausibility in 1966 than in 1964, for a general election was pending and there was no pre-eminent candidate. He was, indeed, the most active player in the second game, as the earlier narrative revealed. He took every opportunity to persuade his colleagues of the value of interim continuity, and some were well-disposed. But he suffered from widespread doubt about his ability to defeat Morarji in a secret ballot and his image as Congress leader in the elections of 1967. Kamaraj and some members of the Caucus were opposed; so too were many of the State leaders; Nanda lacked popularity at all levels. Nor was he aided by reports, unconfirmed, that he was being backed by some business houses and the Left. Had Morarji withdrawn, the fact of his being in office might have been sufficient to keep him there. When a contest seemed certain, however, he was effectively dislodged.

The behaviour of lesser players has been noted. Patnaik followed the pattern of 1964—supporting Morarji at the outset and then throwing his weight behind the coalition candidate. Jagjivan Ram also began by supporting Morarji but ultimately yielded to the consensus. But both were more active in the first game, Patnaik as a key organizer in the Morarji campaign and Ram as close ally and then independent candidate of consequence.

Their influence in the second succession was less important, though one aide claimed that but for their 'defections' Morarji might have triumphed. Among the Chief Ministers, Mishra of Madhya Pradesh was the most active and prominent, welding the State leaders into a cohesive force behind Mrs. Gandhi. The first to raise the idea of Mrs. Gandhi as a suitable candidate was Sukhadia of Rajasthan, as early as Wednesday the 12th. The Left was much less in evidence than in 1964, their activity being more proportionate to their influence in each game. Certainly there was no evidence of support for Morarji at any stage, as widely reported in the first succession. Menon saw Kamaraj daily but disclaimed any other form of activity, and from Sunday the 16th at any rate he made known that he would vote for Mrs. Gandhi. Some participants suggested that both he and Malaviya favoured Nanda at an earlier stage, but this remains conjectural.

Three stages may be perceived in the flow of candidates into the game of 1966. Nanda and Morarji entered at the outset and were so identified as early as the day of Shastri's death; but Nanda did not have to say so, for he held the office, and Morarji refrained from proclaiming his candidacy until the Grand Council meeting on Friday. A flurry of names were floated on Wednesday and Thursday—Kamaraj, Patil, Reddy, and Jagjivan Ram—but none except Ram encouraged the idea. Finally, on Friday evening, the victor stepped forth on to the stage. Stated in different terms, the two persons for whom this was 'now or never'—Nanda and Morarji—jumped in first. The two who have time on their side—Mrs. Gandhi and Chavan—remained cautious and guarded until the direction of events became clear; the former then entered and the latter withdrew from the contest.

Various differences between the successions of 1964 and 1966 have already been noted. Yet there are others which merit attention. To begin with, Shastri was the pre-eminent candidate, whereas Mrs. Gandhi *emerged* from a process of elimination. The Congress President and some Chief Ministers favoured her from the outset, but few regarded her as the obvious outstanding choice. In a sense, Mrs. Gandhi owed her triumph to three persons: Kamaraj, for superb management of the game; her father, for providing the name and mantle; and Morarji, for pressing the issue to a secret ballot. Indeed, it was his insistence that turned the tide in the coalition's ultimate choice; apart from anything else, she alone was certain to win.

It is always hazardous, but intriguing, to assess 'what might have been'. Had the 1964 consensus pattern been repeated, Nanda's prospects would have improved. Despite the Congress President's known opposition, he might have accepted the continuance of the *status quo* for a year—willingly or under Syndicate pressure. Alternatively, he might have favoured the more experienced Chavan, as he indicated privately in mid-stream; the Defence Minister's prestige had risen in the euphoria following the war with Pakistan. And if Kamaraj had yielded to the pressure to enter the contest himself, Mrs. Gandhi would have withdrawn. Thus, Morarji in defeat exerted a profound influence on the outcome of the second game.

The role of the Syndicate and of Kamaraj in the two successions was alluded to earlier: the change in their relationship was not—and it is both revealing and important. In essence, the myth of the Syndicate's power was drastically undermined, if not shattered, by the events of mid-January 1966. Erosion of their influence had already taken place during Shastri's tenure of office. But their inability to block Mrs. Gandhi and, even more, their disunity during the crucial game dramatized the decline in the public view. One astute observer cautioned that they would remain together to fight another day and should not therefore be ruled out as a continuing pressure group in the Congress hierarchy of decision. And one Chief Minister indicated that it would be unwise to alienate them in an election year. Nonetheless, the Caucus suffered a damaging blow.

The influence of Kamaraj, by contrast, is now at its peak. He was the principal figure in both successions, but the second was infinitely more complex: there was no pre-eminent candidate, the Syndicate opposed his choice, and consensus had given way to contest. Hence the Congress President's achievement as king-maker (or 'queen-maker') was of a higher order. Some detractors suggested that his ability is confined to building a consensus or a victorious coalition in moments of political trauma. But even if this is true, and the evidence is by no means convincing, this is an extraordinary skill, and Kamaraj has performed an invaluable service to India's political system.

His success in the second game was partly due to the sustained co-operation of the Chief Ministers, whose role was far more conspicuous than in 1964. Indeed, they replaced the Syndicate as the Congress President's principal pillar of support. More important, the role of the State leaders confirmed and strengthened the trend to decentralization of power in the Indian Union, vividly demonstrated in decision-making over food and language policy. This important strand in the web of Indian politics, long submerged by the charisma of Nehru, has now been asserted in seemingly irrevocable form, with far-reaching implications still to unfold.

A curious feature of the 1966 succession was the inconsequential role of the Congress organizational leaders in the States; rather, it was the State governmental leaders who held the centre of the stage. In fact, the second game was dominated by an alliance between the head of the all-India organizational wing of the Party and the heads of the governmental wing in the federal units; together they overcame the resistance of a pressure group in the organizational wing at the Centre and ensured Mrs. Gandhi's victory. What consequences will flow from this unusual pact will become apparent during the imminent election campaign and beyond.

Another difference between the two successions was the role of the Congress Parliamentary Party: in 1964 it was a mere rubber stamp for a decision reached by the Working Committee; in 1966 it exercised the franchise in a secret ballot. For three days it was the principal object of attention, as both camps canvassed furiously for support. And then, on Wednesday 19 January, the CPP held the centre of the stage. Whether this precedent of relative autonomy—M.P.s were subjected to massive pressure—will transform the Parliamentary Party into an independent power centre remains an open question. But those who aspire to this status and influence have been given a thin wedge with which to assert the claim.   Certainly the CPP cannot be totally ignored in the future.

Stated in other terms, the second succession legitimized decision-making by overt conflict.   This had happened occasionally in elections to the Congress presidency, notably in 1950, when Tandon, Sardar Patel's candidate, defeated Kripalani, who had Nehru's backing; but it had never occurred in the CPP.   It is likely to occur again.   This, too, was Morarji's contribution to the developing pattern of Indian politics.

The decision by ballot had other consequences.   It challenged the myth of unqualified control of blocs of votes by party leaders of national, as well as regional and State, stature notably members of the Syndicate; the size of Morarji's vote showed, among other things, that their ability ' to deliver the vote ' was not absolute. This, in turn, brought into the public view a hitherto-concealed, though not unknown, factor of Centre-State relations: many M.P.s are expatriates from intra-State factional squabbles, ' exiled ' to Delhi by those in power; their factional identity was expressed in dissent from Chief Ministers' ' advice '.   And this was made possible by a secret ballot.   An open contest had laid bare this interplay of diverse loyalties in national and State Congress politics.

To complete this catalogue of differences between the two successions, it may be noted that the Military played no role whatsoever in 1966, nor was there any talk or rumour of its involvement, as there was in 1964; also that there was no organized conclave of Muslim M.P.s, and that the role of the Left was less vocal than in the first game.   A final—disquieting— contrast was the set of criteria applied by the actors in assessing the qualifications of the different candidates.   Shastri was chosen partly because of Party interests—he was considered the man most likely to unify and strengthen the Congress; but much thought was also given to ' national interests '—who would serve India most effectively in a time of trouble.   In 1966, however, the latter consideration was *never* raised, except by Morarji; not once was it mentioned in any of this writer's interviews and discussions with members of the coalition.   The only concerns appeared to be ' to beat Morarji ' and ' to win the 1967 general

election '. In that sense the second succession was much more a
Party affair.

The similarities were fewer in number and can be delineated
more briefly, but they are no less important. One was *tranquillity*,
which indicated an instinctive and intellectual grasp of the rules
of the Congress game. It was the mythology and tradition of
' Mother Congress ' that provided both the ballast for a tranquil
process and the framework for peaceful competition among and
within the key interest groups—the Working Committee, the
Chief Ministers' club, the CPP, and the Syndicate—with a commitment by all not to destroy the symbol or the substance of
unity. Another similarity was *maturity* and *resilience*, accentuated in the second succession by the contrasting method of
political change at the summit in India's counterpart in Africa—
a *coup* in Nigeria.

In both successions, too, *constitutional propriety* was demonstrated. The President filled the vacuum within hours and,
later, appointed as Prime Minister the person elected as Leader
of the Congress Parliamentary Party, though the election was
unanimous in the first and contested in the second. Finally, the
Congress élite managed both processes; they were largely leadership decisions—but the leaders spoke for large and well-defined
constituencies.

Can one anticipate that this dramatic challenge to consensual
decision will shatter the unity of the Congress, or is its resilience
such that it can be absorbed? The answer cannot be definitive,
but the possibility of a split in the near future seems remote—
unless the coalition leaders cause it by *force majeure*, i.e., by
depriving Morarji and his supporters of due representation in
Party and Parliament and of the opportunity to influence policy
and patronage. Two reasons suggest themselves: the mystique
of the Congress, to which Morarji is strongly committed (other
leaders in his position might well respond differently); and the
belief, strongly supported by experience, that withdrawal from
the Congress means the political wilderness; thus far, at any rate,
the path to influence and success in politics has been through the
Congress.

The succession of 1966, like that in 1964, was an impressive democratic process, conducted in the full public view—domestic and foreign—with no qualms about concealing the lobbying and bargaining throughout. Perhaps the most apt comment came from Atulya Ghosh: 'Last time we did it [by consensus] because of our inferiority complex. The British and American newspapers had cried so long, " after Nehru, who? ", and so we yielded to it. There is no need of this any longer. We are politically mature.'

NOTES

I RATIONALE

[1] Dankwart A. Rustow, 'Succession in the Twentieth Century', *Journal of International Affairs*, Vol. XVIII, No. 1 (1964), 105. The information in this and the preceding paragraph is drawn from Rustow's concise and lucid survey.

[2] At the sub-national level, a peaceful change in the governing party occurred in India's State of Kerala in 1957; the Communist Party of India formed a government for two and a half years but it was dismissed from office by the proclamation of President's Rule in 1959, following widespread agitation within the State.

[3] *Jerusalem Post*, 16 May 1965.

[4] For an account of Ben-Gurion's resignation and some implications of Eshkol's succession to the Prime Ministership of Israel in 1963, see Jon Kimche, 'Succession and the Legacy in Israel', *Journal of International Affairs*, loc. cit., 43–53.

[5] On Nehru's diverse roles, see M. Brecher, *Nehru: A Political Biography*, 1959, esp. ch. XX. A thoughtful but unconvincing expression of concern about the future of Indian politics may be found in Selig Harrison, *India: The Most Dangerous Decades*, 1960. On the candidates for succession, see Welles Hangen, *After Nehru, Who?*, 1963.

II BACKGROUND

[Wherever remarks are attributed to individuals, and no source is given, these are derived from interviews conducted by the author. A specific source is given for the first selection from each interview.]

[1] The first widely-reported incident occurred at Longju, in the north-east, on 25 August 1959; the second, at the Kongka Pass, in the north-west, in October of that year. By coincidence or design, the bodies of nine Indian policemen killed by the latter incident were returned to Delhi on Nehru's birthday, 14 November!

[2] Krishan Bhatia, 'Political Commentary', *Statesman*, 3 August 1962.

[3] To this writer in 1964–5, among them, Mrs. Pandit, Krishna Menon, Professor P. C. Mahalonobis, and a score of political and official colleagues.

[4] Interview, New Delhi, 3 December 1964.

[5] Interview, Bombay, 31 July 1964.

[6] *Hindu Weekly Review* (Madras), 20 May and 3 June 1963; *Economic Weekly* (Bombay), 1 and 22 June, 6 July 1963.

[7] There were deeper roots to the malaise and the dramatic response of 1963—subtle changes which were taking place in the Congress in the last phase of Dhebar's presidency (1954–9). These changes are explored in a hitherto unpublished paper by W. H. Morris-Jones: 'The Congress Party: Dilemmas of Dominance', written in 1965.

[8] *Hindustan Times*, New Delhi, and *Times of India*, New Delhi, 6 July 1963. Unless specifically indicated, all data in this study are based on

the comprehensive political reports in the 'Big Four' English-language daily newspapers in India, all of which have Delhi editions: the *Statesman, Times of India, Hindustan Times,* and the *Indian Express.*

9 See also the *Hindustan Times* editorial, 'Outdated', 8 July 1963; and the *Times of India* editorials, 'Tarnished Image', 9 July 1963, and 'Sorry Pass', 10 July 1963.

10 'A Laughing Stock', *Times of India,* 5 August 1963.

11 Brecher, *Nehru,* 502–7.

12 A comprehensive report of the AICC session on 10 August is to be found in the *Times of India,* 11 August 1963.

13 'Party and Power', 10 August 1963.

14 'Reforming the Congress', 11 August 1963.

15 'The Kamaraj Plan', 12 August 1963.

16 'Revitalizing the Congress', 14 August 1963.

17 *Hindustan Times,* 15 August 1963.

18 'Political Commentary', *Statesman,* 15 August 1963.

19 *Hindustan Times,* 14 August 1963.

20 *Hindu,* 12 August 1963.

21 For the text of Nehru's Note to the Working Committee, see the *Times of India,* 25 August 1963.

22 'They Also Serve', 26 August 1963.

23 'Right Note', 30 August 1963.

24 'Ministerial Transfers', 1 September 1963.

25 'The Great Purge', 27 August 1963.

26 'A Great Wind of Change', 27 August 1963.

27 The Prime Minister obliquely acknowledged responsibility for the VOA muddle in a statement to Parliament on 14 August 1963: 'I was consulted on two or three occasions but did not go into the whole matter at any particular stage. The matter was, however, briefly mentioned to me before the agreement was signed and, in that context, I must assume responsibility.' The text is to be found in the *Times of India,* the *Hindustan Times,* and the *Hindu,* 15 August 1963. The decision process on this issue will be analysed in a study of India's foreign policy, now in preparation.

28 See Brecher, *Nehru,* ch. XX, especially 628. According to Prem Bhatia, Shastri chose to leave the Cabinet because of slight friction with Nehru at the time: Shastri allegedly opposed the return of Katju as Chief Minister of Madhya Pradesh and opposed Nehru's reluctance to dismiss Kairon as Chief Minister of the Punjab. 'Mr. Nehru's Illness and an If', *Indian Express,* 17 January 1964.

29 *Hindustan Times,* 8 August 1963.

30 This powerful organ, which supervises the allocation of election tickets, among other things, was enlarged from five to seven members: Shastri and Patil were added; Morarji replaced U. N. Dhebar; and Jagjivan Ram was already a member. *Times of India,* 25 August 1963.

31 See Brecher, *Nehru,* 460–2.

32 'Kamaraj Plan Acquires New Dimensions', *Statesman,* 30 August 1963.

[33] 'Kamaraj Plan Will Strengthen Congress Executive', *Statesman*, 31 August 1963.

[34] 'Kamaraj Plan Lifts Lid Off A Pandora's Box', *Hindu*, 23 September 1963. See also his 'Kamaraj Plan: Effect on Top Leadership', ibid., 7 October 1963.

[35] 'First Fruits of Kamaraj Plan: Disillusionment', *Economic Times*, 7 October 1963.

[36] *Hindustan Times*, 5 September 1963.

[37] 'The Mind of Mr. Nehru', *Times of India*, 28 August 1963.

[38] Reported by K. Rangaswami, 'Reasoning Behind the Kamaraj Plan', *Hindu*, 15 August 1963.

[39] *Hindustan Times*, 25 September 1963. Shastri termed it 'a big step forward', *Times of India*, 12 September 1963; and Jagjivan Ram called it 'a gallant effort to strengthen the Party', *Hindustan Times*, 27 September 1963.

[40] Ibid., 26 and 27 September 1963.

[41] *Free Press Journal*, Bombay, 21 October 1963.

[42] Interview, New Delhi, 30 October 1964.

[43] *Hindustan Times*, 24 April 1964.

[44] For comprehensive reports of the discussion at the AICC session on 29-30 August, see *Hindustan Times*, 31 August 1964, and *Link*, 6 September 1964. See also Nandan Kagal's assessment, 'Party Before Post?', *Times of India*, 2 September 1964; the *Statesman* leader, 'Party and Office', 1 September 1964; the *Indian Express* leader, 'The First Salvo', 1 September 1964; and the *Patriot* leader, 'A Confused Party', 31 August 1964. For an assessment of the Kamaraj Plan's effects on the political situation, see Ranajit Roy, 'One Year's Working of the Kamaraj Plan', *Statesman*, 7 August 1964.

[45] *Hindu*, 1 October 1963.

[46] A message to the Madhya Pradesh Congress *Patrika*, as reported in *Times of India*, 9 August 1964. Of some interest, in this connection, is the fact that, two and a half years earlier, Sanjiva Reddy suggested, in his presidential address to the Congress, that persons who had held office for ten years or more should step down and devote themselves to organizational work—except Nehru. *Hindustan Times*, 7 January 1961.

[47] Interview, New Delhi, 22 December 1964.

[48] Krishan Bhatia, 'Kamaraj Plan: Bouquets and Brick-bats', *Hindustan Times*, 27 August 1964.

[49] 'Kamaraj Plan Acquires New Dimensions', *Statesman*, 30 August 1963.

[50] 'In Perspective: The Mind of Mr. Nehru', *Times of India*, 28 August 1963.

[51] Sanjiva Reddy, interview, New Delhi, 27 March 1965.

[52] The term 'Syndicate' was first used by Inder Malhotra in his 'Political Commentary' in the *Statesman*, on 10 June 1964, but it is generally ascribed to Romesh Thapar, Delhi Correspondent for the *Economic Weekly* (Bombay) and editor of *Seminar*. See his 'Capital View: Shastri and "The Syndicate"', *Economic Weekly*, 13 June 1964,

973-4. The Tirupathi meeting was reported in the *Times of India*, 3 October 1963. The origins of the Syndicate are somewhat earlier. In the autumn of 1962, before the Chinese invasion, senior officials observed that four or five Chief Ministers were regularly discussing issues of national policy and leadership at National Development Council meetings, sessions of the Emotional Integration Committee, and in a number of similar contexts in which State leaders gathered for national purposes.

[53] See chapter VI below.
[54] *Statesman*, 7 October 1963. See also *Times of India*, 7 October 1963.
[55] *Statesman*, 7 October 1963.
[56] Ibid., 8 October 1963.
[57] Sanjiva Reddy interview.
[58] Atulya Ghosh, interview, New Delhi 20 March 1965. The *Hindustan Times* reported at the time (10 October 1963) that Atulya had raised the question and that Nehru and others had approved the proposal, with Shastri, Patil, and Reddy specifically mentioned. Kamaraj himself told newsmen in Madras that he was surprised by the turn of events at the Working Committee meeting. *Hindu*, 16 October 1963.
[59] Sanjiva Reddy interview.
[60] Interview, New Delhi, 12 March 1965.
[61] Interviews.
[62] *Hindustan Times*, 4 November 1963.
[63] *Hindustan Times*, 1 January 1964, and *Patriot* (New Delhi), 10 January 1964. See also K. Rangaswami, 'Congress After Nehru's Illness', *Hindu*, 20 January 1964.
[64] Inder Malhotra, 'New Importance of Congress President', *Statesman*, 31 January 1964. For reports on the Jaipur Session, see *Times of India*, 3 November 1963, and *Hindustan Times*, 4 November 1963. See also S. M., 'The Significance of the Jaipur Session', *Hindustan Times*, 7 November 1963.
[65] Delhi, 27 December 1963.
[66] *Statesman*, 12 January 1964.
[67] *Indian Express*, 14 January 1964. He repeated this a few days later: *Times of India*, 20 January 1964.
[68] 'Mr. Nehru', 17 January 1964.
[69] 'Nehru's Unfinished Tasks', *Hindustan Times*, 16 January 1964.
[70] *Indian Express*, 17 January 1964.
[71] *Statesman*, 15 January 1964 and *Indian Express*, 16 January 1964.
[72] *Hindu*, 23 January 1964. In effect, Sanjivayya was the replacement for Jagjivan Ram, the Untouchable representative in the Cabinet from 1946 until the Kamaraj Plan.
[73] The text of the President's Order is in the *Times of India*, 3 February 1964. There was no reference to the Planning Commission of which Nehru was Chairman.
[74] 'Mr. Nehru's Illness and an If', *Indian Express*, 17 January 1964.

[75] Inder Malhotra, 'New Importance of Congress President', *Statesman*, 31 January 1964.
[76] Quoted in *Hindustan Times*, 23 January 1964.
[77] Quoted in *Hindustan Times*, *Statesman*, and *Times of India*, 24 January 1964.
[78] Reported by H. R. Vohra, *Times of India*, 24 January 1964.
[79] 'The Succession Issue', *Times of India*, 29 January 1964.
[80] 'Collective Leadership: First Phase', *Indian Express*, 31 January 1964.
[81] D. R. Mankekar, *Lal Bahadur Shastri: A Political Biography*, Delhi 1964.
[82] 'Kamaraj Plan ensures Orderly Succession', *Indian Express*, 26 February 1964.
[83] 'Vacuum Persists in Delhi Leadership', *Statesman*, 14 February 1964.
[84] 'Leadership Crisis Persists at Centre', *Statesman*, 13 March 1964. He persisted with this theme: 'Central Leadership Crisis Deepens', *Statesman*, 3 April 1964.
[85] *Indian Express*, 14 February 1964.
[86] 'A Deputy Prime Minister', 15 February 1964.
[87] 'Who's Who', 19 March 1964.
[88] *Indian Express*, 19 March 1964.
[89] *Times of India*, 31 March 1964.
[90] See *Patriot*, 'Deputy Prime Minister', 1 April 1964, and Prem Bhatia, 'P.M.'s Final Verdict about a Deputy', *Indian Express*, 2 April 1964.
[91] An interview with Arnold Michaelis, which was shown on TV in New York, on 18 May. Reported in the *Hindustan Times*, 19 May 1964, eight days before his death.
[92] In January 1965.
[93] The Indian Institute of Public Opinion: Monthly Public Opinion Surveys, 101, 'After Nehru, Who?', Vol. IX, No. 5, February 1964.
[94] Interview, New Delhi, 10 April 1965.
[95] Interview, Bombay, 31 July 1964.
[96] Interview, New Delhi, 9 October 1964.
[97] Interview, New Delhi, 18 August 1964.
[98] *Times of India*, 18 May 1964.
[99] *Times of India* and *Patriot*, 23 May 1964.

III DRAMA

[1] Interview, New Delhi, 10 August 1964. Singh was then Special Secretary in the Home Ministry and later became Home Secretary.
[2] 'My Last Meeting with Jawaharlal Nehru', *Times of India*, 7 June 1964.
[3] *Hindustan Times*, 29 April 1964.
[4] The name given to the Prime Minister's Residence, which stands on Teen Murti Road in New Delhi. On 14 November 1964, Nehru's 75th birthday, it became a Nehru Memorial Museum.
[5] Interview, New Delhi, 25 February 1965.

[6] This account is based on conversations with members of the family and Nehru's personal staff, one of the attending physicians, and many senior members of Cabinet.

[7] Interview with Raghunath Singh, New Delhi, 7 April 1965.

[8] Interview, New Delhi, 17 October 1964.

[9] Interview, New Delhi, 5 December 1964.

[10] Interview, New Delhi, 31 August 1964.

[11] Related by eye-witnesses, who wish to remain anonymous.

[12] Then Assistant Secretary of State for the Near East and South Asia.

[13] Interview, New Delhi, 16 February 1965.

[14] The text is in the *Statesman*, 28 May 1964.

[15] Ibid.

[16] Interview, New Delhi, 12 March 1965.

[17] Interview with Malaviya, New Delhi, 24 March 1965.

[18] See pp. 85–87 below.

[19] For a vivid account of Gandhi's funeral, see Louis Fischer, *The Life of Gandhi*, 1950, ch. I.

[20] An unauthorized but undoubtedly authentic text of Nehru's Will, dated 21 June 1954, was published in *Blitz* (Bombay) in two instalments, 22 and 29 August 1964. An official text has not yet appeared, apart from an extract issued from Delhi as 'Testament of Jawaharlal Nehru', which includes these words.

[21] For a defence of the religious ceremony, see Sri Prakasa, 'Hindu Ceremonies and Nehru's Obsequies', *Indian Express*, 1 September 1964. 'Sentiment both in the family and outside was too strong to avoid all that.'

[22] For a comprehensive survey of secularism in India, see D. E. Smith, *India as a Secular State*, 1963.

[23] For a witty and informative account of Nanda's reliance on the advice of his astrologer, Haveli Ram, see Selig Harrison's article in the *Washington Post*, 11 October 1964.

[24] Chavan interview.

[25] Malaviya interview.

[26] Interview, New Delhi, 17 February 1965. Three years earlier, Ram had been backed by the Left in his abortive contest with Morarji for the Deputy Leadership of the Congress Parliamentary Party! The wheel had turned full circle. More than that, Ram's behaviour, like that of most of his colleagues, reveals the non-ideological character of Congress Party politics.

[27] Morarji Desai interview.

[28] The report emanated from the United News of India (UNI) and appeared in three Delhi newspapers. See *Times of India*, 29 May 1964.

[29] Interview, Bombay, 31 July 1964.

[30] Menon interview.

[31] Malaviya interview.

[32] Chavan interview.

[33] Morarji Desai's Personal Correspondence, 1 September 1956.

[34] Reddy interview.

[35] Patnaik interview.

[36] Based on various interviews, notably with Jagjivan Ram. Shastri's biographer also confirmed this incident. Mankekar, op. cit., 35–36; he termed it ' a red herring '.

[37] Interview, New Delhi, 7 August 1964.

[38] Related by a journalist who wishes to remain anonymous.

[39] See Brecher, *Nehru*, 389–401.

[40] Mankekar, op. cit., 37.

[41] Atulya Ghosh interview.

[42] *Patriot*, 31 May 1964.

[43] Ibid.

[44] The others were Harekrushna Mahtab, former Chief Minister of Orissa, Krishna Kant Singh, and Raja Rameshwar Rao.

[45] K. Rangaswami, in the *Hindu*, 31 May 1964.

[46] Ibid., and *Patriot*, 31 May 1964.

[47] *Patriot*, 31 May 1964.

[48] *Hindustan Times*, 31 May 1964.

[49] Morarji Desai interview.

[50] Some diplomats present in Delhi during the struggle.

[51] See Brecher, *Nehru*, 349.

[52] *Hindu*, 1 June 1964.

[53] Rangaswami, in the *Hindu*, 1 June 1964.

[54] Kamaraj himself, the *Times of India*, 1 June 1964, and some Delhi pundits.

[55] Ram, Nanda, Reddy, Atulya Ghosh, Chavan, and Menon interviews.

[56] *Statesman* and *Hindu*, 1 June 1964.

[57] *Indian Express*, 1 June 1964.

[58] Ram, Chavan, and Nanda interviews.

[59] 1 June 1964.

[60] Menon interview.

[61] Nanda interview.

[62] *Hindu*, 2 June 1964.

[63] Reported in the *Times of India, Indian Express*, and *Hindustan Times*, 2 June 1964.

[64] Morarji Desai interview.

[65] Notably, Subhas Chandra Bose in 1939, Acharya Kripalani in 1951, and C. Rajagopalachari in the 1950s.

[66] Atulya Ghosh interview.

[67] Shastri interview.

[68] Inder Malhotra, in the *Statesman*, 3 June 1964.

[69] *Times of India*, 3 June 1964.

[70] Full accounts of this meeting are to be found in all major Delhi English-language dailies of 3 June 1964.

71 Menon interview.
72 ' Well Begun ', 2 June 1964.
73 ' The New Phase ', 3 June.
74 The new Government was sworn in on 9 June 1964. See the *Statesman*, 10 June 1964.
75 ' New Leader ', 3 June 1964.
76 ' Mr. Shastri's Task ', 3 June 1964.
77 ' A Good Beginning ', 3 June 1964.
78 ' The Middle Way: Premier-Designate Shastri ', *Times of India*, 3 June 1964.
79 *Indian Express*, 3 June 1964.

IV PROCESS

1 Interview, New Delhi, 13 June 1956.
2 See note 91 of chapter II.
3 Mrs. Pandit, Krishnamachari, and Kamaraj interviews.
4 Morarji Desai interview.
5 Patnaik interview.
6 Nijalingappa was apparently told that he had been relieved of the post —even before he took office—by Kamaraj at the last moment; he had just returned to Bangalore to wind up his affairs. Related by a person who wishes to remain anonymous.
7 Morarji Desai's Personal Correspondence, 19 February 1953.
8 Ibid., 23 February 1953.
9 Ibid., 1 September 1952.
10 Ibid., 28 February 1956.
11 Ibid., 20 December 1952, in reply to Nehru's letter of 19 December 1952.
12 Ibid., 6/7 July 1952.
13 Ibid., 9 July 1952.
14 Ibid., 5/6 August 1952.
15 Ibid., 8 August 1952.
16 Ibid., 18 August 1952.
17 Ibid., 21 January 1953.
18 Ibid., 22 January 1953.
19 Ibid., 25 January 1953.
20 Ibid., 29 January 1953.
21 Ibid., 5 February 1953.
22 Ibid., 16 February 1953.
23 LSD (Lok Sabha Debates) (52), cols. 12292–12320, 26 April 1963. The emphasis has been added, except in the case of Mukherjee's remarks.
24 Inder Malhotra, ' Morarji Lost Succession Battle in April ', *Statesman*, 3 June 1964.
25 See note 93, chapter II.
26 ' The Middle Way: Premier-Designate Shastri ', *Times of India*, 3 June 1964.

[27] Morarji Desai interview. Kamaraj, too, justified the consensus procedure in these terms. Kamaraj interview.

[28] Interview, New Delhi, 12 October 1964.

[29] Shastri interview.

[30] The writer is indebted to Neville Maxwell, Delhi Correspondent of *The Times* since 1959, for this apt metaphor.

[31] Shastri interview.

V IMPACT

[1] The eight-point formula was announced on 6 June 1961. See the *Hindu Weekly Review*, 12 June 1961. The eruption of violence began in 1960 and flared up again in 1961. Of its magnitude and causes, Nehru wrote with candour to some of his colleagues: ' . . . the fact remains that fifty thousand or more Bengalee-speaking people of Assam became refugees. . . . The language issue was dominant and yet, surely, it was not merely because of language that these passions were aroused. There were economic causes, more especially unemployment, and the fear of the Assamese that outsiders, and especially Bengalees, got the lion's share of employment in their own State. There was fear of the Bengalees which led so many to leave their homes, and there was fear of the Assamese that they might be submerged in the influx of others and thus almost lose their identity. When fear grips any people, it is difficult to reason. . . .' Unpublished Nehru Letters, July 1960.

[2] See the *Statesman* and *Times of India*, 29 December 1963, ff.

[3] For a sympathetic and perceptive assessment of Shastri, see Pran Chopra, 'Mr. Shastri: A Man of Rich Experience', *Statesman*, 3 June 1964.

[4] Shastri interview.

[5] *Hindustan Times*, 16 March 1964.

[6] Morarji Desai interview.

[7] Interview, New Delhi, 5 December 1964.

[8] Brecher, *Nehru*, 448–66.

[9] Morarji Desai interview.

[10] Krishnamachari interview.

[11] Interviews with various members of Cabinet.

[12] For a full list of the Cabinet, see *Times of India*, 10 June 1964. Changes in portfolio among members of Cabinet and Ministers of State are to be found in *Times of India*, 14 June 1964.

[13] Inder Malhotra, 'Ministry-Making to Suit the Claimants', *Statesman*, 19 June 1964.

[14] 'The Cabinet', 10 June 1964.

[15] *Statesman*, 10 June 1964. Seven weeks later Nanda declared that he had not discussed with Shastri the inclusion of Morarji in the Cabinet or the question of ranking. *Amrita Bazar Patrika*, 1 August 1964.

[16] *Times of India*, 19 July 1964.

[17] Chagla, Chavan, Kabir, Krishnamachari, Nanda, and Patil interviews.

[18] Menon interview.
[19] See chapter VI. For a criticism of their resignation, in terms of 'collective responsibility', see the *Statesman* leader, 'Responsible Ministers', 13 February 1965.
[20] Prem Bhatia, 'Checks and Balances in the Cabinet', *Indian Express*, 26 August 1964.
[21] Interview, New Delhi, 26 September 1964.
[22] See Brecher, *Nehru*, 453.
[23] Jha's experience, from 1942 to 1964, has been entirely in economic affairs; in succession: Supply Department (1942–6), Chief Controller of Imports and Exports (1947–50), Commerce and Industry (1950–6), Heavy Industries (1956–7), Commerce and Industry (1957–60), and Finance (1960–4). Jha acquired impressive expertise in the spheres of planning and foreign aid; he was one of the key Indian officials at the 'Aid to India Club' consortium talks over the years.
[24] Related by officials in the Ministry of External Affairs.
[25] *Times of India*, 16 April 1965. See also the leader, 'Wrong Answer', *Times of India*, 17 April 1965.
[26] The Foreign Service Officers' Association reacted at once by making representations to the Foreign Minister. *Times of India*, 18 April 1965.
[27] See Prem Bhatia, 'Information Pipelines to the PM', *Indian Express*, 12 August 1964.
[28] This term was coined jointly with a diplomat who wishes to remain anonymous.
[29] Menon's role will be explored in a forthcoming study, *Krishna Menon : India and World Affairs*.
[30] This dispute will be analysed in a study on *The Foreign Policy of India*, now in preparation.
[31] Related by persons close to the Prime Minister.
[32] See Brecher, *Nehru*, 238–40.
[33] Ibid., 430–7.
[34] Reddy interview.
[35] For a penetrating analysis of the Congress as the hub of India's political system and of politics within India's ruling party, see W. H. Morris-Jones, *The Government and Politics of India* (1964), 148–54 and 169–80. See also Rajni Kothari, 'The Congress "System" in India', *Asian Survey* (Berkeley, Calif.), Vol. IV, No. 12, December 1964, 1161–73.
[36] Unpublished Nehru Letters, January 1959.
[37] Professor Morris-Jones terms the Shastri-Kamaraj relationship 'the third stage of Congress leadership since 1947', in his perceptive survey of Indian politics in 1964: 'India: Under New Management, Business as Usual', *Asian Survey*, Vol. V, No. 2, February 1965, 63–72.
[38] In the spring of 1965 Reddy publicly repudiated the suggestion that there is a 'gang' or 'syndicate' in the Congress. *Times of India*, 14 March 1965. Atulya Ghosh did the same in the Lok Sabha a few days later.
[39] Patil interview.

[40] Government of India: *Constitution of India* (revised), 1962.
[41] On the concept of 'Bargaining Federalism', see Morris-Jones, *Government and Politics . . .* , 141–4.

VI IMPLEMENTATION

[1] The estimate of a British writer, soon after the close of that century, was 20 million. William Digby, '*Prosperous*' *British India*, 1901.
[2] Raj Krishna, 'Viewpoints on Food—IV: Substantial Scarcity The Real Crisis', *Statesman*, 2 February 1965.
[3] Group discussion with Patil in New Delhi, 23 December 1964.
[4] 'Basic Facts Behind India's Food Crisis', *Statesman*, 14 August 1964.
[5] K. Rangachari, 'Viewpoints on Food—I: Need for Stricter Fiscal and Monetary Discipline', *Statesman*, 21 January 1965.
[6] A. M. Khusro, 'Viewpoints on Food—II: Differences Between Theory and Practice', *Statesman*, 23 January 1965.
[7] P. N. Thapar, 'Viewpoints on Food—III: Making the Best Use of Land Potential', *Statesman*, 1 February 1965.
[8] *Times of India*, 24 December 1964.
[9] Raj Krishna, op. cit.
[10] *Indian Economic Growth: Performance and Prospects*, 1965, Lecture 1: 'The Current Crisis and Agriculture'.
[11] The text is in the *Statesman*, 24 June 1964.
[12] *Statesman*, 4 July 1964.
[13] *Times of India*, 29 July 1964.
[14] *Statesman*, 11 September 1964.
[15] Unpublished Nehru Letters, August 1957.
[16] Ibid., November 1957.
[17] Ibid., March 1958.
[18] Ibid., September 1958.
[19] Ibid., May 1959.
[20] Ibid., August 1960.
[21] *Statesman*, 6 October 1964, ff.
[22] *Hindustan Times*, 27 October 1964.
[23] 28 October 1964.
[24] *Statesman*, 29 October 1964.
[25] The text is in the *Statesman*, 6 November 1964.
[26] *Statesman*, 20 January 1965.
[27] The text is in the *Hindustan Times*, 9 November 1964.
[28] 'The Real Emergency', 12 November 1964.
[29] *Statesman*, 13 November 1964.
[30] *Statesman*, 19 November 1964.
[31] *Hindustan Times*, 20 November 1964 and *Times of India*, 28 November 1964.
[32] *Times of India*, 16 December 1964.
[33] 'Grasping the Nettle', 19 November 1964.

[34] 'State of the Union', 1 December 1964.

[35] 'Irrational', 18 December 1964.

[36] *Statesman*, 30 December 1964.

[37] Group discussion with Subramaniam, New Delhi, 22 November 1964.

[38] To the CPP Executive, on 25 December 1964. *Times of India*, 26 December 1964.

[39] *Statesman*, 28 January 1965.

[40] K. Rangachari, *Statesman*, 24 April 1965.

[41] *Statesman Overseas Weekly*, 3 July 1965. For Sen's views, see *Times of India*, 29 June and 9 July 1965.

[42] *Times of India*, 23 July and 7 August 1965.

[43] Cyril Dunn, 'India Facing Famine Menace' (Ofns), *Jerusalem Post*, 17 November 1965.

[44] See Brecher, *Nehru*, 479–93.

[45] Language Tables of the 1961 Census, released by the Registrar-General and Census Commissioner in February 1965. See *Times of India*, 5 February 1965.

[46] Political Correspondent, 'What Nehru Said—And Said Not', *Statesman*, 23 February 1965.

[47] Unpublished Nehru Letters, December 1957.

[48] As quoted in 'What Nehru Said—And Said Not', loc. cit. The same themes are evident in much of Nehru's writings and correspondence; for example, in an exchange of letters with Rajagopalachari at the beginning of 1958.

[49] Unpublished Nehru Letters, February 1963.

[50] Ibid., January 1958.

[51] Shastri interview.

[52] *Statesman*, 5 October 1964.

[53] 'Changeover', 9 October 1964.

[54] 'Eleven Weeks to Hindi Changeover', *Statesman*, 6 November 1964.

[55] See, for example, his remarks to the Hindi Association of Parliament on the celebration of Hindi Day. *Times of India*, 15 September 1964.

[56] Convocation Address to Visva Bharati, Santiniketan. *Times of India*, 24 December 1964.

[57] *Times of India*, 17 December 1964.

[58] The Delhi Press gave wide coverage to the language explosion in its issues of 11 February 1965 ff. See also *Link* (New Delhi), 21 February 1965, 'The Language Crisis', and, especially, the *Hindu* and *Madras Mail* of that period.

[59] The text is in the *Times of India*, 12 February 1965.

[60] 'The Stake', 16 February 1965.

[61] Kamaraj interview.

[62] Reddy interview.

[63] Panel discussion on 'the language question' at the American International School in New Delhi, 31 March 1965. For a pronounced

Hindi view among the pundits, see Nandan Kagal, ' A Cruel Legacy ', *Times of India*, 3 February 1965.

[64] *Statesman*, 1 April 1965. Noteworthy, too, is the fact that Delhi, with a fraction of the total population of India, has accounted for 8 per cent. of the Services' posts since independence, exceeding the combined share of Andhra, Madhya Pradesh, and Rajasthan, which comprise 20 per cent. of the total population! It is of special interest that the share of Uttar Pradesh, largest State in the Union (and Hindi-speaking), is proportionate to its population ratio. So too with Bengal.

[65] For a comprehensive eye-witness account and analysis of the 1965 crisis, see Robert L. Hardgrave, Jr., ' The Riots in Tamilnad: Problems and Prospects of India's Language Crisis ', *Asian Survey*, Vol. V, No. 8, August 1965, 399–407. See also Nandan Kagal, ' The Gathering Crisis ', *Times of India*, 1 March 1965.

[66] Unpublished Nehru Letters, June 1961.

[67] The text is in the *Statesman*, 18 February 1965.

[68] To newsmen, 16 February 1965. *Times of India*, 17 February 1965.

[69] *Times of India*, 21 February 1965.

[70] Inder Malhotra, ' Total Obsession with the Language Issue ', *Statesman*, 26 February 1965.

[71] The text is in the *Times of India*, 25 February 1965. For an analysis of the pressures affecting the consensus, see *Link*, 28 February 1965, ' Language: Accord or Uneasy Compromise? '.

[72] The text is in the *Times of India*, 26 February 1965.

[73] ' Not Enough ', 26 February 1965.

[74] *Statesman*, 25 February 1965.

[75] *Times of India*, 23 February 1965. See also his article on the occasion of the changeover, ' National Unity Through Hindi ', ibid., 26 January 1965.

[76] *Statesman*, 26 February 1965. By the same evening, another fifteen M.P.s had indicated their readiness to support the move.

[77] Ibid., 3 March 1965.

[78] See, for example, ' Language Evasions ', *Times of India*, 17 March 1965, and Inder Malhotra, ' Delhi Dilly-Dallies on the Language Issue ', *Statesman*, 16 April 1965.

[79] *Times of India*, 23 March 1965.

[80] Ibid., 24 February 1965.

[81] Ibid., 7 April 1965.

[82] The most informative assessment of the bargaining in the Grand Council is the account in the *Times of India*, 2 June 1965.

[83] Text and analysis of the resolution are in the *Statesman*, 3 June 1965.

[84] Ibid.

[85] ' At Last ', 4 June 1965.

[86] ' Collective Thinking Helps on Language Issue ', *Statesman*, 4 June 1965.

[87] *Times of India*, 13 June 1965.

[88] 'Dangers of Three Language Formula', *Statesman Overseas Weekly*, 7 August 1965.

[89] *Times of India*, 15 June 1965.

[90] Ibid., 30 June 1965.

[91] 'Hasty and Clumsy', 3 July 1965.

[92] *Statesman*, 6 August 1965. See also the *Statesman* leader, 'Put It In Writing', 7 August 1965.

[93] Government of India: Ministry of Defence: *Annual Report 1964–65*, 1–2.

[94] For a thoughtful and informative discussion of the role of the Military, see Lloyd I. Rudolph and Susanne Hoeber Rudolph, 'Generals and Politicians in India', *Pacific Affairs*, Vol. XXXVII, No. 1, Spring 1964, 5–19.

[95] These are explored in breadth, for the first time, in Myron Weiner, *The Politics of Scarcity*, 1962, a pioneering study of interest groups in the Indian political system.

[96] *Times of India*, 4 June 1965.

VII LEGACY

[1] A partial text is in the *Statesman*, 25 March 1965.

[2] From a speech at an Independence Day ceremony in Bombay, 15 August 1964. As quoted in Nandan Kagal, 'State of the Union', *Times of India*, 20 August 1964.

[3] As reported by the Political Correspondent, *Statesman*, 3 April 1965.

[4] Interview, New Delhi, 10 April 1965. K. D. Malaviya, among others, expressed similar views.

[5] 'A Question of Confidence', *Times of India*, 24 March 1965.

[6] Reddy interview.

[7] Atulya Ghosh interview.

[8] 'The Heart of the Matter', *Indian Express*, 9 November 1964.

[9] S. M., 'Mr. Shastri's Six Months', *Hindustan Times*, 9 December 1964.

[10] 'Assets and Liabilities for the New Leader', *Statesman*, 11 June 1964.

[11] 'Pessimism a Greater Danger Than Prices', *Statesman*, Republic Day Supplement, 26 January 1965.

[12] 'One Year in the Saddle', 8 June 1965.

[13] 'The First Year', 9 June 1965. See also 'Mr. Shastri's Economics', ibid., 10 June 1965.

[14] Political Correspondent, *Statesman*, 10 June 1965.

[15] B. G. Verghese, 'Poverty of Politics', *Times of India*, 22 April 1965.

[16] See the *Times of India* leader, 'Disturbing', 21 August 1964.

[17] Prem Bhatia, 'A Political System in Grave Danger', *Indian Express*, 14 April 1965.

[18] Pran Chopra, 'Congress—II: Time to Remedy the Absence of Policy', *Statesman*, 13 April 1965.

[19] Inder Malhotra, 'Making Friends Nearer To Home', *Statesman*, 16 October 1964.

VIII THE SECOND SUCCESSION

[1] This analysis is based upon personal observation, interviews with many of the prominent actors, and a careful reading of the Indian Press during the nine-day succession drama. Valuable insights and data were derived from interviews with Congress President Kamaraj; the two principal candidates for the succession, Mrs. Indira Gandhi and Morarji Desai; the three leading members of the 'Syndicate', Atulya Ghosh, S. K. Patil, and Sanjiva Reddy; the Chief Ministers of Madhya Pradesh (D. P. Mishra) and Mysore (Nijalingappa); former Union Cabinet Ministers, Jagjivan Ram, K. D. Malaviya, Krishna Menon, and T. T. Krishnamachari; Orissa Congress leader, Biju Patnaik; many M.P.s, some civil servants, and some Indian political analysts.

Factual material, the source of which is not specifically cited, has been drawn from six daily newspapers: *Hindustan Times, Indian Express, Patriot, Statesman,* and *Times of India* (all from Delhi), and the *Hindu,* from Madras.

[2] A senior civil servant, who was a member of the Indian delegation in Tashkent, remarked two days after the agreement was signed that the image of deadlock conveyed to the outside world was inaccurate and that, to many of the participants, there was no doubt that some measure of agreement would be achieved.

[3] A permanent invitee to the Congress Working Committee meetings.

[4] Inder Malhotra, Political Correspondent of the *Statesman.*

[5] Mrs. Gandhi interview, 16 January 1966. Parenthetically, she recalled her attitude to the 1964 succession and clarified the question of her alleged support for Nanda at that time: 'Nanda came to me and said he would like to continue for at least a month. He seemed so terribly keen that I made a special effort to wrench myself from the numbness that I felt and said to Kamaraj and others, " why not let him continue for a month or so; there can be no harm in this, and he is so keen ". They bawled me out for suggesting that sort of thing.'

[6] Kamaraj interview, 21 January.

[7] Patil interview, 16 January.

[8] Atulya Ghosh interview, 21 January.

[9] Mishra interview, 19 January.

[10] Based on the diary of appointments with Kamaraj at his home, kindly made available by Congress General Secretary Manaen. All subsequent references to persons who met the Congress President are derived, in the first instance, from this diary.

[11] Morarji Desai interview, 13 January.

[12] Nanda's plea for continuity was noted in the *Statesman,* 13 January. The words quoted above are the English translation of Kamaraj's Tamil version of Nanda's request, conveyed to a confidant.

[13] This informal and negative ' decision ' was confirmed by at least two participants. Atulya, who was not present, dissented. He added the revealing comment: ' Morarji was never excluded. In all my discussions Morarji's name was never mentioned, not by a single person.'

[14] Atulya Ghosh interview.

15 Nijalingappa interview, 20 January.
16 Rajaji made his suggestion at a condolence meeting in Madras. *Statesman*, 13 January. Malaviya implied his preference in a conversation on 13 January.
17 In an interview on Thursday night, 13 January, Jagjivan Ram replied to questions as follows: 'Is it true that you have become a candidate?' 'Some people have mooted my name.' 'Are you encouraging them?' 'I am not discouraging them.'
18 'Choosing a Successor to Mr. Shastri', *Statesman*, 14 January 1966.
19 'Choosing a Leader', *Hindustan Times*, 14 January.
20 Patnaik interview, 14 January.
21 Atulya Ghosh interview.
22 Kamaraj interview.
23 Morarji Desai interview.
24 Nijalingappa interview.
25 This was suggested by the Political Correspondent of *Organiser* in his account, 'The Full Story of Indira's Election', Republic Day issue, 1966, pp. 7, 8, 45.
26 Mishra confirmed the account of his and Jagjivan Ram's 'mission to Morarji', noted on p. 50 above.
27 An effort to discover who had called on him was unsuccessful, perhaps because of concern about possible victimization by the victors.
28 The seven M.P.s were: J. B. Kripalani, N. C. Chatterjee, A. B. Vajpayee, Prakash Vir Shastri, H. V. Kamath, Abdul Gani, and Dayabhai Patel.

INDEX